Studies in Trans-Disciplinary Method

This groundbreaking and innovative text addresses the deep ontological and epistemological commitments that underpin conventional positivist methods and then demonstrates how "method" can be understood in much broader and more interesting ways.

Drawing on a broad range of philosophical and methodological theory as well as a wide variety of artistic sources from fine art to cinema and from literature to the blues, leading contemporary thinker Michael Shapiro shows the reader how a more open understanding of the concept of method is rewarding and enlightening. His notion of "writing-as-method" is enacted throughout the text and offers a stimulating alternative for students to positivist social science methods.

This is essential reading for all students and faculty with an interest in post-positivist methods.

Michael J. Shapiro is Professor of Political Science at the University of Hawaii.

Interventions
Edited by
Jenny Edkins, *Aberystwyth University* and
Nick Vaughan-Williams, *University of Warwick*

"As Michel Foucault has famously stated, 'knowledge is not made for understanding; it is made for cutting.' In this spirit the Edkins–Vaughan-Williams Interventions series solicits cutting edge, critical works that challenge mainstream understandings in international relations. It is the best place to contribute post disciplinary works that think rather than merely recognize and affirm the world recycled in IR's traditional geopolitical imaginary."

Michael J. Shapiro, University of Hawai'i at Mãnoa, USA

The series aims to advance understanding of the key areas in which scholars working within broad critical post-structural and post-colonial traditions have chosen to make their interventions, and to present innovative analyses of important topics.

Titles in the series engage with critical thinkers in philosophy, sociology, politics and other disciplines and provide situated historical, empirical and textual studies in international politics.

Studies in Trans-Disciplinary Method

After the aesthetic turn

Michael J. Shapiro

LONDON AND NEW YORK

First published 2013
by Routledge
2 Park Square, Milton Park, Abingdon, Oxon OX14 4RN

Simultaneously published in the USA and Canada
by Routledge
711 Third Avenue, New York, NY 10017

Routledge is an imprint of the Taylor & Francis Group, an informa business

British Library Cataloguing in Publication Data
A catalogue record for this book is available from the British Library

Library of Congress Cataloging in Publication Data
Shapiro, Michael J.
Studies in trans-disciplinary method : after the aesthetic turn /
Michael J. Shapiro.
   p. cm. -- (Interventions)
   Includes bibliographical references and index.
   1. Political science--Research--Methodology. I. Title.
   JA86.S52 2012   320.01'1--dc23
   2012006902

ISBN: 978–0–415–78355–2 (hbk)
ISBN: 978–0–415–69294–6 (pbk)
ISBN: 978–0–203–10150–6 (ebk)

Typeset in Times New Roman
by Bookcraft Ltd, Stroud, Gloucestershire

Printed and bound in Great Britain by the MPG Books Group

To Cleo Cherryholmes

Contents

List of figures

Acknowledgments

The names of people whose help and/or inspiration I wish to acknowledge include those to whom I am indebted for the lecture and meeting panel invitations that prompted the prototypes of chapters, those who inspired me by reading and responding to drafts, those who inspired me in general by example (some of whom I served with on panels at professional meetings), those who encouraged me in discussions about my ideas for the book, and students who helped me formulate my approach to political analysis as I discussed it in my courses. I am grateful to: Florentina Andreescu, Ivan Asher, Jane Bennett, Brenna Bhandar, Didier Bigo, Bettina Brown, Bill Callahan, Bill Carroll, Terrell Carver, Melisa Casumbal, Sam Chambers, Chairat Chareoen-o-Larn, Cleo Cherryholmes, Bill Connolly, Jodi Dean, Mick Dillon, Tom Dumm, Jenny Edkins, Kathy Ferguson, Kennan Ferguson, Jon Goldberg-Hiller, Brianne Gallagher, Olivia Guaraldo, Alex Hirsch, David Howarth, Anatoli Ignatov, Laura Junka, Rohan Kalyan, Krishna, Garnet Kindervater, Chuck Lawrence, Isis Leslie, Luis Lobo-Guerrero, Catherine Malabou, James Martel, Fabiano Mielniczuk, Fred Moten, Martin Nitsche, Joao Nogueira, Sam Opondo, Davide Panagia, Paul Passavant, Richard Powers, Sami Raza, Julian Reid, Lorenzo Rinelli, Kam Shapiro, Jon Simons, Nevi Soguk, Manfred Steger, John Sweeney, Lars Toender, Irina Velicu, Ritu Vij, Rob Walker, Cornel West, Geoffrey Whitehall.

I would like to especially acknowledge my editors at Routledge, Craig Fowlie and Nicola Parkin, for their friendship, and support. One could not wish for better attention from publishers.

This book is dedicated to Cleo Cherryholmes, a life-loving friend who has battled adversity without complaint, and in retirement from academia, is still growing and changing.

Preface

The title of this book is inspired by Harold Garfinkel's classic collection of investigations, *Studies in Ethnomethodology*.[1] His *Studies* ..., aimed at "learning how members' actual, ordinary activities consist of methods to make practical actions, practical circumstances, common sense knowledge of social structures, and practical sociological reasoning analyzable," effect a methodological approach that contrasts radically with the traditional philosophy of inquiry and established procedures of social science investigations. Rather than beginning with concepts, translating them into measurement protocols, and treating them as variables to test causal explanations, Garfinkel conceives the meaning of a concept as an accomplishment that emerges at the *end* of an investigation – as an outcome of a group's deliberations when it is charged with the task of implementing the concept. Thus in his investigation of suicide, in which he observed the decision-making practices of the staff at the Los Angeles Suicide Prevention Center, charged with coding whether or not unattended deaths were suicides, he analyzed what he calls the "practical reasoning" and "artful practices" through which "suicide" as a coding is accomplished.

As Garfinkel summarizes it, "the term ethnomethodology [refers to] the investigation of the rational properties of indexical practical actions as contingent ongoing accomplishments of organized artful practices of everyday life."[2] As applied to his investigation of suicide, his ethnomethodological approach was focused on the interactive decision process – the collective artful practices – through which the staff accomplished the coding of deaths as suicides, given the equivocalness of "suicide" versus other kinds of death. Garfinkel's actors are thus epistemological subjects. Involved in knowledge production tasks, they achieve the meanings of concepts and phenomena through their collective decision-making in practical everyday life settings. Garfinkel therefore refigures the methodological approach of social science practitioners, substituting for social science investigators, social actors who pursue concepts as the ultimate achievement of their inquiries. Those achievements are politically framed inasmuch as those social actors operate within structures of accountability. While deciding how to classify episodes, they are always already in a future scene of justification. In Garfinkel's words, "Decisions [have] an unavoidable consequentiality."[3]

In contrast with Garfinkel, my investigations in the studies in this book focus on the protagonists of artistic texts rather than on decision-making groups. Instead of task-oriented subjects involved in practical reasoning, my subjects are what I call aesthetic subjects. They are characters in texts whose movements and actions (both purposive and non-purposive) map and often alter experiential, politically relevant terrains. To provide an initial sense of the difference, I turn briefly to one of Philip Roth's protagonists, Simon Axler, a theater actor in his novel *The Humbling* (2009). Despairing at having lost his ability to perform convincingly on stage, and having attempted suicide as a result, Axler commits himself to a psychiatric clinic, where he gets acquainted with the clinic's other would-be suicides. At one point, feeling discontent with the clinic staff's approach to treatment, he gathers his fellow patients to give them his view of suicide as an artistic performance:

> The one thing everyone wants to do with suicide is explain it. Explain it and judge it … Some people think of it as an act of cowardice. Some people think of it as criminal, as a crime against the survivors. Another school of thought finds it heroic and an act of courage … [instead, he argues] Suicide is the role you write for yourself … You inhabit it and you enact it. All carefully staged – where they will find you and how they will find you … But one performance only.[4]

Through Axler's statements and actions, Roth generates a suicide *dispositif*, which consists of (among other things) a "heterogeneous ensemble consisting of discourses, institutions … scientific statements, philosophical, moral and philanthropic propositions … the said as much as the unsaid … the elements of the apparatus."[5] And he subjects that *dispositif* to critique by having Axler oppose a self-fashioning aesthetic of suicide to the explanatory apparatuses of suicide. Like Garfinkel's approach to concepts, Roth renders suicide as an "artful practice." However in this case, the artful practice belongs both to the author who invents his subject and to the subject/protagonist who enacts the artfulness. And whereas the meaning of suicide is rendered as an accomplishment by Garfinkel's epistemological subjects – whose actions consummate the institutional tasks to which they are assigned – Roth's aesthetic subject paralyzes the institution in which he is situated. Like Herman Melville's character, Bartleby (in his story "Bartleby the Scrivener," whom I introduce in Chapter 5), whose formula, "I prefer not to," disrupts the work of an attorney's law office, "erod[ing] the attorney's reasonable organization of work and life,"[6] Roth's character disrupts the clinic's therapeutic functioning.

Certainly there is a critical aspect of Garfinkel's approach in that he sees the outcomes of the "artful practices" of his epistemological subjects as "contingent accomplishments."[7] For Garfinkel, "suicide," rather than being an already stabilized phenomenon to be explained, emerges as an artifact of the organization of the task aimed at accomplishing it. To the extent that there are stabilities associated with such accomplishments, they result from achievements of "common sense," which develop from the deliberations of the institutionalized groups undertaking the tasks. Although I too depart from the traditional explanatory orientation of empiricist, explanation-seeking social science, my analyses mobilize "uncommon sense." Following Gilles Deleuze's suggestion that common sense involves merely recognizing the representational practices that already exist within the *doxa*,[8] or, as I have put it elsewhere, from the "unreflected upon acceptance of the world of actualities that exist in everyday, banal discourses,"[9] my studies seek to displace institutionalized forms of recognition with *thinking*. To *think* (rather than to seek to explain) in this sense is to invent and apply conceptual frames and create juxtapositions that disrupt and/or render historically contingent accepted knowledge practices. It is to compose the discourse of investigation with critical juxtapositions that unbind what are ordinarily presumed to belong together and thereby to challenge institutionalized ways of reproducing and understanding phenomena. My approach to inquiry therefore accords with Maurice Blanchot's notion of the purpose of literature, which is "to interrupt the purposeful steps we are always taking toward a deeper understanding and a surer grasp on things."[10]

However, my investigations are not aimed at disruption alone. To *think* rather than reproduce accepted knowledge frames is to create the conditions of possibility for imagining alternative worlds (and thus to be able to recognize the political commitments sequestered in every political imaginary). It is not, as is the case for Garfinkel, to administer *the* world within which collective tasks can be made to make sense. Articulated in this way, my methodological approach is in accord with Jacques Rancière's version of critical artistic practices, which he sees as "ways of doing and making that intervene in the general distribution of ways of doing and making."[11] They are practices that function within what he calls the "aesthetic regime of the arts," practices that "disturb" accepted relationships between "the sayable and the visible" and that effectively repartition the "distribution of the sensible."[12]

The pursuit of thinking with artistic texts rather than generating and testing explanations is neither a retreat into abstractions that lack contact with the world nor an avoidance of ethical and political concerns. It is a practice of critique that should be understood both as a challenge to epistemological certainties and as a positive engagement with actual experiences and issues pertaining to them. That practice requires one to resist the institutionalized knowledge that contributes to coercive structures, to – in Foucault's terms – make those knowledge practices "fragile, temporary [and thus to turn those practices into] events, nothing less than events."[13] As for the ethico-political force of critique: writing about critique-as-method in another place, I put it this way: "Critique … is ethical as well as political. In my various explorations of domains of political exclusion, for example, modes of identity and security politics that reject various forms of movement, both substantive (for example, immigration flows of the 1990s) and symbolic (such as migrating sexualities), I seek to encourage a hospitality towards ambiguous, protean and unsettled modes of selfhood and community."[14]

Critique in this sense is therefore empirically grounded. In contrast with the kind of "accomplishments" foregrounded in Garfinkel's ethnomethodological investigations, where what is "empirical" emerges from the accomplishments of collective, common sense-creating tasks, the empirical grounding of my approach resembles what Louis Althusser calls "the materialism of the encounter."[15] In contrast to what he calls "a materialism of necessity and teleology, that is to say, a transformed, disguised form of idealism," Althusser's "*materialism of the encounter*" draws on a philosophy of "the aleatory and of contingency."[16] His substitution of contingency for necessity is reminiscent of Garfinkel's similar substitution, inasmuch as Althusser suggests that within his philosophical perspective, "one reasons ... not in terms of the necessity of the accomplished fact, but in terms of the contingency of the fact to be accomplished."[17] However, in rendering facticity as a contingent event of encounter rather than (like Garfinkel) seeing it as the outcome of institutionalized tasks, Althusser draws attention to the historical contentiousness of what gets constituted as facticity. As he adds, "History here is nothing but the permanent revocation of the accomplished fact by another indecipherable fact ... only a provisional encounter, and since every encounter is provisional even when it lasts, *there is no eternity in the 'laws' of any world or any state*."[18]

In order to illustrate more elaborately the epistemological value of encounter and the artistic media genres that stage them, I turn to some insights offered by the Mexican writer, Carlos Fuentes, which I have analyzed elsewhere.[19] Fuentes reports a conversation that took place while he and friends were lost while on a driving trip in the Morelos region of Mexico. Assuming that the local map had a unitary set of addresses, he asked a local *campesino* the name of the village where they had stopped. The *campesino*'s reply astounded him: "That depends, we call the village Santa Maria in times of peace. We call it Zapata in times of war."[20] In reaction to the surprising answer, Fuentes reflected upon the plurality of temporal presences in the contemporary world. As he reports, "the old *campesino*" possesses a knowledge that "most people in the West have assiduously ignored since the seventeenth century: that there is more than one time in the world, that there is another time existing alongside, above, underneath the linear calendars of the West."[21] Fuentes proceeds to reflect upon the significance of encounter for his vocation as a novelist and finds himself asserting that the novel is especially attuned to multiplicity, to the plurality of presences or spatio-temporal ways of being in the world. Literature, according to Fuentes, can bring to presence "our forgotten self [because] ... the West, through its literature, internally elaborated a plurality of times in stark contrast to its external, chosen adherence to one time, the future-oriented time of progress."[22]

In effect, Fuentes' *campesino* precipitated an "event" in Foucault's above noted sense, for it has rendered a dominant mode of temporality fragile and also in the sense in which Deleuze conceives it when he states that the event "'hovers over' the bodies that it expresses."[23] Accordingly, rather than conceiving of Fuentes' experience in the encounter with the *campesino* as one in which a subject accomplishes the meaning of a concept/object (multiple co-existing temporalities in this case), we should recognize that there was, in Deleuze's terms, a "virtual field," a "problematic presiding over the genesis of the object."[24] What is to be discerned from Fuentes' brief commentary is the way such encounters actualize subjects, who in this case belong to alternative temporalities. While it is the case that "the fluid ways in which interpretations of time's passage become the idiom and the accent of the nation's trajectory,"[25] there are alternative subjects to the citizen-subject familiar in nation state-centric discourses. They emerge in encounters. So, unlike Garfinkel's studies in which already formed subjects accomplish meanings, an event-oriented perspective sees subjects as the non-volitional accomplishments of historical moments. As a result, critical analysis must involve what Deleuze calls "the counter-actualization" of the event or "counter-effectuation" of accepted facticities.

To appreciate what a counter-actualization implies, one must recognize the Kant-inspired – but reinflected – approach to empiricism that is central to Deleuzean philosophy. In contrast with Kant's transcendental idealism is Deleuze's transcendental empiricism, based on his concept of the virtual in which every actualization of experience brought into discourse is one actualization among other possible ones.[26] As Deleuze and Guattari put it, "the state of affairs actualizes a chaotic virtuality."[27] Crucially, to distinguish Deleuze's transcendental empiricism from the familiar social science approaches in which ideas/concepts are accorded representational measurement protocols, a given actualization is not a *representation* of the virtual. Rather, it is one kind of "repetition of the virtual" – an order extracted from a chaos – so that the politically relevant question becomes not one of whether it is a faithful representation but is instead one of "how a particular actualization becomes sedimented ... fixed over a period of time."[28] And to show how radically contingent a given actualization is, Deleuze suggests (in one of his early texts) that the discourses and/or texts that effectively counter-actualize such fixities do so by repeating or mimicking a given actualization in order to "double the actualization ... to give the truth of the event the only chance of not being confused with the only actualization ... to liberate it for other times."[29] Subsequently, he and Guattari attribute such a critical effect to the way that the characters in texts – both "conceptual personae" (involved in generating the "powers of concepts") and "aesthetic figures" (involved in generating "the powers of affects and percepts") – produce "thought events"[30] that achieve that counter-actualization.

Although my approach to such figures and the "thought events" in which they are involved is elaborated in my introductory chapter, I want to elucidate Deleuze's non-representational image of thought here by providing an illustration of a politically pregnant articulation of "other times" actualized in a current piece of literature. To do so, I follow briefly a character in a contemporary novel that functions as both a conceptual persona and an aesthetic figure. The character, Lenny Abramov, is an employee of a "life extension" enterprise in Gary Shteyngart's novel *Super Sad True Love Story* (2010).[31] Lenny, an unassertive, unsophisticated and unprepossessing young Russian Jewish émigré, begins the narration thus:

> Today I've made a major decision: *I am never going to die.* Others will die all around me. They will be nullified. The light switch will be turned off. Their lives, their entirety, will be marked by glossy marble headstones bearing

false summations ("her star shone brightly," "never to be forgotten," "he liked jazz"), and then these too will be lost in a coastal flood or get hacked to pieces by some genetically modified future-turkey.[32]

Lenny's conceit that such a "decision" is available to him is based on his employment, "as the Life Lover's Outreach Coordinator (Grade G) of the Post-Human Services division of the Staatling-Wapachung Corporation," which purports to be on the verge of perfecting the technology to offer its clients immortality.[33] While posted in Italy, Lenny describes his work to an old family friend, "I work in the creative economy ... indefinite life extension. We're going to help people live forever. I'm looking for European HNWIs – that's High Net Worth Individuals – and they're going to be our clients. We call them 'life lovers'."[34]

Implausible though the corporation's service may be (it eventually gives up life extension and becomes a lifestyle boutique), it trades on two aspects of the human condition, one enduring and one contemporary. The former is the ontological depth of life/death, a virtuality that has always hovered over every human aspiration, great and small. The latter is an "event," a historic shift in command structures. Corporate capitalism has attenuated the cultural authority of religion's symbolic and practical control over life/death. If we go back historically and look at the dawn of the approach to life and death that salvation-oriented religions have conceived and propagated, we discover a search that contrasts markedly with Lenny's. Instead of a corporate search for "high net worth" clients, there was an intense, wide-spread search for saints and sorcerers – both of which were alleged to be "intimate with the divine" – as people sought details on what they could expect from an afterlife.[35]

Jumping to a text that reflects on a futuristic rather than an ancient concern with life extension, we can contrast a fictional reflection on an articulation between enterprise and religion, Philip Dick's invention of a historical moment in which corporate control over life/death assimilates a religious motif. In his popular novel *Do Androids Dream of Electric Sheep?* and especially in Ridley Scott's film version of it, *Blade Runner*, corporate capitalism and religion are inter-articulated. A large private enterprise, the Tyrell Corporation, presides over life and death by making artificial people to help manage a dystopic world. They are "replicants" with built-in termination dates (a four-year life span). The film's imagery renders the Tyrell Corporation as a giant temple, and toward the end of the film, one of its products, Roy Batty, comes to "meet his maker," the corporation head, Eldon Tyrell, saying, "I want more life fucker!"[36]

The corporate control of life/death in Shteyngart's novel functions in a future in which religion has been wholly displaced by private enterprise. In contrast with the God-like Eldon Tyrell, whose products are the people he makes, the Staatling-Wapachung Corporation functions in a futuristic, neo-liberal world that, except for some advanced surveillance practices and technologies, looks a lot like the present. Death-avoiding life extension services are to be available to those who can afford them (subjects that neo-liberal economic practices have made – the HNWIs that Lenny Abramov has been hired to solicit), those for whom immortality is allegedly an available but costly commodity.

My assemblage of a historical trajectory of textual renderings of control over life/death constitutes a rough genealogy, an approach familiar in the late investigations of Foucault. As his investigations have indicated, a politically oriented genealogy of control over life and death is marked by a shift from the sovereign's absolute power over life to the state's concern with the management of life, effectively a governmentalization of life/death. Within this latter historical phase, the "event" in question is the historical emergence of a problematic and thus a new subject, the "population" As Foucault puts it, "Governments perceived that they were no longer dealing simply with subjects [those whose lives were under the control of the sovereign], or even with a 'people,' but with a 'population,' with its specific phenomena and its peculiar variables: birth and death rates, life expectancy, fertility, state of health, frequency of illnesses, patterns of diet and habitation."[37] As Foucault notes elsewhere, that new collective subject reflects a different "governmentality," one in which governance is less concerned with making sure that the will of the sovereign remains unopposed than with the use-value of people, with the human resources available as the state seeks to manage its economy and war machine.[38]

Shteyngart's novel effectively registers a new historical event, the neo-liberal privatization of the power over life and death, one in which a new kind of subject has emerged, "high net worth individuals" (HNWIs), who, when they like Ridley Scott's Roy Batty "want more life," can seek it in a private sector whose services are not available to LNWIs (low net worth individuals). The novel accomplishes its political analysis through the experiences of its "aesthetic subject," Lenny Abramov, who is both a "conceptual persona, generating concepts, and a literary figure, generating affects and percepts." And although the life extension corporation ultimately fails to deliver the services its high net worth clients seek (in the end "nature simply would not yield"),[39] the subjects its practices have created constitute part of a contemporary event; they reflect the emergence of a neo-liberal world that generates new forms of human capital. Moreover, it is not only a world that harbors an extreme level of social inequality but also a hyper-securitized world (revealed when Lenny has difficulty avoiding scrutiny on returning to the U.S. from Italy because the computerized interviewing icon – an onscreen animated otter – renders his statement that he befriended "some Italians" as "Somalians"). The world that Lenny's trajectory through the novel maps is in effect what Deleuze would refer to as an "actualization" of a contemporary problematic. Moreover, and crucially, Shteyngart's novel, whose characters and situations mimic that world, operates as critique, as a counter-actualization of the event it discloses and reflects.

In the chapters in this book, I canvass a variety of artistic texts that enact the kind of critical effect found in Shteyngart's novel, beginning with Chapter 1, which, influenced by neo-Kantian philosophies of aesthetics, treats a variety of artistic texts that offer critical forms of uncommon sense. I begin that chapter with a brief reprise of the significance of the Kantian revolution in philosophy for two reasons: first because traditional social science methodologies remain largely innocent of its implications, and second because it has shaped the critical perspectives that inform my methodological conceptions and applications throughout the studies in this book. After treating the implications of the Kantian revolution, the chapter sets up the rest of the book's studies by introducing and illustrating (with treatments of a variety of artistic genres) my primary methodological actants, diverse aesthetic subjects.

1 Philosophy, method and the arts

Prelude: the Kantian revolution

Considered in terms of their main tendencies, political science and political studies remain in a pre-Kantian epistemological slumber. Presuming that the world is responsible for what is perceived, they have slept through Kant's (self-described) Copernican Revolution, a change in the way to raise questions about the experience of the object world. Within a pre-Kantian philosophical framing, experience is engendered by that which appears, as opposed to that which lies behind appearance ("the intelligible essence").[1] To simplify at the outset, "appearances" constitute the data for empirical/explanatory analysis and "the intelligible essence" references the object of some versions of hermeneutic/interpretive analysis. What Kant contributed is a shift that enfranchises post-empiricist and post-hermeneutic modes of inquiry: "phenomenon will no longer at all be appearance."[2] Kantian epistemological orientations privilege *the conditions of possibility* for something to appear, an innovation in the philosophy of experience that puts critical pressure on the way that political inquiries have construed issues of method. Heeding that innovation in the midst of the "behavioral revolution" in political science in the mid-twentieth century, the political theorist Sheldon Wolin addressed himself to the implications of Kant's philosophy. Seeking to redeem the "tradition" of political theory, Wolin indicted the behaviorist trend in political science for its "methodism," for exhausting the space of political education with a preoccupation with methodological techniques, to the neglect of a historically informed and politically engaged knowledge.[3] Invoking the Kantian revolution in philosophy, Wolin asserted that "method" [in the sense in which empiricists construct it] "is not a thing for all worlds. It presupposes a certain answer to a Kantian type question, what must the world be like for the methodist's knowledge to be possible?"[4]

Although Wolin does not elaborate on this brief but pregnant Kantian aside, his provocation is well attuned to the Kantian contribution. Without going into elaborate detail on Kant's first critique: in overturning traditional philosophy's focus on the extent to which what appears can be reliably observed, Kant substitutes a productive mode of consciousness for mere passive perception and rejects a search for the essence or thing in itself behind the appearance. He introduces a subject who is no longer subjected to the object. Philosophically, it is a

phenomenological rather than an empiricist subject, one which retains a recep-
tive sensibility but also has an active understanding that legislates and reflects; a
subject responsible for constituting the conditions under which things can appear
as things. Consequently, within the Kantian philosophical frame, inquiry into
how one has the world requires elucidation of the structures and dynamics of
subjectivity. Moreover, rather than a concern with relationships among existing
objects of knowledge (an explanatory syntax), Kant's philosophical revolution,
as it has been elaborated in a variety of post-Kantian perspectives, encourages
inquiry into the forces that have brought such objects and their interrelations to
one's attention.[5]

Certainly Kant-inspired post-Kantian philosophy has yielded compelling alternatives to the consciousness-privileging Kantian subject. Among the most significant are the subject's involvement in the world and thus the "how" rather than
the "what" of subjectivity (the perspective of Martin Heidegger); the subject's
lack of unity – its conflicting multiplicities, rendered as the "which one" rather
than the what or how of subjectivity (a philosophical trajectory running from
Friedrich Nietzsche to Gilles Deleuze); and the subject who emerges as epiphenomenal to discursive practices, one located in the discursive formations within
which alternative subjectivities are possible (the perspective of Michel Foucault).
And while Kantian philosophy presumes the conditions of possibility for a
common sense (a *sensus communis*) and enframes that common sense within a
juridical figuration, critical post-Kantian philosophy – especially as exemplified
by Deleuze, Lyotard and Rancière – emphasizes dissensus and discord (drawing
on Kant's reluctant discovery in his "analytic of the sublime" that the sublime
evokes "pain, opposition, constraint, and discord," which makes it difficult to
achieve the "subjective necessity" that legislates in favor of common sense).[6]
Nevertheless, the Kantian legacy, with its focus on the conditions of possibility
for the emergence of what is perceived, encourages a recognition of multiplicity,
of alternative worlds (containing differently implicated subjects) within which
things can emerge as objects of knowledge.

The most perspicuous post-Kantian effects discernible in inquiry treat historically emerging modes of subjectivity rather than assume a timeless, universal
subject, conceived as a structure of apprehension. For example, in an application
of Kantian philosophy in an architectural treatise, Irwin Panofsky shows how
the subject fashioned in the emerging scholastic thought world was material-
ized in the design of the Gothic cathedral (beginning in the twelfth century).
In the former "mental habit," realized in the Romanesque cathedral, faith was
insulated from reason in a design that enacted in stone an ontological divide
between the reasoning/experiencing faculties and spirituality. In contrast, the
Gothic cathedral constituted a realization of "aesthetic subjectivism," mate-
rialized as a series of homologous spaces within which a subject with vision
could gain clarity about the interrelations of reflective thought and spirituality
as that subject moved through the cathedral's spaces.[7] Similarly, to consider a
more recent historical subject, Michel Foucault suggests that Édouard Manet
bears significant responsibility for the emergence of the "modern viewer."[8]
Manet's canvases, he observes, "played with the place of the viewer"[9] in such

a way that, in contrast with a world of fixed or immobile subjects, the spectator became "an individual exiled from his certainties regarding his place in the world."[10] Jonathan Crary offers a similar insight into Manet's disturbances to the formerly stable viewing subject. In an analysis of Manet's *The Balcony* (1868), he suggests that, "Manet's painting takes us outside the stable circuit of visuality to an arrangement in which neither eye nor objects in the world can be understood in terms of fixed positions and identities."[11]

With these post-Kantian challenges as background – the implications of which I elaborate and illustrate throughout this chapter – I want first to review the pre-Kantian methodological protocols of social science by revisiting my graduate school methodological training, which summoned instructional materials predicated on the assumption that we are in a unified, subjectively shared world within which inquiry's objects are those already residing in familiar political discourses. One implication of that assumption is that one has to heed only technical issues of measurement, reliability and validity and then test explanatory models to make inferences about relations among politically relevant objects. As a discourse of inquiry, the empiricist, pre-Kantian orientation prescribes a causal grammatical syntax that contains no problematic dimensions of subjectivity. As I will suggest, there are alternative, more politically attuned, grammars of inquiry.

The grammar of problems and the political assets of inquiry

In the mid-1960s, I was enrolled in a course designed to edify beginning political science PhD students about social science methods. One of the texts in the course, the multi-authored *Research Methods in Social Relations* by Claire Selltiz *et al.*, provided a basic narrative of the research process, introducing that process with a list of the "major steps in research":

1   A statement of purpose is made in the form of *formulating the problem*;
2   A description of the study design is given;
3   The methods of data collection are specified;
4   The results are presented;
5   Frequently, there follows a section on *conclusions and interpretation*.[12]

In retrospect, two aspects of the text's instructions are especially striking: its distribution of coverage and its assumption about the reading/evaluating constituency of the research. Both issues emerge in beginning sections. The "formulating the problem" discussion is a bit less than five pages and is exemplified in the sentence, "The formulation of the topic into a research problem is the first step in a scientific inquiry and, as such, should be influenced primarily by the requirements of scientific procedure."

Thereafter, the text devotes the rest of its 587 pages to steps 2 through 5, with most of its emphasis on step 3, "methods of data collection." As was the case with most of the methods approaches in social science in the mid-twentieth century, research design and causal inference occupied the bulk of the text's terrain of inquiry (and with few exceptions, "political research" methods books continue this tradition of coverage[13]). There is no attention to the historical context of inquiry, for example the methodological concern with why particular problems emerge at particular historical moments. Thus for example, Selltiz *et al.* don't acknowledge that their research agenda has been produced in the midst of what Paul Gilroy aptly terms "the color-line century."[14] Arguably, the twentieth century is a period of the hardening of a racial-spatial order in the U.S., especially as it is manifested in urban space. As Robert Crooks suggests, the violence that took place on America's western frontier (an inter-nation frontier) during the nineteenth century, shifted to urban frontiers – in his terms, a "transformation of the frontier from a moving western boundary into a relatively fixed partitioning of urban space ... a racial frontier."[15] However, the racial and ethnic fault-lines within social orders, which affect the differential assets deployed for alternative constituencies or assemblages by different formulations of research problems, are not noted by Selltiz *et al.* as relevant to the "formulation of the research problem."

I choose the word, "asset," because less than a decade after being exposed to *Research Methods in Social Relations*, I encountered Michel Foucault's most method-oriented work, *The Archaeology of Knowledge*, and have since been especially attentive to his remarks about the value of statements, where he writes, "To analyze a discursive formation is ... to weigh the value of statements. A value that is not defined by their truth, that is not gauged by the presence of a secret content; but which characterizes their place, their capacity for circulation and exchange." Foucault goes on to suggest that statements should be regarded as "assets" and to note that to interrogate statements is not to seek to discover either the fidelity of what they are about (the empiricist focus on representation) or their intelligibility when their silent context is disclosed (a hermeneutic focus on disclosure), but to note the way they pose "the question of power" because the statement is "an asset that ... poses the question of power [and is thus] ... by nature, the object of a struggle, a political struggle."[16]

In contrast to Selltiz *et al.*'s exclusively technical approach to inquiry – where the only judgments solicited are from a scientifically oriented research constituency – Foucault's remarks on discursive formations offer a way to articulate inquiry into historico-political encounters with concrete "assemblages" (entities constructed through very specific historical processes:[17] with something at stake in the way inquiries approach explanation, interpretation or critique. To give Foucault's suggestion that discursive formations deploy assets a concrete historical example (one that resonates with Gilroy's expression, "the color-line century"), I offer a brief illustration supplied by Clyde Woods in his analysis of the racial partialities in the history of social science. Investigating an "arrested development" in the Mississippi Delta, which resulted from economic policies during the New Deal period in American politics, Woods contrasts "plantation bloc explanation" with "blues epistemology." He points out that the plantation system has persisted not only as an exploitive agricultural capitalism but also as an ontology and way of knowing.

Woods' analysis emphasizes the way the plantation perspective has been articulated through social science explanation, as a "world view," one in which "the planter [is] the heroic master of a natural ethnic, class, gender and environmental hierarchy." The "plantation movement in social science," inaugurated in the late nineteenth century, developed a model of the "Negro problem," wherein "racial friction," based on (allegedly) natural antipathies, stood in the way of the economic and political progress that agricultural capitalism promises.[18] To that social science-assisted epistemological framing, Woods juxtaposes "blues epistemology," which articulates a history of African American practices of knowing and assembling that contest the ontological and epistemological hegemony of the plantation bloc. As he puts it, blues epistemology serves as a resource for the "constant reestablishment of collective sensibility in the face of constant attacks by the plantation bloc and its allies." It reaffirms "the historical commitment to social and personal investigation, description, and criticism present in the blues."[19] He points out that, while the blues developed "as a theory of African American aesthetics" and as a form of social criticism, "social science remained unscathed."[20] They have been collusive with "the planters' mythical ethno-regional system of explanation."[21]

Doubtless for those attuned to the familiar social research paradigms, the political register of blues is hard to discern. What may appear to some as mere entertainment – for example Bessie Smith's song "Crazy Blues" (1920) – registers itself among much of the African American assemblage as "an insurrectionary social text ... contributing to an evolving discourse on black revolutionary violence in the broadest sense ... black violence as a way of resisting white violence and unsettling a repressive social order."[22] Although racial antagonisms and the bases of white hegemony have receded significantly since Bessie Smith was lyrically addressing herself to racial divisions, fault-lines with historical depth remain. Thus to appreciate the force of Woods' contrast between "plantation bloc explanation" and "blues epistemology," is to recognize that the "social" component of "socio-spatial relations" contains sharp divisions, based on (among other things) differences in the historical trajectories of arrival into social space of different historical groups, especially as coerced versus voluntary labor. Those modes of arrival have had a lasting legacy with respect to the value of social knowledge that the ahistorical protocols of traditional social research methods cannot acknowledge.

There are also inquiry-relevant fault-lines that exist across societies and nations. For example, to cite another politically attuned critique of social science's historical inattention to the constituencies that its technically-oriented method-obsessive focus enfranchises, we can heed the philosopher/poet from Martinique, Aimé Césaire's reflection on the way Euro America has located the Hitler phenomenon in fields of knowledge. As I have noted elsewhere, the Hitler experience shaped two major dimensions of post-World War II political science. One was a political psychology that sought to discover the cognitive features of the fascism-sympathizing personality (for example, the investigations of Theodor W. Adorno and associates, Milton Rokeach, and H. J. Eysenck, among others).[23] Another was "comparative politics," a sub-discipline whose inquiries were predicated on a fear of political instability and an assumption that a fascist-proof political system must institutionalize structural impediments to office-holding by partisans with extreme or marginal political agendas. Both dimensions of political inquiry were predicated on the assumption that the Hitler phenomenon (understood as racist and/or ethnocidal violence) was a historical aberration.[24]

Césaire, who emphasizes the global fault-line separating Europe from its former colonies, suggests a radically different historical narrative for understanding the Hitler phenomenon. Incorporating that phenomenon within a history of what he calls Western European barbarism, he suggests that the peoples of Europe have failed to appreciate that what they suffered during the Nazi period – if viewed historically and from the point of view of the former colonies – was not a singular phenomenon. Certainly it was "barbarism," he writes, but:

> Before they were its victims, they were its accomplices; that they tolerated Nazism before it was inflicted on them, that they absolved it, shut their eyes to it, legitimized it, because, until then, it had been applied only to non-European peoples; that they have cultivated that Nazism, that they were responsible for it ... European man's [complaint against Hitler is not Hitler's] *crime* in itself, *the crime against man*, it is not *the humiliation of man as such*, it is the crime against the white man, the humiliation of the white man, and the fact that he has applied to Europe colonialist procedures which until then had been reserved exclusively for the Arabs of Algeria, the coolies of India, and the blacks of Africa.[25]

As these two illustrations suggest, if, rather than focusing on the technical aspects of inquiry we want to recognize the alternative knowledge constituencies – predicated on alternative ways of becoming part of the world – that inquiry can serve, we have to turn our attention to past moments of individual and collective encounter. Such a focus encourages inquiry into the historical context of "problems" and thus into the different worlds in which those problems have been made to appear. When viewed from a historico-political perspective, the concepts formulated in theoretical inquiries call for more than measurement and validation protocols. Rather, as Gilles Deleuze and Félix Guattari suggest (in Kantian philosophy-edified terms), concepts articulate a "zone" or "neighborhood" that is connected to the historical development of the "possible worlds" within which concepts and their attendant problematics emerge.[26]

What then is the appropriate grammar for referencing the multiplicity of worlds and acknowledging the diverse stakes for alternative assemblages within those worlds? Foucault provides relevant instruction on the historicity of problems by pointing to the historical moments in which alternative subjects emerge within different historical worlds. It is a strategy he employs in order to achieve distance from familiar "problems." As he puts it at the outset of his second volume on the history of sexuality, in order to attend to "the history of successive forms" and appreciate how peculiar the contemporary form is, he had "to stand detached from it, bracket its familiarity, in order to analyze the theoretical and practical context with which it has been associated."[27] He achieves that detachment by looking at periods in which there have been different problematizations of sexuality. The grammatical shift from "problem" to "problematization" effects a change from a static thing to the connotation of a historical process of thing-making. Using this altered grammar, Foucault shows for example that, "starting from the modern era, and proceeding back through Christianity to antiquity, one finds certain activities and the pleasures that attach to it, an object of moral solicitude." By asking "why and in what forms was sexuality constituted as a moral domain?" and "why this 'problematization'?"[28] he is able to point to historical forces sequestered within what are ultimately represented as problems and thus to allow one to "learn to what extent the effort to think one's own history can free thought from what it silently thinks, and so enable it to think differently."[29] Similarly, when asked about his decision to emphasize the emergence of the prison as the primary practice of punishment, Foucault again emphasized the need for detachment from the now all-too-familiar use of imprisonment. "It's a matter," he states, "of shaking this false self-evidence, of making visible not its arbitrariness, but its complex interconnection with a multiplicity of historical processes, many of them of recent date."[30]

Clearly, Foucault's historical analysis of the emergence of confinement as the primary mode of punishment – which he elaborates to include the historical development of a wide variety of carceral apparatuses (agencies of care as well as coercion and confinement) – provides a *critique* that is not an asset for those who enjoy a class privilege in which their economic activities, whether benign or predatory, are not criminalized. Predicated on the assumption that a history of punishment is articulated with systems of domination, or at least struggle, Foucault's analysis of the development of the prison shows convincingly that modern apparatuses for levying penalties are less politically significant in terms of what they manage to punish than in terms of the practices they either enable or inhibit. As he puts it:

> Penalty would ... appear to be a way of handling illegalities, of laying down the limits of tolerance, of giving free rein to some, of putting pressure on others, of excluding a particular section, of making another useful, or neutralizing certain individuals and of profiting from others, In short, penalty does not simply 'check' illegalities; it 'differentiates' them, it provides them with a general 'economy'. And, if one can speak of justice, it is not only because the law itself or the way of applying it serves the interests of a class, it is also because the differential administration of illegalities through the mediation of penalty forms part of the mechanisms of domination.[31]

Foucault's insight into the class privilege-related politics of penalties can serve to differentiate between a typical social science approach to criminality – for example one that seeks causal explanations of the different types of persons who end up involved in illicit practices[32] – and a critically oriented investigation that seeks to identify the historically emerging authority-sanctioned privileges that authorize what is licit versus illicit. For example, recognizing that "drugs" are among the world's primary commodities and that "there is no hard-and-fast alkaloidal or natural distinction between illicit drugs and other drug-like goods," one critically oriented inquiry has focused on the differential policing (interdiction, prosecution, sentencing, versus trade assistance from governmental agencies) of drug flows in order to discern precisely what Foucault has addressed: whose activities in regard to the flows have been enabled and whose have been subject to "the day-to-day dirty work of policing."[33] As the investigator points out, once we look at the way drugs as commodities are differentially enabled versus policed, our investigation becomes *"historically* deeper; it helps interrogate how illicit drugs were 'made' during the dual process of forming early modern world capitalism and modern nation states."[34]

The "critical attitude"

The prison for Foucault is at the center of what he calls a power/knowledge-related "regime of truth," a discourse on criminality that has privileged places for certain speaker/judges (jurists, forensic psychiatrists, prison administrators, social workers, and other disciplinary agents), whose control over truth is occasionally challenged when, for example, prisoners "confiscate, at least temporarily, the power to speak on prison conditions."[35] Crucially, for the purpose of approaching a philosophy of method, Foucault's investigation of the history of punishment and its eventuation in what he terms "the disciplinary society" is an implementation of a "critical attitude," an epistemological mentality that he addresses in his reflections on Kant's brief response to the question "what is enlightenment?" (published in the journal, *Berlinische Monatschrift*, in 1784).

I turn here to that reflection (which I also address briefly in the Preface) because the "critical attitude" that Foucault derives and re-inflects from his reading of Kant implies that the "assets" deployed by theoretical discourses empower a critical – as opposed to a partisan or identity – politics. Rather than merely serving particular social segments or disempowered groups, such an attitude is designed to "understand the present" in terms of its difference of today "with respect to yesterday." In this respect, the constituencies that critical inquiries are designed to serve are all inclusive. The critical attitude presents a challenge to identity politics in general: it encourages self-reflection rather than capitulation to the already-institutionalized identity spaces available within prevailing power arrangements – even those on which some challenging social movements are predicated. In Kant's perspective, the critical attitude is designed to give people a "way out" of their capitulation to authority or, in his terms, their "self-imposed immaturity,"[36] thereby encouraging them to dare to engage in unhindered participation in public reasoning. In Foucault's terms, expressed once he takes leave of his explication of the Kantian answers, "enlightenment" involves the "permanent reactivation of [the critical] attitude … that is, of a philosophical ethos that could be described as a permanent critique of our historical era." Its political implications inhere in the way it deprives the present of its necessity.[37] To summarize in Foucault's terms, "criticism" is neither aimed toward finding "formal structures with universal value" nor toward "making metaphysics possible." Rather, it's aimed at treating "the instances of discourse that articulate what we think, say and do." It is to be a "historical ontology of ourselves."[38] Such an ontology is an antidote to submitting unreflectively to coercive forms of knowledge by revealing the "effects of power they generate."[39]

Foucault's "philosophical ethos" is predicated on three intimately interconnected axes that must be analyzed: "The axis of knowledge, the axis of power, and the axis of ethics."[40] Accordingly, the politics of the "critical attitude" to which he refers follows the Kantian challenge to resist the modes of subjectivity that authorities impose (and are subsequently self-imposed). As he puts it elsewhere, "We need to promote new forms of subjectivities by renouncing the type of individuality that was imposed on us over several centuries."[41] Félix Guattari offers a similar version of that philosophical ethos, which he enacted in his therapeutic practice. Faced with an "ethical choice," he had decided that rather than "scientise subjectivity" and impose a search for the etiology of the patient's abnormality, he sought to grasp subjectivity in its "processural creativity." Which, as applied to his psychiatric practice, implies developing a scenario that gives the patient space for "multiple strategies of subjectivation" or self-fashioning.[42] Guattari's practice, like Foucault's critical attitude, derives from a perspective on philosophy as a practice of creativity rather than discovery.

The relevant implication of such a philosophical ethos for my purposes is how it orients an approach to inquiry. While empiricist philosophies of social science have been preoccupied with questions of the validity and reliability of knowledge claims, a critically oriented philosophical ethos encourages an aesthetic mode of apprehension: articulated as the invention of new concepts deployed on a variety of genres of expression, rather than the acceptance of existing conceptualizations of familiar "problems." Jacques Rancière refers to this mode of apprehension as "aesthetic experience," which disturbs authoritative distributions of social identity. In his words, "Aesthetic experience has a political effect to the extent that ... it disturbs the way in which bodies fit their functions and destinations ... It has a multiplication of connections and disconnection that reframe the relation between bodies, the world where they live and the way in which they are 'equipped' for fitting it."[43]

For the purpose of illustration, I turn here to an example I have addressed elsewhere in a critical re-inflection of the concept of fear. In social science, fear has usually been conceptualized as a problem of individual and collective psychology – for example, the conceptualization used by psychologists in several military-sponsored studies aimed at helping soldiers overcome their fear in battle.[44] To conceive of fear in a way that gives it political and epistemic status instead of rendering it as a psychological attribute, we have to distance ourselves from its current mode of problematization. For that purpose, I evoke a historical moment in which "fears" were juxtaposed to "beliefs" in an encounter that took place in the arctic region in 1924 (reported by the writer, Barry Lopez). Lopez writes, "A central Eskimo shaman named Aua, queried by Knud Rasmussen, a Danish anthropologist, about Eskimo beliefs, answered, 'We do not believe, we fear'."[45]

Instead of attributing the shaman's answer to misunderstanding, Lopez's discussion encourages inquiry into the genealogy of our concern with such cognitive concepts as beliefs. Rather than being concerned with the validity and reliability of statements about beliefs, the question that would direct such an inquiry would pursue the forces that have made the concept of belief so central to a social science, such as anthropology. As I put it elsewhere, "With such a questioning, we are set on a track that helps to disclose the contemporary politics of fear."[46] Aua's response reflects the Eskimo way of problematizing security. In their everyday lives, they practice an epistemology of fear in order to protect themselves from (for example) marauding polar bears or frenzied walruses during a hunt. To feel fear is to be constantly alert to imminent danger. By contrast, "we" (in contemporary industrial/commercial societies) practice an epistemology of belief because for us, security is mediated by various agencies – insurance companies, the Defense Department, the police, the army, and so on. Belief is a cognitive category that attracted scholarly scrutiny because security-related institutions and agencies that have needed to legitimate their practices wanted to know if their ways of managing danger, reported through a variety of media, were being positively received. In short, beliefs "are phenomena that are intimately connected to a variety of institutionalized interests and procedures involved in indirect influence."[47]

Here I want to extend that observation with reference to a specific project. Although not all social science approaches to belief serve particular security agencies, my example represents a typical type of cold war-influenced inquiry, designed to aid Defense Department policy-makers. In the mid-1960s – at a time when "military contract research organizations [sponsored] … massive volumes of psychological and other types of work for the DOD"[48] – that agency, along with other federal agencies, funded a "defense beliefs" project run by the Oakridge National Laboratories, a research institution that began with a mandate to do research on "civil defense." Focusing on the consequences of a nuclear attack on the U.S. it was eventually decided that "the research also required understanding the reactions of people under stresses that would accompany emergency use of underground shelters … the Laboratory hired its first social scientists."[49] The research of the social scientists ultimately expanded to the treatment of U.S. citizens' reactions to defense and military policies as a whole. To note one example: in an investigation entitled, "Dimensions of Defense Opinion: The American Public" (funded by the Atomic Energy Agency, the Office of Civil Defense, and DARPA, the Advanced Research Projects Agency of the Defense Department), the researchers on the Laboratory's social science staff focused on "public opinion on national security matters," and investigated attitude configurations. They found that, among many other things, the American public's support for various kinds of military hardware is largely unrelated to "the believed desirability of disarmament."[50]

If our focus is on social science's twentieth-century romance with psychological attributes such as attitudes and beliefs, the constituencies for the research are more interesting than the findings. Certainly, as I have suggested, the sponsoring agencies were interested in the reception of security policy. And the research – which employed the then popular attitude scaling research technique, factor analysis – was pitched to methods-interested social science practitioners as well. As the authors conclude, "The purpose of this paper has been less to test specific hypotheses that to explore the explanatory potential of concepts in the literature for handling defense opinion variance."[51] Thus, the findings, equivocal though they were, about the "defense thinking" of American psychological subjects, were designed to have value for both policy-makers and social scientists.

Aesthetic subjects

What I want to note at this point is that there is a way to challenge the philosophical ethos of social science's romance with the psychological subject and at the same time pursue a "critical attitude" with a different kind of subject – what I call an "aesthetic subject." Aesthetic subjects are those who, through artistic genres, articulate and mobilize thinking. For example, the value of conceiving subjects aesthetically rather than psychologically becomes evident in Pierre Vidal-Nacquet's reading of Aeschylus's tragedy, *Seven Against Thebes*. He points out that some commentators have been perplexed by the behavior of the tragedy's main protagonist, Eteocles, the king of Thebes. Eteocles seems to have a disjunctive personality, changing from "a man who is 'cool' and at ease, ready-witted and concerned for the morale of his people" at one point in the tragedy to a man "driven and out of control, seemingly finally overcome by the curse imposed on his lineage by the Oedipus saga" at another point. However, attempts to impose a unified personality on a character in a tragedy who seems reasonable at one stage and unreasonable at another, are not sufficiently genre-sensitive. As Vidal-Nacquet points out, "Eteocles is not a 'human being', reasonable or otherwise ... He is a figure in a Greek tragedy ... the values that stand in contrast to each other [at various points in the tragedy], the values of the *polis* and those connected with the world of the family, are not states of mind."[52]

The inquiry implications of displacing psychological subjects with aesthetic subjects are also well illustrated when we consider another genre: romantic film. In Leo Bersani and Ulysse Dutoit's analysis of Jean-Luc Godard's *Contempt* (1963) – a film in which a couple becomes estranged as the wife, Camille (Bridget Bardot), has her feelings for her husband, Paul (Michel Piccoli), turned from love to contempt – they note that Godard's focus is not on "the psychic origins of contempt" but on "its effects on the world." In the context of cinema, that shift in focus is conveyed by "what contempt does to cinematic space ... how it affect[s] the visual field within which Godard works, and especially the range and kinds of movement allowed for in that space." Like Aeschylus's Eteocles, Godard's Camille and Paul are best understood as aesthetic rather than psychological subjects. Their movements and dispositions are less significant in terms of what is revealed about their inner lives than what they tell us about the world to which they belong.[53]

We can also look at aesthetic subjects to treat the "security" issue that prompted the Oak Ridge social science division's investigations. A turn to the arts – rather than to the psychological framework of social science – yields a different kind of political apprehension of security, framing it within a different political ontology and a different spatial imaginary. To return to Barry Lopez's account of the conversation between Knud Rasmussen and Aua, I want to emphasize the way it recovers a moment of encounter between two incommensurate knowledge cultures. At the particular moment that the encounter took place, knowledge-and information-seeking about the security practices of an exotic group – rather than coercion – was on the social scientist's agenda. However, rather than deepening our understanding of exotic belief systems, the encounter tells us about the historical moment in which a developing, security-oriented knowledge problematic shaped the inquiry.

Ultimately, if we want to pursue the encounter implications of alternative security knowledge cultures, we have to recognize that "security" operates within a relational economy – the security of one party is intimately connected with the insecurity of another. For example, during the first Gulf War in the 1990s while social scientists were analyzing the conflict within a geo-strategic frame as a post-cold war reorientation of international antagonisms, a comparative literature scholar, Rob Nixon, was turning to literature to provide his students with a way of conceiving the conflict from a different point of view. Pointing out that "few subjects resist a national frame as self-evidently as oil," and desiring to emancipate the students from "the self-enclosed stories that the United States tells itself," he selected works by non-Americans that give the "oil story historical depth and geographical reach" in order to transform the class's "inner geography."[54] Among the course's readings was a quintet of novels, *Cities of Salt*, written in the mid-1980s by the Jordanian writer Abdelrahman Munif. The novels deal with the 1930s, when Americans came and found oil, which not only produced catastrophic effects on the environment but also displaced a group of Bedouins, who "found themselves at the violent end of another cultural novelty: a police force, instructed to beat to death, if necessary, any nomads who refuse to leave their oil-rich lands."[55] In contrast with the geopolitical view of oil, which emphasizes its strategic significance in the context of global antagonisms, Munif's story mobilizes diverse aesthetic subjects who try in vain to stop the local emir from allowing predatory oil companies to destroy the oases that constitute their world. When the emir tells a delegation from the oasis known as Wadi al-Uyoun (which was ultimately leveled by heavy equipment) that by allowing the oil exploration they "will be among the richest and happiest of all mankind," the leader of the delegation responds "As you know, Your Excellency … money is not everything in this world. More important are honor, ethics, and our traditions."[56] But the Bedouins' entreaties fall on deaf ears. By the end of the novel, most of them are dead or dispersed.

Like the story of oil, the story of rubber yields insights into the way the securing of a life style in one place produces radical insecurity in another. One version of that story is told by Sven Lindqvist, who begins with that seemingly benign moment in 1887, when "the Scottish surgeon, J. B. Dunlop hit upon the idea of equipping his small son's bicycle with an inflatable rubber tube."[57] Ultimately (with of course several steps in between), driven by the growing trade and profitability of rubber, the "natives [in Belgium's African colonies] were obliged to supply both rubber and labor," and after pockets of labor resistance developed, King Leopold's policing agents engaged in "wholesale slaughter in several districts."[58]

From a methodological point of view, more significant than the disturbing substance of the story Lindqvist tells is the innovative structure of his textual approach. To tell the story of the extermination of much of Africa's native population by Europeans in the nineteenth century, Lindqvist fashions *himself* as an aesthetic subject. He enacts a travel story as he visits the extermination sites to reflect on the violent nineteenth-century European–African encounters, while at the same time interspersing archival material to rehearse the rationales used to justify the slaughters. Rendering his investigation a "story of a man [Lindqvist] traveling by bus through the Sahara desert while simultaneously traveling by computer through the history of the concept of extermination, he provides a view of Europe's encounter with Africa that is largely fugitive within traditional geo-political narratives. In small, sand-ridden desert hotels, his investigation is driven by one sentence in Joseph Conrad's *Heart of Darkness:* 'Exterminate all the brutes'."[59] Textually, Conrad accompanies Lindqvist in his travels, through the many references Lindqvist provides from the story of Conrad's famous novel. However, rather than critique it as European literature on the colonial experience in Africa, I want to break away at this point from Lindqvist's compelling story and let African writers tell their stories, as they produce aesthetic subjects with trajectories of movement and interpersonal engagement that render insights into the multiplicity of spaces, temporalities and role types that now constitute the African reality.

Resisting "the invention of Africa"[60]

As is well known, the mainstream social science approach to the African continent has been dominated by the concept of political development. Usually operating at a macropolitical level – for example a focus on the ideological cast of the leadership in diverse African states – many U.S.-initiated inquiries have been concerned with how to interpret the extent to which African states can be relied on to further U.S. economic and security interests. One such inquiry is exemplary, Crawford Young's *Ideology and Development in Africa*, which was sponsored by the "African Project of U.S. Council on Foreign Relations." Canvassing various kinds of regimes and their "development pathways": "Afro-Marxist," "Populist Socialist," and "African Capitalist," Young's investigation is explicitly "designed to focus both on Africa and on the significance for the United States."[61] Looking back on that kind of inquiry, Achille Mbembe notes that there has been "hardly ever any discourse about Africa for itself":

> In the very principle of its constitution, in its language, and in its finalities, narrative about Africa is the mediation that enables the West to accede to its own consciousness and give a public account of its subjectivity. Thus there is no need to look for the status of this discourse; essentially, it has to do at best with self-deception, and at worst with perversion.[62]

Briefly, Mbembe (as is the case with some other African scholars) provides a different, more realistic locus from which one can discern the multiplicity that has hitherto been condensed into the (racialized) territory thought to be "Africa." As he puts it, "there is no African identity that could be designated by a single word or subsumed under a single category. African identity does not exist as a substance."[63] In accordance with Mbembe's observation, I want to illustrate the methodological insights that derive from the way that what he calls "African self-writing" effectively juxtaposes an aesthetic subject to social science's ideological, regime-oriented subject. The self-writing to which Mbembe refers displaces the moribund macropolitical concern with "development" (social science's version of the civilizing mission in which Africa is always understood in terms of what it lacks) with a micropolitical concern with the complexities that constitute Africa; complexities that exist in the form of, among other things, fractionated subjectivities.[64] As Mbembe points out, what is now observable as "Africa" is based on a variety of intersecting historical tempos, a "multiplicity of times, trajectories, and rationalities" which are sometimes "local" but are also characterized by "rhythms heavily conditioned by European domination."[65]

Many African authors, writing in English, capture the multiplicity to which Mbembe refers. But it is "a new English [that is] still in communion with its ancestral home but altered to suit its new African surroundings."[66] For example, as Sam Opondo suggests, in contrast with the Africa that emerges in the Danish settler/writer, Isaac Dinesin's, autobiography (a romanticizing of "authentic Africanness") is the Africa that emerges in Marjorie Oludhe Macgoye's poem *Song of Nyarloka*, "a poetic venture into the everyday rhythms and practices [which] … achieves important insights into the plural character of citiness and Africanness [while it] … resists developmentalist and statist representations of the African city."[67] While there are numerous other examples of African "self-writing" that provide realistic aesthetic challenges to the statist developmental paradigm, I want to focus on one novel – Ben Okri's *The Famished Road* (1991) – because of the way its protagonist (its primary aesthetic subject named Azaro, who functions as a mythological "concept-metaphor") is paradoxically realistic *because* he is mythical. Azaro is an "Abiku," an in-between subject, a child with a connection to the living and to the dead spirit world at once. The Abiku subject's "in-betweenness" devolves from the reality that many children "succumb to illnesses within their first year of their birth." Their situation therefore "lends meaning to unbearable loss."[68] The use of a subject who exists in the present, while at the same time carrying memories of the past, reflects the ways in which the society has a socio-historical culture that contains layers of time. As Jorge Fernandes puts it, "The Abiku's subjectivity is marked by an antecedent that colors his experience of the present, suggesting that all subjectifications are always already haunted by a history of previous encounters."[69] The use of a mythical protagonist is therefore not a departure from realism but rather its affirmation. The Abiku subject affirms the existence of a particular form of cultural understanding. Against those who would locate his novel as merely magical rather than realistic, Ben Okri points out that "everyone's reality is superstitious (the scientist's because her/his "view of the world … is provisional"; "the atheist's view … because of the way it excludes," etc.).[70] Moreover, as a child who is among other things "a bundle of impulses, sensations, emotions and perceptions,"[71] Okri's Azaro is a quintessential aesthetic subject inasmuch as *aisthitikos* – the ancient Greek word/concept from which aesthetics is derived – refers to the pre-linguistic, embodied, or feeling-based aspect of perception.

In addition to its affects and percepts, Okri's novel contains a cultural inter-discursivity – a charged meaning inter-articulation that reflects both a history of African superstition and Africa's assimilation of European superstitions. There are moments when Azaro functions within a narrative that observes the present world of objects and other moments when there is a sudden shift to "the mythopoetic description of the 'other reality'."[72] For example, there is a scene in Azaro's parent's house which is followed by a magical one, shifting from a family household to the world of kindred spirits:

> One moment I was in the room and the next moment I found myself wandering the night roads, I had no idea how I had gotten outside. I walked on the dissolving streets and among the terrestrial bushes. The air was full of riddles. I walked through books and months and forgotten histories. I was following a beautiful woman with a blue head. She moved in cadenzas of golden light. She floated in the wind of a royal serenity.[73]

With what is effectively a mythic narration, Okri "clears a space for the texture and structure of African folkloric narrative."[74] And because that narrative colors the everyday lives of the people who are the referents of the novel's characters (in *The Famished Road* as well as in his other novels), the stylized mythos Okri creates constitutes "the real." As Fernandes aptly puts it, Okri's novels "are nodes where histories and styles intercept. As an author, he is thus as much a creator as he is a medium through whom history, languages, and cultures flow." His "intertextual gestures" challenge the discourses within which African identities have been simplistically territorialized and substitutes a complex process of contending positionalities.[75] What, then, can we say about the epistemic status of such fictional texts? To answer this we need to inquire into authorial subjectivity.

Writing: the politics of fiction

What is the difference between the social science investigator – whose text reports and interprets the results of interview protocols or other data collected from or about individuals and collectives – and the fiction writer who invents her/his subjects and their experiential data? In one crucial epistemologically relevant sense they both stand at a distance from their materials. However, among their differences is the presumption of the social science researcher that her/his subject position is irrelevant to inquiry. By contrast, the fiction author practices a mobile subjectivity that develops in the writing process. The genre theorist, M. M. Bakhtin, conceives that mobility with reference to the way authors are open to themselves by seeing themselves as "unconsummated," as subjects who are always becoming: who are, as he puts it, "axiologically yet-to-be." That mode of self-recognition articulates itself through the ways they fashion the "lived lives" of their protagonists as dynamics of accommodation to a complex world.[76]

Frantz Fanon famously applies such insights about the fragility and mobility of authorial subjectivity to the historical implementation of race difference. Describing his experience of the rift between his practice of self-identification and the way he was interpolated by the "white other," when, as he puts it, "the corporeal schema crumbled [and] its place was taken by a racial epidermal schema,"[77] Fanon writes:

> I had sketched a historico-racial schema ... The elements that I used had been provided not by 'residual sensations and perceptions primarily of a tactile, vestibular, kinesthetic, and visual character.' But by the other, the white man, who had woven me out of a thousand details, anecdotes, stories. I thought that what I had in hand was to construct a physiological self, to balance space, to localize sensations, and here I was called on for more.[78]

To pursue the methodological implications of the historical intimacy between blackness and whiteness to which Fanon's "epidermalization" – his experience of becoming "black," against his own self-fashioning assumptions – attests, I contrast a typical social science investigation with two literary enactments of that historical intimacy. First, the social science version: Keith Reeves's *Voting Hopes or Fears?* is an investigation that adheres assiduously to scientific protocols. It is an inquiry into the "latent racial effects" of "white" voting preferences in connection with, among others, the 1982 California Gubernatorial Race.[79] Carefully wrought and cogently argued, his research shows a marked decrease in "white" voting preferences for "black" candidates as the election campaigns proceed. Employing the typical syntax of social science explanation – an emphasis on "what causes what"[80] – Reeves attributes the decrease in "white" support for "black" candidates over the course of the campaigns to the way the media emphasizes the racial backgrounds of the candidates. He interprets the change as a racial bias that is amplified by media-generated racial awareness.

Although within conventional social science protocols Reeves's data support his interpretations, from a more critical conceptual perspective with historical depth, we can interrogate the limitations of his use of the reified identities of what he calls "white respondents" and "black candidates." Hortense Spillers famously addresses such reifications effectively in her critique of the famous Moynihan Report on "The Negro Family" (which attributes the cause of African American poverty to the frequent absence of African American fathers). The Report, she suggests, constructs "the white family, by implication, the Negro family by outright assertion, in a constant opposition of binary meanings."[81] She goes on to connect the Report's ascription of ethnicity to a temporal strategy: "Ethnicity in this case freezes in meaning, takes on constancy, assumes the look and affects of the Eternal."[82]

The two literary treatments of "racial" encounters I want to review avoid freezing racial identity. The movement trajectories of their protagonists show how racial identity emerges from a historically evolving set of relationships and encounters, not a set of individual attributes. The first such treatment is Russell Banks' *Continental Drift* (1985), a novel in which two moving bodies – those of Bob Dubois, an oil burner repairman from New Hampshire, and Vanise Dorsinville, a Haitian refugee – meet off the coast of Florida (on Bob's boat that is running Haitian refugees to Florida) after both have struggled through dangerous and emotionally fraught experiences of adaptation to their changing environments. The novel constitutes a challenge not only to reified racial identities but also to a fixed view of geopolitical space. The stories of Bob and Vanise – two diasporic bodies: both with French surnames, which reflect earlier migrations – provide a view of the planet that privileges flows rather than geopolitical units and demonstrate the contingency of encounter rather than affirming a linear narrative in which states represent the political completion of the human community. Their stories suggest that what is known as the "people" of the United States is a product not of the evolution of a natural community but rather of "overlapping diasporas" and identity-shaping encounters.[83]

Most significantly for our purpose, is what Bob's encounters with racial difference reveal about whiteness. He had not experienced himself as white until he got to Florida and for the first time recognized himself as a color-coded outsider in a space populated by "racial" others, whose attractiveness and seemingly comfortable adaption to Florida's spaces made him feel dislocated from his usual assumptions about *his* belonging and the superiority of whiteness. As Bob's discomfort is articulated in the novel, looking at "the American blacks … the Jamaicans and Haitians [and] … the Cubans – these working people who got here first … Bob is embarrassed by his lateness, [and] He feels ugly in his winter-gray skin."[84] Having become thus disoriented, when he becomes intimately involved with a "black" woman, Marguerite, he "falls to contemplating the love of a Southern black woman and the kind of Northern white man it will make of him,"[85] Ultimately, in addition to its privileging of movement rather than fixed settlement, Banks's novel – focused on the relationality from which whiteness emerges – makes it evident that, phenomenologically, "race" is a function of identity becomings that result from historically contingent encounters, rather than being a trait derived from fixed essences. Moreover, in accord with the mobile subjectivity that attends the fiction writer's creative experience, Banks attests that his sense of obligation to the human community developed *as* he engaged in writing: "I was so self-destructive, so angry and turbulent, that I don't think I could have become a useful citizen in any other way." And, specifically as regards the thematic in his *Continental Drift*, Banks's becoming-a-citizen-through-writing was a process of becoming active: "If you are a member of a society or culture that is racist and sexist – as ours is – and you don't offer an ongoing critique of that as part of your daily life, then you're inevitably going to end up participating in it."[86]

The second illustration, which I am taking from Hari Kunzru's novel *The Impressionist* (2002), lends more historical depth to the understanding of the encounters that give rise to racial becomings. It begins its narrative of a process of becoming white at an earlier historical juncture – one that is crucial to the formation of "racial" division. The setting of the novel is colonial India during the period in which the colonial experience played a major role in the shaping of what came to be understood as whiteness. Kunzru's protagonist (and primary aesthetic subject) begins his life as Pran Nath Razdan, who is represented by his mother as her wealthy Indian husband's child but is actually the product of her earlier, brief encounter with a "white" English scientist, who drowned in a flood shortly after they co-habited. When his putative Indian father dies and it is discovered that he is not the true heir, the fifteen-year-old Pran is pitched into the street and barred from the estate. In desperation, he realizes that becoming white by managing impressions, which is a possibility given his very light skin tone, is his best shot at survival.

Here Georg Lukács's approach to the protagonist of the historical novel is instructive. He shows how the novel's thematic has been historically implicated in implementing the construction of "historical-social types" and in displaying the "subject events" and "performative forces governing the acts of individuation that anchor their narrative organization."[87] Accordingly, as Kunzru's "historical-social type," Pran sets about inventing himself (and thus confronting the forces that make performative demands on those seeking an altered subject position). His first step in the direction of his whiteness project is facilitated by an English Major, Privett-Clampe, to whom he is assigned as a sex servant in a palace that contains both colonial functionaries and agencies that service them. Although Pran gained entry to be groomed as a sex servant, the Major becomes more interested in making him literate than in having sex with him. He gives Pran reading lessons, so that eventually Pran acquires the major's English idiom and style of pronunciation.

However, once he escapes from the palace and ends up as a servant in a Christian mission, Pran's locutionary style, as he "tries to hold Privett-Clampe's voice inside his mouth,"[88] is still inadequate to allow him to escape his identity as a "blackie white." But he is only temporarily stymied. Yearning to make his way into colonial English circles – to become unambiguously identified as an Englishman and thus as "white" – he becomes a dedicated observer of the English colonials' body language, costuming, social interacting styles – and even their odors. Pran's story therefore has a striking similarity to Franz Kafka's short story (which Kunzru's humorous irony closely models) about an ape which acquires enough human language and etiquette to be able to give a speech to a scientific academy. When asked how he achieved his comportment and language ability, the ape says that he was so desperate to escape from captivity he assiduously studied human behavior in proximity to his cage and, in time, "managed," as he puts it, to "reach the cultural level of an average European."[89]

Like Kafka's ape, Pran, in his desperation, hones *his* observational skills. And as his becoming white proceeds – his "walking into whiteness," as Kunzru puts it at one point[90] – the novel provides insights into the way whiteness is historically constituted by the colonial encounter. In addition to being a style of enunciation, whiteness turns out to be a kind of odor, to which Pran adapts by changing his diet. It also turns out to be a mode of bodily comportment, which he learns when he encounters a woman of mixed background who has already succeeded in becoming white. Finding her compellingly beautiful, Pran (who has adopted the name Bobby at this point) stalks her. When she finally confronts him and tells him to leave her alone, she tells him that she knows what he is because she has been there: "Look. I know what you are. You may think you're pretty good, but I can see through you."[91] She then leaves him with some advice about his bodily comportment: "Don't do that with your head. It's a dead giveaway. The two cardinal rules are never to waggle your head, and never let them see you squatting on your heels. Allright?"[92]

Such setbacks only strengthen Pran's resolve to complete his whiteness project. However, Pran's impressionist trajectory from his (assumed) father's house to his ultimate (also false) identity as the Englishman Jonathan Bridgeman (after he assumes the identity of a deceased English heir he meets in India), has an ironic twist. By the time he is Jonathan, he has learned all too well how to perform whiteness. Thus when the English woman he loves jilts him for a "black" man, and he is at pains to try and win her back by explaining that he is not as white as he may seem, his claim is not credible to her because his white performance has become so polished. However, Pran's unhappy fate aside, from a critical inquiry standpoint his life drama is less interesting as a personal saga than for what its insights into the production of whiteness reveal.

The novel embeds whiteness in a historical account of how it has developed as a result of colonial encounter. However fascinating the novel's players may be – Indian Rajahs, servants, English colonial bureaucrats and administrators, prostitutes, pimps, soldiers, hunters, and so on – what is compelling from a political inquiry standpoint is the way the novel presents the historical and structural forces at work during the colonial period – its rendering of the conditions of possibility for the performances and identity ascriptions produced throughout the history of colonial encounter. Moreover (and crucial methodologically) the novel's various encounters show that a critical investigation of the politics of identity is gained not by analyzing the success or failure of individual status striving, but through demonstrations of the contingent events of encounter from which identities emerge and devolve over time. As is the case for Banks, for Kunzru writing has become a part of his own complex becoming. Understood as "half Indian, half English," Kunzru's identity reflections, articulated in his writing, were initiated by his experience as one who "didn't fit securely into anybody's gang. I grew up with a real sense of disconnection because of it. People are authenticity freaks, and if you're mixed you're not 100% anything."[93]

Ultimately, as both novels show, identities are not attributes of individuals, a lesson that has failed to gain much traction in social science. Nevertheless, there have been some under-appreciated conceptual contributions. For example, in a critical treatment of the research on equality/inequality, Alan Garfinkel shows why an inquiry that embraces a methodological individualism as a premise reaches the "paradoxical and puzzling conclusion" that "variations in economic status among individuals are caused by nonsystematic factors: varieties of competence … the ability to hit a ball thrown at high speed, the ability to type a letter quickly and accurately" and so on.[94] As Garfinkel points out, economic wellbeing involves a relationship. What are to be explained are not individuals' holdings: "If we look at a particular history which led to an individual's economic holding, we find that it is typically unstable: small perturbations would have qualitatively changed it."[95] However, what seems chaotic becomes an intelligible pattern when we recognize that wellbeing is a relationship; some people are rich *because* some are poor (and vice versa). Moreover, this pattern of identity/difference constitutes an interdependency – a relationship between those who are privileged to be able to avoid burdensome work and those who are not so privileged. Garfinkel makes that point by suggesting that what are to be investigated are not the fates of individuals but the pattern of social positions. Each social identity can thus be understood as a "structural property."[96]

An alternative philosophy of inquiry

While Garfinkel's analysis of the structural predicates of identity and his critique of methodological individualism are edifying, his approach lacks Kunzru's historical depth and dynamism: he produces no scenarios of encounter that effectively enact his insights into identity/difference. In contrast with single narrator analyses, novels and other artistic genres create subjects-in-process who emerge as subjects while they are mobilized and affected by their encounters. However, to appreciate the methodological implications of shifting from the theory-building and hypothesis-testing protocols of social science investigations of individual respondents, to literary enactments that mobilize aesthetic subjects and stage encounters, we have to discern the epistemic contribution of the arts by recasting the relationship between philosophy and inquiry. In particular, we have to see philosophy's role as an innovative, idea- and concept-creating practice, rather than as a set of logical tools for moving from concepts to measurements and for deriving propositions and functions.

Empiricist philosophy of social science's role with respect to empirical inquiry is relatively uniformly conceived. A primary issue for the philosophical basis of behavioral science is whether or not human actions can be reliably measured and whether regularities can be discovered and validated. In short, such a philosophy of social science concerns itself with the cogency of explanations, which is a function of logics of representation, discovery and inference. However, before such logics can be invoked, a problem has to be evinced for which an explanation can be sought. By contrast, when philosophy is conceived as conceptual invention, rather than as norms for truth testing and validation, it becomes hospitable to the epistemological contributions of those genres of the arts that challenge hierarchies of sense-making and entrenched models of intelligibility from which "problems" tend to be unreflectively presumed. To pursue that difference, I turn to another illustration in which pragmatic political concerns can be shown to hover around a particular pursuit of explanation adequacy and then contrast this pursuit with an artistic invention which is governed by an aesthetic sensibility.

In the early 1970s, the Australian government became concerned with the high infant mortality rate of its Aboriginal population. After commissioning studies by social scientists, the government's policy paper "explained that '*the semi nomadic life of some of the Aborigines*, which has aspects not compatible with normal health standards, *is a contributing factor*'" and went on to refer to the psychological and social recalcitrance of Aborigines to sound health practices.[97] The politics of the government's explanation – however reliable may have been the social scientists' measuring devices and inferences from their data – should be evident. They adopt an assimilationist perspective rather than acknowledging that Australia is a bicultural state. Instead of an explanation of the problem as an Aboriginal "failure to assimilate to our norms," another explanatory option was available – for example, an investigation of what created the rigidity of a health care delivery system that had failed to adapt to a nomadic segment of the population. The government's policy paper assigned "culpability" to "transients" rather than the dysfunctional health bureaucracy – for example "the dichotomy in the allocation of health functions as between the Health Department and the Welfare branch."[98]

Certainly, there is another more critical, historically sensitive way of locating the "politics of Aboriginal health" if we adopt a genealogical approach. Heeding Foucault's way of investigating the history of problematization, the inquiry would concern itself with Australia's participation in the contemporary "governmentality" in which governance is no longer primarily concerned with reactivating the sovereign power of its rulers but is concerned with managing its "population" – a modern object of governance. As Foucault puts it (here I repeat a passage from the Preface):

> One of the great innovations in the techniques of power in the eighteenth century was the emergence of "population" as an economic and political problem: population as wealth, population as labor capacity, population balanced between its own growth and the resources it commanded. Governments perceived that they were not merely dealing simply with subjects, or even with a "people," but with a "population."[99]

The governmentalization of health has been part of the management of "populations." Moving up one century to the nineteenth, Foucault points to the convergence that developed between "the requirements of *political ideology* and those of *medical technology*."[100] It was a development in which the medical gaze operated in the service of the state's concern with the vitality of its population. As a result, medical knowledge, increasingly managed by the new public health services and bureaucracies, turned away from a focus on the peculiar maladies of individuals and concerned itself instead with "the collective life of the nation."[101] Ill health was increasingly observed in terms of its "frequency."[102] Foucault's analysis of the emergence of the population as the target of governance has a crucial methodological implication. The "population" was not a collection of juridical subjects from whom obedience could be extracted but "a set of elements" to be managed in order to achieve concrete assets for advancing the circulation crucial to emerging commerce and to supply bodies for advancing state security. Consequently, "we have," as Foucault puts it, "a whole field of new realities in the sense that they are pertinent elements for mechanisms of power, the pertinent space within which and regarding which one must act."[103] Thus, whereas the traditional social sciences seek knowledge *about* elements of populations, seeking to lessen the volume of the existing *terra incognita*, Foucault's historically sensitive accounts map the changes in the terrain within which knowledge issues arise; for example, the conditions through which the "field of economic theory" expanded to include "this new subject-object" (the population).[104] In this study – as in Foucault's other investigations – he is not attempting total explanation. Moreover, he has produced neither a philosophical tract nor a comprehensive study in history. Rather, in his words, such investigations are "at most philosophical fragments put to work in a historical field of problems."[105] The political effect of those "fragments" inheres in the way they disrupt institutionalized knowledge that cedes forms of power and authority unreflectively. Heeding Foucault's methodological project and recognizing that critically effective fragments are among the main contributions of cinema to political thinking, I turn to a further example of my critique of the politics of Australia's encounters with its Aboriginal population.

Inquiry as mobilized thinking: cinematic political thought

> Only those who know how to take the time to photograph the clouds also know how to take the time not only to look at what is beneath those clouds, but also to construct the artistic forms best suited to engendering a different way of looking at humanity …
>
> Jacques Rancière

Foucault's critical method produces a politically perspicuous shift from the "problem" of Aboriginal health to a historically sensitive analysis of problematizaton, which identifies the forces that direct attention to "Aboriginal health." However, I want to illustrate a critical perspective that adds local context – an aesthetically-oriented political gloss on aboriginality that is available in a film by Ivan Sen, a part Aboriginal filmmaker/director. Sen's film *Beneath Clouds* (2002), allows me to offer "micropolitical" insights into Australia's inter-ethnic political situation by focusing on Aboriginal identity struggles rather than the macropolitical issue of governmental policy. Crucially for my purposes, the film provides an illustration of how philosophy can serve political thinking, when it is conceived as a creative process that articulates with the arts rather than as a logical discipline attuned to scientific inquiry.

Sen's *Beneath Clouds*, which is based on Australia's indigenous experience, is a road movie. The film's dramatic narrative is uncomplicated. Lena, the daughter of an Aboriginal mother and absent Irish father leaves her rural home to find her father in Sydney. Her skin tone and blonde hair allow her to pass as "white," and she is initially intent on having that part of herself exhaust her identity. Vaughan is a Murri boy who looks unmistakably Aboriginal and is headed to see his ill mother. Events throw them together on the road as they head toward the city, catching rides together along the way. Despite their disparate initial perspectives, they become close – Lena headed she hopes toward whiteness and Vaughan seeing himself as a victim of Australia's racial hierarchy. Their encounter with each other and with those they meet along the way, especially an old "Aunty" who asks Lena, "Where're your people from girl?", encourage them to reflect on the ambiguities and fragilities of racial coding.

Figure 1.1
Lena

Figure 1.2
Vaughan

While as a narrative the film reaches no dramatic conclusion, the film's landscape and close-up face and body shots carry the burden of its political thinking. Sen's concatenation of shifting images transcends the plot as his shots and editing show both the emotionally charged and complex ethnic mix of Australia by focusing on eyes and the historic ethnic fault-line between Euro and Aboriginal Australians by cutting to panoramic and deep focus landscape shots. The close-ups of eyes – some blue (belonging to a mixed, Irish-Aboriginal teenage girl) and some dark brown (belonging to a Murri teenage boy) – illustrate the complexity of Australia's ethnic landscape. The cuts from eyes to landscape shots – some of which show vast expanses devoid of activity, some of which show industrial interventions into the landscape, and one of which shows a looming mountain, filtered in a way that spiritualizes it – demonstrate the multiplicity of ways in which the land is occupied, both experientially and symbolically. It becomes clear that the landscape is worshipped by Aborigines when at one point Vaughan tells Lena, as they walk past a cliff-face, that they are moving past a "sacred site."

Ultimately, through his camera work Sen mounts a cinematic challenge to a history of Euro-Australian landscape imagery, especially the Euro-Australian landscape painting tradition, which is largely oriented toward showing "the construction of a new land" in the light of "the ambivalent background of the Aboriginal presence."[106] Insofar as Aborigines show up in the history of Euro-Australian landscape painting, the tendency has been to represent them as peripheral to the work of nation-building – for example representing them "at home in the sublime [and as] … strangers to the world of work, as it is conceived by the settler."[107] However, Sen does not privilege a single viewpoint. Shots taken from those of the different characters – alternating through cuts and juxtapositions, with images that often contradict their expressed viewpoints – show that subjective perception is not what commands interpretation. And with his depth of focus shots of the landscape and his panning shots that locate his characters and interactions in spatial contexts, Sen lends "spatial expression" to his drama to develop political implications that exceed the particular moments experienced by the bodies moving across the landscape.[108]

In Sen's film Australia, as space, is not merely the domain of sensations to which the characters are meant to react. His way of rendering the landscape is central to how his film thinks about the history of Australia's inter-ethnic politics. And crucially, if we follow Deleuze's insights about the deployment of philosophy in cinema, Sen's *Beneath Clouds* is best thought of as a cinema of seeing, rather than dramatic action. In Deleuze's terms, "the viewer's problem becomes 'What is there to see in the image?' (and not now 'What are we going to see in the next image?')."[109] Of course, cinema has not always been a critical medium. As Siegfried Kracauer noted early on the development of the medium, some films are intended to make you believe rather than see critically because they deal primarily in "corroborative images."[110] However, cinema became an increasingly critical medium throughout the twentieth century. As Deleuze points out, in contrast with early cinema, in many post-WW II films there is no centered commanding perception. Characterized by direct images of time – where time is a function of the cuts and juxtapositions of the editing rather than linear flowing of the movement of the characters – they manifest a critical capacity by deprivileging the directionality of centered commanding perception, allowing the disorganized multiplicity that is the world to emerge. As Deleuze puts it, "Instead of going from the acentered state of things to centered perception, [we] could go back up towards the acentered state of things and get closer to it."[111]

Sen's *Beneath Clouds* recovers an Australian multiplicity with its shifting viewpoints and depth of field shots, which allow for sheets of the present and the past to coexist. As a result, the film's *mise en scène* is more telling than its storyline. The landscape shots usher in historical time as they locate the viewers in "spatial and temporal positions" that are "distinct from those of the characters."[112] And, finally, as a road movie *Beneath Clouds* is organized around what Bakhtin (in his treatment of time in diverse novelistic genres) refers to as a "chronotope of encounter": "On the road the spatial and temporal series defining human fates and lives combine with one another in distinctive ways ... [making possible] new departures."[113] However, inasmuch as *Beneath Clouds* is a film rather than a novel, images are more important than dialogue – the testimony of the changing landscape is more telling than the verbal exchanges between the protagonists. The time images in landscape shots combine with the images of Lena and Vaughan to create a critical exchange between the biographical time of the characters and Australian settler national time. In the process, the film thinks through the medium of Sen's writing-through-image-editing about the identity struggles of those who manifest varying degrees of aboriginality to accommodate to a place where aboriginality has been largely over-coded by the signs of Euro-Australian settlement. The film reminds us that critically oriented writing is not merely informational. Rather, writing and critical thinking are radically entangled, a position I elaborate in my next section.

Poiesis as method and the politics of aesthetics

From the point of view of an explanatory social science, the writing aspect of inquiry is informational. The researcher reports on what has been explained and on the procedures of data gathering and validation that assign confidence to the results of the inquiry. From the point of view of critical artistic work, thinking through writing rather than presenting information is involved. As in the case of Ivan Sen's film *Beneath Clouds,* that thinking takes place through the imaginative staging of encounters that disrupt rather than affirm institutionalized and familiar versions of worlds. As Deleuze has noted, cinematic depth of focus shots articulate sheets of time (especially notable in the films of Orson Welles and Alain Resnais in which "sheets of past coexist and confront each other")[114] to produce a critical temporal multiplicity that challenges both humanist and sacred models of unitary time. Such a cinematic effect, which yields a disruptively original sense of spatio-temporality, encourages one to think (as I suggested in my analysis of Sen's film *Beneath Clouds*).

However, the novel can also challenge entrenched models of temporality. For example, Carlos Fuentes has made that case: "the novel is the literary form that, with most complexity, permits us to reappropriate time."[115] Fuentes's provocative remark about the novel's articulation of times other than a universally shared linear historical time – which as I noted in the Preface, he ascribes to the genre's ability to render a multiplicity of presences – helps to situate the relevance of writing performances to a politically oriented mode of inquiry. To proceed with a more elaborate, inquiry-related illustration of Fuentes's suggestion, I want to return to the Europe–Africa relationship and treat a Portuguese novel – António Lobo Antunes's *The Return of the Caravels* (2002) – because the way it re-appropriates time provides an exemplary illustration of the contribution of creative writing to political apprehension. The novel registers an author-in-process, Lobo

Antunes, who experienced Portuguese colonialism as a doctor in a military hospital during "The Angolan War" and subsequently wrote a series of critical anti-colonial novels as he processed his growing interest in death and otherness and his disaffection with Portugal's colonial violence.[116]

A consideration of the political impetus of Lobo Antunes's novel – which deals with the drama of the return to Lisbon of descendants of Portuguese colonialists fleeing the post-independence former colonies – is especially appropriate at this historical moment because of a remarkable reversal in the relationship between Portugal and its former colony, Angola. Portugal's African colonies were once treated as places from which to extract wealth, while their populations were either enslaved or otherwise economically exploited (in Angola, "the average white employer earned between ten and one hundred times more than his African employees"[117]). However, Portugal – going through a serious economic downturn in the first decade of the twenty-first century – was now "increasingly placing its hopes of recovery on Angola, a former colony that has established itself as one of the strongest economies in sub-Sahara Africa." Among other things, Angolan students came to account for almost a fifth of the students enrolled at the University of Lisbon.[118] Three philosophically derived analytics help to disclose the critical political thinking in Lobo Antunes's novel. As I summon them to an engagement with the novel, my analysis constitutes what Cesare Casarino calls philopoesis, "which names a certain discontinuous and refractive interference between philosophy and literature."[119] That "interference" is one between an "'art of forming, inventing, and fabricating concepts'" (philosophy) and an art constituted as "the production of a 'bloc of sensations … a compound of percepts and affects'" (literature).[120] With Casarino, I want to note that the political force (or perhaps better, the meta-political force) of a philopoesis derives from the interference between philosophy and literature because: "in questioning each other, philosophy and literature put the whole world into question."[121]

The first philosophical engagement with the novel is drawn from Deleuze's analysis of the method of the painter Francis Bacon. Turning to Bacon's canvases to provide insights into aesthetic comprehension, Deleuze points out that, in Bacon's case, one should not assume that the artist "works on a white surface." Rather, "everything he has in his head, or around him is already on the canvas, more or less virtually, before he begins his work."[122] To resist "psychic clichés" and *"figurative givens,"* the artist must "transform" or "deform" what is "always-already on the canvas."[123] (Sandro Bernardi discerns a similar aesthetic problem to which Roberto Rossellini addressed himself in his films. As he puts it, "Rossellini's work … consisted above all of a 'cleansing of the eyes', an attempt to free cinema, vision and therefore knowledge from the stereotypes accumulated over time, over centuries … [as he] used cinema to think.")[124] For my purposes, it is especially apropos that Deleuze turns for illustration to the paintings of Francis Bacon, because Bacon's canvases manifest not only the explicit aim of deforming rather than reproducing figurative givens but also are in accord with what I have noted as the implications of the Kantian revolution – a focus on the conditions under which things appear. As Bacon testifies, "what I want to do is to distort the thing far beyond the appearance, but in the distortion to bring it back to a *recording* of appearance [my emphasis]."[125]

As was the case with Bacon's canvases and Rossellini's films, Lobo Antunes's novel enacts a disfiguration or deformation. One commentary on Antunes's writing makes his deforming practice explicit: "Instead of taking some specific facts or general topics on which he may write a novel, Lobo Antunes clearly prefers to inculcate his personal views on these topics and to deform those facts."[126] The "given" to which *The Return* is a disfiguring response is Luís de Camões's epic poem, *The Lusiads* (1572), which valorizes the first voyages of Vasco da Gama, as it performs a "celebration of the deeds of a nation."[127] Whereas Camões's protagonists are heroic noblemen (*barões*), Lobo Antunes's are anti-heroes: "clergymen, Genoese astrologers, Jewish merchants, governesses, slave smugglers, [and] poor whites"[128] whose livelihoods in the colonies depended on the hegemony of the colonizing Portuguese state. They are the novel's *retornados*, who reverse the direction of Camões's heroes and find themselves back in Lisbon. However, unlike Camões's epic, which narrates a particular historical moment, Lobo Antunes's novel inter-articulates historical and contemporary time: the anti-heroic figures are temporal hybrids who combine historical characters – for example Pedro Alvares Cabral, who departed from Lisbon to Africa in the fifteenth century and returns from Luanda to Lisbon after Angolan independence in the 1970s. Making use of fiction's powerful capacity, "the defeat of time" – "A century of family saga and a ride up an escalator can take the same number of pages"[129] – Lobo Antunes writes in a way that insinuates the past into the present, while also "contaminating the earlier historical time," as Cabral is invented at both the moments of his departure and his return (the caravel of his leaving in the fifteenth century becomes an airplane on his return to Lisbon in the twentieth).[130]

While Lobo Antunes' rewriting/disfiguring of Camões's heroic epic is part of the novel's political impetus, a second philosophical engagement, drawn from Jacques Rancière's neo-Kantian approach to aesthetics, effectively situates the novel's politics of aesthetics. In contrast with Camões's aristocrats – who manifest a fully formed and unambivalent identity – Lobo Antunes's *retornados* are dynamics of becoming, as they reflect on and "gradually adopt ... the perspective of the colonized."[131] For example, one of his *retornado*/narrators reveals his level of moral insensitivity to his African wife – "thirty-one years and seven months younger than I" – whom "I swapped with my chum for an airplane ticket to Lisbon: 'You keep her and the furniture and just give me the little piece of paper for the flight'."[132] By turning its aesthetic subjects, the *retornados*, into vehicles for reflection on the moral degradation of the colonial experience, the novel evinces an anti-colonial impetus. It is in this respect that the novel's reflections comport with Rancière's perspective on the politics of aesthetics: Lobo Antunes's aesthetic subjects manifest more than mere attitudes. They have reconfigured colonial sensibility; or in Rancière's preferred mode of expression, they have engaged in a repartitioning of the sensible by reordering their relationship with the history of the colonial experience.[133] At the moments in which they express sympathy with the experience of the colonized (in contrast with

Camões's unambivalent colonial "heroes") their mouths become "organ[s] of disfiguration." No longer merely expressing perceptions, the enunciating mouths alter the disposition between the two bodies – those of the colonizer and colonized – to enact "a new and temporary partition of the sensible."[134]

The third philosophical engagement with the novel is drawn from the methodological implications that Walter Benjamin derives from his recasting of Kant's philosophy of experience and his applications in several of his writings, especially his *Arcades Project* and his essay "The Work of Art in the Age of Mechanical Reproduction."[135] Without going into the many tensions, complications, and contradictions in Benjamin's project of (as he puts it) sorting out "which elements of the Kantian philosophy should be adopted and cultivated,"[136] two aspects of his refiguring of Kantian philosophy influence my reading of the novel. One is the lexical idiom: Benjamin displaces the Kantian configuration of the faculties with the configurations immanent in the conditions of legibility. This alteration presumes not a static subject who merely apprehends the world but a historically conditioned, active or mobile subject who *reads* the world at hand – especially the urban world, which manifests a dense and complex sensorium.[137] Moreover, inasmuch as there is a plurality of historically embedded subjects, the active perceptions involved in the reading process produce a multiplicity of configurations.[138] The philosophically conceived configuration-reading subject of experience serves Benjamin as a predicate for the sense that his aesthetic subject, the city dwelling *flâneur*, makes of urban life ("botanizing on the asphalt" as Benjamin famously puts it). It is a subject at the center of Benjamin's critical method.

Benjamin's other reconfiguration of Kantian philosophy is articulated through his concept of shock. To appreciate the Kantian legacy of that concept, we have to recall that, for Kant, both beautiful and sublime objects/events – which cannot be subsumed within laws that govern either understanding or desire – throw the subject back on itself, provoking moments of reflection (in encounters with the beautiful) and a sense of autonomy (in encounters with the sublime in which the subject is freed from the attraction of the object and is able to engage its own subjectivity as it considers the coherence of the relationships among its diverse faculties and its freedom from the world of necessity). Benjamin applies those insights to works of art that, having lost their aura (or ritual power), shock – or at least distract – the spectator, giving her/him autonomy. In particular, Dadaist art – and its successor, film – shock the viewer (especially though such mechanisms as collage and rapid montage) in such a way that she/he is diverted from the object and pushed toward reflection and critical thinking. Rodolphe Gasché has captured this aspect of Benjamin's neo-Kantian politics of aesthetics: "[T]he object character of the artwork recedes entirely, and thus a radical diversion from what attracts ... has been effectively achieved. An aesthetics of shock is thus non-objective. In it the object has become diverted and deflected. It thus has all the allure of the Kantian aesthetics with its subjective bent."[139]

Thus first, if we turn from Benjamin's re-inflection of the Kantian philosophy of experience in his various treatments of philosophy and perception to the collection of fragments that constitute his *Arcades Project*, we have the basis for situating the radical implications of Lobo Antunes's *The Return*. Lobo Antunes's aesthetic subjects, his *retornados*, wander around Lisbon as they offer interpretations of the now time of the city, in the context of the forces that generated Portugal's colonial experience. Because the novel's bi-temporal subjects enact the significance of a particularly political fraught historical moment, the text functions in accord with Benjamin's suggestion that an artwork is not to be understood as a realization of a mental intention but as "a constructed intervention into a historical moment."[140] And, as Benjamin insists, to understand that moment one must embrace a "methodological objective" that abandons "the idea of progress."[141] To read the present in terms of the relation of the "what-has-been to the now" [for] ... the image that is read – which is to say the image in the now of its recognizability – bears to the highest degree the imprint of the perilous critical moment on which all reading is founded."[142] And crucially, "In order for the past to be touched by the present instant ... there must be no continuity between them."[143] In a remark that effectively situates Lobo Antunes's non-linear approach to historical time and his critical mixing of characters who exist simultaneously in the past and present, Benjamin sees his critical method as an injunction to "carry over the principle of montage into history," which has the effect of breaking with a "vulgar historical naturalism."[144] Second, if we want to understand the impact of Lobo Antunes's text, we also have to consider the ways in which the rapid cutting back and forth between historical and present moments and diverse, non-heroic characters prevents the reader from comfortably incorporating the text into a traditional national narrative. While, as an anti-history, the novel disturbs the temporal structure of the national story, as a form it distracts the reader from applying traditional modes of intelligibility. Its cuts and juxtapositions throw the reader back on her-/himself to provoke critical reflection rather than allow for mere recognition or understanding.

Conclusion: aesthetic inquiry

The philosophically informed analytics that I have summoned to engage Lobo Antunes's novel all have the effect of showing how his writing disrupts a particular national narrative by mobilizing diverse aesthetic subjects with conflicting perceptual orientations and by confounding traditional linear temporalities. Certainly, the approach I have taken to the text is not empiricism's focus on explanation. However, I want to add that neither is it traditional hermeneutics: it is not an interpretive as opposed to explanatory method. Rather, the approach is effectively "post-hermeneutic," where "post-hermeneutics," activates an epistemology that allows for "theorizing and analyzing ways of sense making that perhaps no longer include effects of meaning and reference."[145] It is an approach that – as David Wellbery has cogently rendered it – "abandons the language game and form of life defined by the hermeneutic canons of justification and enters into domains of inquiry inaccessible to acts of appropriative understanding."[146] For example, referring to discourse analyses by the media theorist, Friedrich Kittler, Wellbery notes that they "delineate the apparatuses of power, storage, transmission, training, reproduction, and so forth that make up the conditions of factual discursive occurrences." [147] In this sense, post-hermeneutic analysis is Kant-inspired inasmuch as the emphasis is not on the relationship between word and referent or on signification (how the text can be understood in terms of the hidden content it discloses) but on the forces – languages, genres, apparatuses, and so on – that are involved in "the production of presence." [148]

If not explanation or traditional hermeneutics, what constitutes an aesthetic approach to knowledge? As I have already noted, in its original connotation aesthetics – *aisthitikos*, from the Greek[149] – referred to the sensory aspect of perception. And it is this sense that governed Kant's Third Critique. However, aesthetics in contemporary critical work has come to refer not primarily to corporeal sensibility but to the arts. Although there is a wide variety of ways in which the original and Kantian versions have been articulated with arts criticism, Rancière's neo-Kantian applications (like Benjamin's, which I have already noted) offer a promising methodological opening to a critical approach to artistic texts. As Rancière points out (and as I have already noted), because – as Kant shows in his analytic of the beautiful – the beautiful object is "neither an object of cognition, subjecting sensation to the law of the understanding, nor an object of desire, subjecting reason to the anarchy of sensations," the beautiful object's "unavailability ... with respect to any power of cognition or desire allows the subject to feel an experience of autonomy, a 'free play' of the faculties." [150] Influenced by this Kantian perspective, Rancière and other post-Kantian philosophers focus on encounters that disrupt "habitual conditions of sensible experience" and thereby solicit critical thinking.[151] Deleuze renders the disruptions of encounter this way, "Something in the world forces us to think. This something is an object not of recognition but of a fundamental encounter." [152] At a minimum, whether the disrupting encounter is with a work of art or with something else, what constitutes the aesthetics of knowledge from both Rancière's and Deleuze's perspectives has to do with the way the encounter leads to an alteration in sensible experience. In Rancière's words, "artistic practices take part in the partitioning of the perceptible insofar as they suspend the ordinary coordinates of sensory experience and reframe the networks between spaces and times, subjects and objects, the common and the singular." [153] And inasmuch as politics for Rancière is rendered as "a way of re-partitioning the political from the non-political," [154] because rather than merely "an exercise of power or struggle for power, politics is first of all the configuration of a space as political, the framing of a specific sphere of experience," [155] aesthetics and politics are homologous. Rancière's perspective engenders a politics of aesthetics in which a critical work of art *constitutes* a politics. Here I extend an earlier quotation – one of Rancière's most important statements about the political effects of aesthetic encounters (which describes succinctly much of the methodological orientation which I refer to as "the aesthetic turn"):

> Aesthetic experience has a political effect to the extent that the loss of destination that it presupposes disturbs the way in which bodies fit their functions and destinations. What it produces is no rhetoric of persuasion about what has to be done. Nor is it the framing of a collective body. It is a multiplication

of connections and disconnections that reframe the relation between bodies, the world where they live and the way in which they are 'equipped' for fitting in it. It is a multiplicity of folds and gaps in the fabric of common experience that change the cartography of the perceptible, the thinkable and the feasible. As such, it allows for new modes of political construction of common objects and new possibilities of collective enunciation.[156]

Although I am tempted to conclude this chapter by providing a counter-list to the one I quote from Selltiz *et al.*'s mid-twentieth century *Research Methods in Social Relations* near the outset, I shall instead offer some reflections on the writing–inquiry relationship, as it is deployed on aesthetic practices and texts in the diverse investigations that follow this chapter. The value for me of the texts I select is not a result of their consolidating and/or validating particular explanations of phenomena. Rather, their value inheres in the way my encounters with them summon critical thinking. And because those encounters are ultimately articulated in how I write, I need to say something about the style of the chapters/essays.

My approach to composition (writing-as-method) is inspired in part by Benjamin, who, when he reflected on *his* method as a writer, noted that it is "literary montage": "I needn't *say* anything. Merely show. I shall purloin no valuables, appropriate no ingenious formulations. But the rags, the refuse – these I will not inventory but allow, in the only way possible, to come into their own: by making use of them."[157] Following Benjamin's concept of montage-as-critique, I prefer to avoid argument-marking meta-statements and let my juxtapositions carry much of the burden of the analyses. Benjamin's remark about his writing comports well with another of my inspirations, Rancière's rendering of political art: "Political art ... means creating those forms of collision or dissensus that put together not only heterogeneous elements but also two politics of sensoryness."[158] Accordingly, my analyses proceed by putting together a variety of disparate references from diverse texts or genres of expression. The overall methodological injunction behind such a "putting together" is what Rancière refers to as indisciplinary thought; it is the kind of thought that breaks disciplines in order to deprivilege the distribution of (disciplinary) territories that control "who is qualified to speak about what."[159] Casarino makes a similar point in his treatment of the interference between philosophy and literature when he asserts that thinking becomes possible when the interference between genres opens up "emergent potentialities that disrupt the status quo of the history of forms."[160]

Following Rancière's and Casarino's perspectives on dissensus and disruption, the inquiries in the chapters that follow deprivilege social science's disciplinary norms and at the same time disrupt the conceptualizations that reinforce the political status quos from which social science researchers have tended to select their "problems." Finally, where Selltiz *et al.* suggest that the process of inquiry should begin with, "A statement of purpose ... in the form of *formulating the problem*," my investigations begin instead by presuming (rather than explicitly stating) the following questions: Given the general area in which you are interested – war, justice, urban politics, border violence, and so on – what is the origin (in terms of the array of shaping forces) of the *doxa*, the currently dominant way of formulating problems? What are the forces at work that allow those formulations to persist? What are the costs and benefits for various constituencies of the mode of problematization that commands thinking and inquiry in the domain of your inquiry? Whose perspectives on problem(s) gain recognition and whose perspectives fail to rise above the threshold of recognition? And, finally, what conceptions, juxtapositions, and soliciting of alternative subjects and thought worlds will disrupt the dominant modes of intelligibility and open up spaces for new political thinking with empowering implications for new forms of subjectivization, for the welcoming of new kinds of (in-process or becoming) subjects into politically relevant space?

Because this is a methods book, there is of course a degree of pretension in my efforts. It is my hope that the opening-up I am advocating, through a commitment to an aesthetically thought, politically oriented trans-disciplinarity, will be methodologically contagious.

2   The moralized economy in hard times

Introduction

In this chapter I engage the moralizing of economy by bringing it into an encounter with political perspectives that displace moralizing with critical, philosophical and ethical thinking. Taking as the initiating provocation the U.S. government's bailout of the American auto industry during the recent financial crisis, my analysis focuses on the ontological depth of automobile culture in the U.S. and proceeds not through direct argumentation but through interpretations of a series of artistic genres – a television drama, a comic strip, a series of novels, and a film – all of which deal in varying degrees with aspects of "automobility" (the economy, culture, and car–driver complex of automobile transportation) as it developed throughout the twentieth century.[1] I am not concerned with explaining why the American auto industry was on the brink of failure. Rather, my investigation is an exercise in thinking about the place of automobility in American culture in the context of a society-wide event that re-inflected relationships between moral and political economy. Accordingly, the temporal context of the inquiry is crucial; it is encompassed in the expression "hard times," which references periods of an intensification of the process through which some people experience misfortune while others achieve financial gain. While "moral economy" is constituted as institutionalized inhibitions to certain kinds of exchange, a "moralized economy" is a specific historical event in which there is publicly visible contention about the morality of a new or altered kind of economic activity or policy. To enact the conceptual orientation I pursue, I begin with an analysis of two episodes of a television drama that is situated in a particularly eventful period in the development of American capitalism and end by analyzing a film about economic hard times in the Ukrainian city of Kiev, shortly after the disintegration of the former Soviet Union, when licit and illicit forms of predatory capitalism are accompanied by violent animosities that have all but displaced conviviality and friendship. Although a swerve to a film situated in Kiev runs the analysis mostly off the road, a car that is featured in the film narrative plays a key role in the way the film thinks. Moreover, as an object of analysis, the film has two virtues. The Kiev cityscape it explores offers a useful contrast because it does not appear to be a well-developed motorscape (unlike most major cities), and the way the film renders tensions between exchange and friendship allows me to stress the kind of ethico-philosophical thinking (as opposed to moralizing) discernible in cinema.

Mad Men, automobility, and the racial order

The AMC television channel's *Mad Men* (2008–2010) follows the professional and personal lives of a group of men and women who work at Sterling Cooper, a fictional, early 1960s Madison Avenue advertising firm. As each episode makes evident, by the 1960s the American economy had become so focused on the identity-vulnerability of the consumer that selling images rather than things had become widely accepted. In comparison with the beginning of the century – when it was deemed immoral to seek to arouse desire for commodities – no moral obloquy seems to afflict the personnel of Sterling Cooper, whose executives and staff, as well as their clients, take for granted the shift in the economy from the production of things to the production of desire. As Lawrence Birken aptly puts it: in the new economic paradigm (well entrenched by the era of *Mad Men*), "commodities themselves were not so much material goods as desired objects."[2] By mid-century, "the land of desire" had developed to the point where mass production had been unapologetically accompanied by "mass consumer entice-ments that rose up in tandem to market and sell the mass-produced goods."[3] And the Sterling Cooper advertising firm, in which the "mad men" toil, has as its main "product," enticement. Nevertheless, even in the era in which enticement had begun to displace production as the main driving force of economy, there remained inhibitions. As Fernand Braudel points out in his monumental treat-ment of the history of commerce, as systems of exchange have expanded, culture has served as a form of inertia or inhibition.[4] Two episodes of *Mad Men*, which reflect some of the tensions between culture and economy in the U.S. of the mid-twentieth century, are especially pertinent to an analysis of moral economy. The first deals with the identity stakes involved in the development of automobile culture in America's post-World War II period; the second, the inhibitions to commerce of America's racial order.

The first inhibition is articulated through *Mad Men*'s main protagonist, Don Draper (Jon Hamm), who harbors a secret he tries zealously to protect. As an episode in the series' second season opens, the camera zooms in on the white sidewall tires of a luxury automobile. There are expensive-looking, well-shined shoes visible below the car from the opposite side. As the visual narrative begins, the viewer sees that the shoes belong to Don Draper, who is walking around the car. Having distinguished himself as a creative director at Sterling Cooper, he is urged by one of the company's executives, Roger Sterling, to visit a Cadillac dealership. The salesman, who has an upper-class English accent, seeing the well-dressed, affluent-looking Draper appearing tentative as he circles the vehicle, says, "Afraid you'll fall in love?" Adding, "I can see you have good taste," the salesman describes the car as a "1962 Coupe de Ville that does everything but make breakfast." When Don replies, "I have a Dodge," the salesman, without missing a beat, says, "Those are wonderful when you want to get somewhere, this is for when you've already arrived." As the salesman's pitch continues, playing

Figure 2.1 Draper and the car salesman

on the "sign function value" rather than the utility of the Cadillac (specifically on the appearance of success it confers on its owner), he delivers a remark that triggers Don's identity insecurity: "I'd bet you'd be as comfortable in one of these as you are in your own skin."[5]

Don Draper is not "comfortable in his own skin" because he is actually Dick Whitman. While serving in the Korean War, he switched identities with his commanding officer, Donald Draper, who was killed in an explosion that made Draper's appearance unrecognizable and seriously wounded Whitman. While in an army hospital, recovering from his injuries, Dick discovers, as he awakes from a coma, that he is thought to be Don Draper. He decides not to disabuse the hospital staff of their incorrect identification, seemingly because leaving his convalescence as Draper allows him to escape from his former stigmatized life (as the son of a prostitute, raised by an unloving couple who mocked and denigrated his origin) and begin a new life with the alias. As the Cadillac salesman heads off to get the car keys to take "Don" for a test drive, "Draper" spies a man in a brown suit looking at another car. That image triggers a flashback to a similar image in 1952, when Dick Whitman (as Don Draper) was working as a car salesman.

While the "Don" in the flashback, dressed in a much less classy outfit (a poorly tailored jacket with non-matching pants), is trying to pitch a used car to a young man, whose skeptical father is there to "make sure when you shake his hand, you don't take his fingers," a woman approaches from behind the man and son. Don leaves the pair temporally to engage the woman, assuming that she is also a potential customer. However, she turns out to be the widow of the real Don Draper. After "Don" says, "Can I help you madam," she asks, "Are you Donald Draper?" When he responds, "I am" and extends his hand, she replies, "You're a hard man to find ... You're not Don Draper." After a close-up of "Don's" troubled look, the scene cuts back to 1962 in the Cadillac agency. As the salesman returns with the keys and says "Let me take you for a ride," "Don" replies, "No thank you" and leaves. His recollection, emotionally freighted with the disparagement of car salesmen in general and specifically with the exposure of his secret, has rendered him too inhibited to make the purchase.

Harboring a "biographical idiosyncrasy," paired with a morally suspect occupational history, "Don Draper" has found *himself* "a hard man to find."[6] As the scene makes evident, for the successful marketing of a commodity, the targets of the enticement have to be able to evince relative certainty of their identity or at least be able to recognize themselves within the frame in which the commodity is being coded. However, in complex societies identity certainty is often fugitive. They are societies in which, "a person's social identities are not only numerous but often conflicting," where, as Igor Kopytoff puts it, one is likely to encounter a "drama of identities – of their clashes, of the impossibility of choosing between them ... the drama, in brief, lies in the uncertainly of identity."[7] However, 1962 is a peak year for the automobile's centrality to both economy and culture. Cars had become both the primary mass-produced product and the primary object of mass consumption. Thus for example the success of Ford's middlebrow entry, the Mercury, coincided with the "arrival of an American middle class that responded to its aspirational message,"[8] while the Cadillac appealed to a higher class which was encouraged to make its already-achieved success conspicuous.

In a later scene in the same episode, a still shaken "Don" is told by Roger Sterling that he should buy the Cadillac because he can afford it and because the gesture is status-confirming; it is "invigorating [to be able to] write a check for $6500." Shortly thereafter, Don is ushered into the office of Bert Cooper (the firm's CEO), where he's congratulated for his performance in securing a large new account and told he is now to be one of the company's primary representatives. Cooper tells him that he is "going to be wearing a tuxedo a lot more" and adds that he will be among those "people who get to decide what will happen in our world." It would appear that the tuxedo and what it implies (the security and confidence conferred on one asked to represent the world he has adopted) alleviates "Don's" discomfort in his own skin and alleviates his identity uncertainty. The encounter has made him a more stable subject, one who feels morally eligible as well as economically equipped for the purchase. After leaving Cooper's office, he goes back to the dealership and buys the Cadillac. There follows a family idyll; the episode connects automobility with traditional family domesticity as Don and his wife and children drive out for an outdoor picnic in the new Cadillac.

In season three of *Mad Men*, we are introduced to another identity inhibition. The hyper-ambitious marketing assistant to Draper, Pete Campbell (Vincent Kartheiser), has decided to pitch the "Negro" consumer to the executives of the Admiral Television Corporation. Accompanied by charts of sales and samples of publications (the magazines *Ebony* and *Jet* and the Harlem newspaper, *Amsterdam News*) – "by Negroes for Negroes," as he puts it – Pete points out that advertising space in these publications is less expensive than in the ones in which the corporation is presently advertising. And he shows data that indicate flat sales among "white" customers and growing sales among "Negroes." He suggests that Admiral's ads, if pitched to a "Negro market," would do "more good": "a 5% increase in the Detroit market will make you more than a 2%

increase system wide." Moreover, he continues, "ads on television pitched to this market will have a double the effect." Asked by one of Admiral's executives if he is suggesting that they double their advertising, Pete responds to the contrary: "Do them together, integrate them." Addressing the remark's fraught political resonances, one of the Admiral executives says, "I don't think that's legal." Pete responds, "Of course it's legal." However, ultimately the Admiral executives reject his pitch. It's evident that they sit unambivalently within "the color-line century" and would rather affirm the inhibitions of America's racial order than sell more television sets.[9]

Such moments of inhibition notwithstanding, arguably the emergence of African Americans as consumers accelerated the process through which they became civic participants. Despite the speed bump demonstrated in the *Mad Men* episode, African Americans were being increasingly welcomed as consumers by the mid-twentieth century, especially as consumers of automobiles. In effect, the expansionary drive of American capitalism helped to break down the fault-lines in the racial-spatial order, as it broke down other impediments to exchange. As Jonathan Crary succinctly summarizes it, "capitalism unleashes a process [that] uproots and makes mobile what is grounded, clears away that which impedes circulation, and makes exchangeable what is singular."[10] As was the case with African Americans, many Native Americans revalued themselves by purchasing automobiles – in their case symbolically becoming participants in modernity rather than remaining as icons of former times.[11] And as is well known, the automobile and the open road contributed to freeing women from the confines of the household – in their ordinary everyday lives (as they joined the ranks of active consumers, ranging some distance for commodities) and in extraordinary situations (well represented in Ridley Scott's film *Thelma and Louise* (1991), in which Louise's sporty green Mustang is the escape vehicle).[12]

Most significantly for the purposes of this analysis, although initially such changes in the economy – which reorder the social matrix and revalue subjects – tend to produce moralistic responses, as people become vexed by challenges to their assumptions about relationships between subjectivity and exchange, the changes tend ultimately to enjoy positive moral sanction, especially after persons with cultural authority endorse the changes. In such situations, a moralized economy is displaced by a moral economy – by an alteration in the structure of inhibitions, which proceeds to becoming familiar and relatively uncontentious. Thus, while moral economy constitutes an inhibition, it can also play a role in the overcoming of inhibition. In particular, with respect to the diminution of America's racial fault-lines, the development of the automobile culture looms large. As Paul Gilroy suggests, the automobile developed "as a kind of *ur*-commodity lodged at the meeting point of moral and economic relations" (where "moral" for Gilroy refers to the ways in which lives are valued). He goes on to point out that, as certain kinds of lives become valued because of their role in the economy, some inhibitions to exchange become abrogated. Accordingly, he demonstrates the critical interconnection between moral and political economy, as it was mediated by automobile culture: "The value of life is persistently specified along racial lines and car ownership remains an unspoken prerequisite for the exercise of citizenship."[13] In short, *Mad Men*'s Pete Campbell was in step with the economic forces that helped draw African Americans into civic life as they were drawn into economic life.[14]

A similar process can be observed in the commoditization of music. Early in the twentieth century, various genres of "black music" (for example blues and jazz) were regarded by the "white" establishment as morally degrading.[15] Among those who were morally outraged by the increasing participation by African Americans in the American soundscape was the auto magnate, Henry Ford, who reacted by using his chain of automobile dealerships to sponsor "old time" (read "white") music.[16] However, eventually (by 1920) black entrepreneurs managed to convince the record companies that "black Americans are manic consumers of their own popular culture." Thereafter, "the white men making up their new business [recognized] that Negroes had something in their pockets worth reaching in to take [and soon] more than a dozen small companies were started, including four upstart black-owned labels."[17] By the early 1960s – the time when the fictional Pete Campbell was attempting to "integrate" ad campaigns pitched at white and black consumers – "black music" had already achieved "cross-market success."[18]

Although African American consumption of a variety of products was getting the attention of producers and advertisers by the mid-twentieth century, a focus on the automobile provides an exemplary window into the consumption–civic life relationship. As Gilroy suggests in his analysis of black consumption patterns, "the automobile supplies the best tool for all attempts to understand both their behaviour as consumers and their diminishing distance from citizenship."[19] Pointing out that by the end of the twentieth century, African Americans constituted roughly "30 percent of the automotive buying public" while they constituted "only 12 percent of the U.S. population," he surmises that "it is hard to resist the idea that the special seductions of car culture have become an important part of the overdeveloped countries to the most mainstream of dreams."[20]

African American car consumption was inflecting America's *moral* economy, weighing positively not only on white perceptions of the value of the African American population but also and especially on African Americans' own sense of self-worth, based on the achievement of a mobility articulated both symbolically and materially (as they enjoyed an "auto-autonomy" after a fraught history of "brutal confinement and coerced labour"). At the same time, automobile culture was also at the center of *political* economy.[21] Bradford Snell's 1974 report on "American Ground Transport," described the political dynamic through which the automobile came to dominate American transportation. Central to the process was the power of General Motors, "whose common control of auto, truck, bus and locomotive production was a major factor in the displacement of rail and bus transportation by cars and trucks [so that ultimately] a monopoly in ground vehicle production ... led inexorably to a breakdown of this nation's ground transportation."[22] After General Motors had diversified into city bus and rail businesses and closed down electric rails systems in order to promote GM buses, they effectively "motorized the city." And subsequently, "together with Standard Oil of California, Firestone Tire, and two other suppliers of bus-related products, [they] contributed more than $9 million to [a] holding company for the purpose of converting electric transit systems in 16 states to GM bus operations."[23] Of course thanks in part to the "radical monopoly" of transportation by the big three automobile companies – GM, Ford, and Chrysler – the automobile's transportation dominance was consummated when the Congress passed the Federal Highway Act of 1956, which spurred the interstate highway system.[24] Among what followed was not merely that system's role in expanding vehicular access to interstate commerce but also a proliferation of cultural genres – especially road movies and television series – involved in the romanticization of automobile culture. The "Rust-belt" economy became dwarfed by that of the "Sun-belt", "and [as] internal migration … from east to west continued unabated … Route 66 [portrayed in films and television series] found new life as a symbol of life on the road."[25] At the same time, the space of the city was attracting different cultural as well as economic meanings. Like the inner migrant heading west, the city dweller had increasingly become a traveling subject.

A brief genealogy of the moral economy of city space can help us appreciate the institutionalized mentality accompanying the motorizing of city space. "Throughout the eighteenth and nineteenth centuries," as Jennifer Bonham points out, "the division and regulation of street spaces in Amsterdam, Paris and London were debated in relation to the health, safety, morality, and economic well-being of the population."[26] By contrast, the city – as the domain of transport – had enfranchised a wholly different city space *dispositif* as the city inhabitant became a traveling subject. Instead of an urban design based on agencies and discourses of health, safety and life-style morality, agencies and discourses associated with automobile-oriented economy dominated the design of urban space. Travel within the city – and thus the design of urban space – was to be organized around a "transport discourse."[27] The city, whose boundaries had once been shaped by a walking subject, was transformed into one accommodating a subject-in-motorized-transit.[28] By the first half of the twentieth century, "the street was entrenched as a site of economical travel and travelers disciplined to this order of movement,"[29] thereby enabling the rapid growth of automobile manufacturing.

Hard Times

The dramatic expansion of Detroit's automobile industry in the twentieth century was not continuous. In the early 1930s, the industry experienced hard times – due in part to the shut-down of Ford plants while there was a changeover from the Model A to the newer V8 models in 1931 and thereafter to a Detroit banking crisis in 1933. Because Detroit was effectively a one-industry city, its employees were prey to economic downturns. Moreover, its banking crisis (as the Guardian Group bank, set up by the auto companies, participated in the nationwide banking failure) contributed to the national economic crisis as a whole.[30] What are "hard times?" In its ordinary usage, the expression refers to historical moments when social segments or enterprises that were once thriving (or at least surviving) economically are experiencing financial failure or extraordinary deprivation. When Charles Dickens famously addressed himself to the implications of hard times, he had them migrate well beyond the hard facts of economic deprivation.

His eponymous novel attacks not only the smug self-satisfaction of the economically privileged – while expressing sympathy for the under-privileged – but also
the thinking that prescribes austere, rationalistic models of political economy.
Attending a circus or reading poetry is anathema to those in the novel – Messrs
Gradgrind and Bounderby, for example – who value utilitarian, profit maxi-
mizing practices. And the novel juxtaposes the bloodless calculating mentalities of those with economic power and moral authority with the sympathetic,
embodied character of the underclass, whose exchanges of support are expressed
as very physical forms of caring.[31]

Dickens's *Hard Times* is thus a profoundly ethical work, where an ethics
of caring is juxtaposed with the moralizing crotchets supportive of rapacious
entrepreneurial practices during the hard times associated with the drudgery of
factory work. Of course, such hard times have always affected people and enterprises differentially. While some suffer, others thrive. For example, an article in
the *International Herald Tribune* reports a growing investment in wine during
the recent "hard financial times," pointing out that high-end wines are drawing
investors – among whom are bankers and financial managers – because "wine
gives greater return, even than shares."[32] The repositioning of wine as increasingly an object of investment speaks to some of the major consequences of
"hard times"; such times encourage changes in the way *things* are valued and
changes in the allocation of favorable financial opportunities to particular kinds
of *persons*. That financial types are disproportionately able to take advantage of
hard times reveals something about the controversial advantaging of particular
locations within the system of exchange.

That's why, as the banking crises drove the economic downturn, a U.S. Senate
committee scrutinized the Goldman Sachs financial corporation, which apparently exploited the recent (2007–2009) mortgage crisis. Goldman Sachs executives
were called to account in the panel's hearings for "their aggressive marketing of
mortgage investments at a time when the housing market was already starting to
falter."[33] Pointing out that the legality of Goldman's actions would be addressed
by the SEC (the Securities and Exchange Commission), Senator Carl Levin from
Michigan – who chairs the permanent subcommittee on investigations – made it
clear that his panel was concerned with moral economy rather than illicit transactions. He said that, while the SEC suit and the courts would address the legality
of its activities, "the question for us is one of ethics and policy: were Goldman's
actions in 2007 appropriate, and if not, should we act to bar similar actions in the
future?"[34] Historically, commercial life has often created disturbances in what
is regarded as ethical life. As Hegel famously put it, from the point of view of
the ethical life, the commercial life is both necessary and destructive, so that the
relationship between the two is "tragic."[35]

Although Hegel's generalization applies frequently, the tragedy genre does
not exhaust the complexities of the relationship. In particular, for purposes of
critical political analysis, it is crucial to identify those historical moments when
economies are moralized and to discover which voices (articulated through
which media) participate in the discursive exchanges. "Moral economy" is an
inter-discursive field in which cultural imperatives and ongoing negotiations

shape what is regarded as acceptable versus unacceptable forms of exchange and what kinds of persons are eligible as licit traders and/or consumers. Igor Kopytoff captures that field in part when he refers to the norms determining exchangeable things: "Out of the total range of things available in a society, only some of them are considered appropriate for marking as commodities."[36] I want to add that, parallel with the process through which certain culturally marked *things* become commodities, as they transcend their singularities to become exchangeable, is the process through which the range of *persons* morally eligible to participate in commodity exchange expands: for example, the above noted welcoming of African American-owned enterprises into the music industry. Accordingly, I turn next to two historical moments when moral economy is on the agenda, i.e., when the economy becomes contentiously moralized as the roles of persons and things take on different values because their moral eligibilities are in transition.

Destabilizing times

In her investigation of the society–economy relationship in seventeenth-century England, Joyce Appleby addresses a historical moment that remains instructive. Noting that the seventeenth century witnessed the end of "the old European order," as sustained economic growth took place, she contrasts the old "moral economy" of "production and sustenance" – in which men and women were involved in "the daily round of tasks" subsumed by a divine rationale – with an emerging capitalism in which "the individual had become subsumed in a depersonalized aggregation [such that] his decisions were not only hidden from the examiner but, more important, the decisions were divorced from their consequences."[37] Not surprisingly, the dramatic change induced varying degrees of moralistic response. For example, in defense of the prior "moral universe," one writer (a religious pamphleteer) described the moral context in which economic activities must be judged thusly: "governours must of necessity and in all reason provide for the preservation and sustenance of the meanest members." The writer's case was in effect that "the freedom to set prices was a petty, pretentious assertion, incompatible with the laws of man and God."[38] But, as Appleby points out, the old moral economy was "in retreat." While some clergymen – for example, Roger Fenton – railed against the usurer, other clergymen – for example, Joseph Lee – "admire[d] the control over natural forces and the motive of self-interest represented by the improving farmer."[39] As Appleby ultimately demonstrates, the outbreak of moralizing was a short-term event, a response to a dramatic shift "as the principle of competitive pricing spread to every element of the economy, replacing custom or authoritarian direction with the market's aggregation of individual choices."[40] Eventually, the preponderance of treatises written by those with moral authority endorsed the new economy, finding ways in which it could be interpreted as "moral," which in that century amounted to its conforming to "the natural order of things."[41] And once the new economic structure had been institutionalized as the norm, moralistic treatises on economy became infrequent.

Roughly a century later, the emergence of the sentimental novel coincided with and morally endorsed another aspect of exchange: the exchange of sentiments. The model of family life depicted in ("sentimental") novels by Henry Fielding and Samuel Richardson, among others, reflected a period in which "family lineage gave way to family life."[42] As a marriage bond based on exchanges of sentiment displaced the "fading patriarchal and lineage-oriented" marriage of class contract, legal interventions ensued, connecting the moral economy of the family with the political economy of the nation (as the Parliament became aware of the nexus between family and economic life).[43] During the passage of the 1753 Marriage Act, one of the act's defenders summarized the necessity of governmental intervention in family life: "The happiness and prosperity of the country depends not only on having a great number of children born, but on having always a great number of well brought up and inured from their infancy to labour and industry."[44] As was the case in the prior century, when moralizing erupted over changes in the subject-exchange nexus, the parliamentary debate featured a clash of moral discourses whose context involved entanglements between social life and economic practices.

As the two examples from England show, socially invested symbolic economies run parallel with the more rationalistic aspects of economic exchange; a co-occurrence to which the sociologist, Georg Simmel, famously addressed himself. With a concentration on the connections between social bonds and economic relations, Simmel shows how a morally fraught history of economy is bound up with changes in the relationships between inter-subjective patterns and monetary relations. Among the most intense historical moments, according to Simmel, are those in which the "interdependence of personality and material relationships, which is typical of the barter economy, is dissolved by the money economy."[45] Simmel's insight implies that people attach some of their ontological anxieties to a concern with finding firm warrant for the value of money, not only to protect their wealth but also to reconnect their exchanges to a foundation with collective symbolic guarantees. In what follows, I extend this observation to the case of automobility in order to assess the historical and contemporary moralizations associated with automobiles, which have functioned both as commodities and as objects bound up with social identity.

Hard times for the automobile industry: too ontological to fail

To appreciate the ontological anxieties evoked by the potential failure of America's auto industry we have to inquire into America's attachment to – its virtual romance with – the automobile. It's an extended romance reflected in a wide variety of media and genres. Here I analyze two series of texts in which the primary protagonists, who are intimately involved with the economy and culture of the automobile, age in real historical time. One is Walt Wallett, the patriarch of the garage-owning Wallett family in Frank King's syndicated comic strip, *Gasoline Alley*. Walt's comic strip family story was launched in 1921 and is still going. The other is Harry Angstrom, aka Rabbit, the protagonist in John

Updike's "Rabbit Quartet": the novels *Rabbit Run* (1960), *Rabbit Redux* (1971), *Rabbit is Rich* (1981), and *Rabbit at Rest* (1990). However, before treating some of the relevant aspects of those aesthetic subjects, whose changing life experiences parallel changes in the economy and culture of the automobile, I want to provide a broader analysis of the basis of automobility's ontological depth within American society.

As John Urry notes, "automobility" is a term that references various dimensions of the dominance of automotive transit, among which is the car as a *machinic complex:*

> constituted through its technical and social interlinkages with other industries, car parts and accessories; petrol refining and distribution; road building and maintenance; hotels, roadside service areas and motels; car sales [the vocation of Updike's Harry Angstrom] and repair workshops [the vocation of King's Walt Wallett]; suburban house building; retailing and leisure complexes; advertising and marketing; urban design and planning.[46]

However, as Urry goes on to point out, those linkages – which reflect the way the car is embedded in a complex socio-economic network – are accompanied by a car–body linkage, a "machinic hybridization of the car-driver … a kind of libidinal economy [that] has developed around the car, in which subjectivities get invested in the car as an enormously powerful and mobile object."[47]

Urry's suggestion about the connection between the car-driver and libidinal economy is suggested in a couple of novels. For example, in his novel, *Middlesex* (2002), Jeffrey Eugenides' character – the photographer, Maurice Plantagenet – markets images in which female bodies are associated with automobiles: "The formula was straightforward: women in lingerie lounging in cars …. Plantagenet teased out all the harmonies, between a buttock's curve and a fender's, between corset and upholstery pleats, between garter belts and fan belts."[48] However, the connection is much more dramatically enacted in J. G. Ballard's earlier novel *Crash* (1973), which turns America's romance with the automobile into an erotic attachment to its deadly potential. The novel's three protagonists – Vaughan, Ballard and Catherine – seek the "erotic delirium"[49] of the car crash; motivated in part by their obsessions with the historic connection between automobiles and the deaths of iconic celebrities: James Dean, Albert Camus, Jane Mansfield, and John F. Kennedy. They seek arousal by staging potentially deadly car crashes. And Vaughan, a TV scientist, who initiates the others to the eroticism of car crashes, has become especially obsessed with the ultimate deadly/erotic accident – a head-on collision with a car carrying the actress Elizabeth Taylor. He creates photographic montages of accident victims in which mutilated body parts are fused with car parts:

> In several of the photographs the source of the wound as indicated by a detail of that portion of the car which had caused the injury: beside a casualty ward photograph of a bifurcated penis was an insert of a handbrake unit; above a close-up of a massively bruised vulva was a steering-wheel boss and its

manufacturer's medallion. These unions of torn genitalia and sections of car body and instrument panel formed a series of disturbing modules, units in a new currency of pain and desire.[50]

Vaughan's photographic art rubs off on the novel's narrator, Ballard's perceptions: "I saw the interior of the motor-car as a kaleidoscope of illuminated pieces of the bodies of women. This anthology of wrists and elbow, thigh and pubis formed ever changing marriages with the contours of the automobile."[51] Ultimately, the novel (as does David Cronenberg's subsequent film version of it) encourages reflection about way the vulnerability of automobiles to deadly accidents evokes an intimacy between death and Eros – which undoubtedly contributes to the ontological depth of automobile culture.

A. R. Stone provides an analytic that elaborates the ontological implications of Urry's observations about the "machinic hybridization of the car-driver" and Ballard's and Cronenberg's eroticizing of it. Rather than the mechanical prostheses of the industrial age, Stone analyzes the communication prostheses of the information age to assay the implications of the body's "prosthetic sociality" (as it is involved for example in phone sex). Using the concept of "machinic desire" to characterize the body's technological hybridity as it is extended to distant desired objects, Stone shows how new versions of the "intelligible body" acquire acceptance.[52] He suggests that a "citizen," who is "socially apprehensible is a collection of physical and discursive elements," remains socially apprehensible through "warranting," which is the process through which a prosthetically altered citizen acquires a fiduciary recognition of the agency of his or her acts. Just as warranting was problematic during the mechanical age – when there were qualms about agency because labor was increasingly mediated by mechanical prostheses that extended the physical body, so that the "body–machine complex" had to be "warranted" (i.e., morally negotiated)[53] – the "post mechanical age and the beginning of the virtual age" have rendered warranting "problematic."[54] Stone goes on to address himself to the warranting process that ultimately tempers the moralistic exchanges over agency that info-technology-inspired "machinic desire" has provoked.

The emergence of automobile culture during the mechanical age was also accompanied by moral anxieties, which were articulated in a variety of media – especially newspapers, where they dominated headlines. Automobiles were often greeted by a "storm of indignation:" among other things because of the way they frightened horses and constituted a disturbance to the outdoor soundscape.[55] In 1906, "Tennessee Representative Thetus Sims channeled rural and working class antipathy to the horseless carriage in his House-floor tirade against the 'rich, reckless, dare-devil young men, driving automobiles simply for pleasure'."[56] And the writer Henry Adams famously referred to the automobile as a "nightmare at a hundred kilometers an hour, almost as destructive as the electric tram which was only ten years older; and threatening to become as terrible as the locomotive steam engine itself."[57] Nevertheless, the car–driver assemblage rapidly acquired warranting throughout the twentieth century. As social space became structured as "auto space," and the landscape increasingly became a motorscape, the car–driver complex became absorbed into the temporal rhythms of daily life.[58] Ultimately, "car-drivers" and "car-passengers" entered civil society as familiar and unproblematic "quasi-objects."[59] Moreover, as work and family life increasingly ontologized the automobile – inasmuch as cars served as a habitus and mode of dwelling along with the home and work place – diverse genres of popular culture warranted the entanglement of the automobile with the spaces and rhythms of a life world in which automobiles symbolized freedom of movement for a collective that had come to interpret 'the good life" as, in part, the product of a "citizenship of mobility."[60]

Gasoline Alley

Frank King's *Gasoline Alley* articulated two dimensions of the world that together helped his comic strip participate as a warranting medium for automobile culture. *Gasoline Alley* began as a strip about the automobile fad and eventually developed a storyline that treated "the human concerns of love, marriage, happiness, and family."[61] Walt began as a confirmed bachelor, but King's strip slowly absorbed him into traditional family life. First, in the February 14, 1921 strip, Walt became "Uncle Walt," after he found a baby abandoned on his doorstep. The baby, named Skeezix ("cowboy slang for a motherless calf")[62] is adopted by Walt and ends up aging along with Walt, beginning in the garage as a worker and then manager, fighting in World War II, marrying and having children, and existing finally as a retired grandfather. He, like Walt and the rest of the strip's characters, age in historical time. Then, to further develop the strip as a family saga, King has Walt meet Phyllis, whom he marries in 1926. Subsequently, as family members arrive through birth, courtship and marriage, the strip inter-articulates the idealized hetero-normal American family with the economy and culture of the automobile.

　Gasoline Alley therefore became a family romance that merged with America's romance with the automobile. That merging is figured early on. In the January 5, 1921 edition, someone in a business office is overhearing his colleague, Avery, on the phone talking about "Betsy," whom he had filled with alcohol on the way to a restaurant, "But she died just before we got there." When the eavesdropper says, "Gosh Avery, that's awful! Who was Betsy?" Avery replies, "Betsy? Oh, that's my car."[63] And the metaphors connecting sentimental human attachments with the automobile work in the reverse direction as well. In that same year, in the February 25th edition Walt is trying unsuccessfully to give the bawling Skeezix his bottle feeding. To overcome the baby's resistance to the bottle (or vice versa), he heats a sewing needle and inserts it in the bottle's nipple to enlarge the hole and says, "No wonder, the vacuum system wasn't working right! We've got to enlarge the intake; here's my motto – when things don't work OK adjust the carburetor."

　However, the attracting power and image-pervasiveness of the automobile goes beyond its interpenetration with sentimental attachments. It also serves as a counterforce to traditional institutions. In that same year – in the January 15th edition – the character Doc draws a warning for working on his car on a Sunday morning, as Walt and a couple of his friends kibitz over the fence while Doc is laboring. One of them says "you'd better get your car in shape on Saturdays! When they pass the blue laws, they'll jail you for doing it Sunday mornings!" Doc responds, "Aw that's bunk. Any time they can put over any fool laws like that, I'll beat it for Cuba." And in an edition two months later (March 16th), Avery's old car is the subject of a conversation in which it is seen as a historical archive. After Avery states that "it would have made an interesting story if I'd kept a diary of that car of mine Walt. It's seen life!" Walt notes that the "fluted fender tells the tale of the day in 1912 you tried to beat Percy Ford to the corner," and the two others – Doc and Bill – chime in about the stories that other dents and bruises could tell. The sense of that episode – that the bonds of friendship are radically entangled with a passionate interest in the automobile – is continuously repeated in subsequent editions. Throughout the years of the strip, in which three cartoonists have succeeded King (Bill Perry, Dick Moores, and the strip's current cartoonist, Jim Scancarelli), the trajectory of family life – in effect a cartoon soap opera – has been accompanied by a chorus of friends (Walt, Doc, Avery and Bill), all engaged in car talk. The 16 March 1921 episode reflects the way the auto as object had migrated from mere transportation to a "quasi-technical hobby." Subsequently, as Reuel Denney notes, "the auto – as it evolved between 1920 and 1945 – had passed through a stage of existence symbolized by the comic strip 'Gasoline Alley.' As auto, it had lost much of its old novelty as transportation; in order to retain glamour, it had to become, in differentiated forms, a kind of daily apparel" – yet another way to figure the ontological depth of automobility.[64]

Updike's "Rabbit"

Although John Updike's Rabbit quartet occupies a briefer historical period – the 1960s through the 80s – than *Gasoline Alley*'s continuing narrative, the texts also participate in a reflection on America's automobility. However, while the *Gasoline Alley* strip enacts a more or less smooth articulation between an idealized American family life and a valorized development of automobility, Updike's American family is a prey to disintegrating pressures: his country's romance with the automobile is as much a hostage situation as it is a boon to everyday life. While Walt and family run a garage, Updike's Rabbit runs a Toyota sales franchise. Motorscapes and car–driver complexes appear frequently, and at one point, in the most automobile-oriented novel in the series, *Rabbit is Rich*, Updike provides a brief genealogy of the American road as it had changed in Rabbit's experience throughout the first three novels of the quartet: "When Rabbit first began to drive the road was full of old fogeys going too slow and now it seems nothing but kids in a hell of a hurry, pushing."[65]

However, the American automobile economy and culture are in crisis in *Rabbit is Rich*. Whereas "hard times" for rural America stemmed from drought conditions (Jefferson's rural-oriented democracy is long past by the time Updike's American is being narrated), the American democracy had become a "dromocracy" – an urbanized society characterized by movement and acceleration rather than a checkerboard of farms[66] – and "hard times" are imposed by energy crises rather than bad weather. Specifically, the novel opens in the period of the oil crisis of the early 1970s and has Rabbit reflecting on the advantages of his car dealership, which sells fuel-efficient Toyotas: "The fucking world is running out of gas. But they won't catch him, not yet, because there isn't a piece of junk on the road gets better mileage than his Toyotas ... the great American ride is ending. Gas lines at ninety-nine point nine cents a gallon and ninety percent of the stations to be closed for the weekend."[67] Yet, from Rabbit's point of view, the success of his Toyota franchise is a mixed blessing because he identifies with the U.S.'s traditional automobile supremacy. Seeing the gas crisis as a symbolic crisis as well, Rabbit is concerned that his country is becoming less recognizable. Talking to a customer, he says, "here we're supposed to be Automobile Heaven and the foreigners come up with all the ideas. If you ask me Detroit's let us all down, two hundred million of us."[68] As Rabbit's remark suggests, there has been a strong ideational connection between national allegiance and the consumption of American cars.

As with *Gasoline Alley*, the economy and culture of the automobile pervades Updike's Rabbit quartet. However, Rabbit's family saga does not live up to the romantic regulative ideals displayed in *Gasoline Alley*. Rather, drug problems, adultery and other aspects of marital stress – the vicissitudes of financial insecurity and success – and generational conflicts plague the family history. In particular, the schism between Rabbit (Harry) and his son Nelson is reflected in their different views about the Toyota franchise that has been the basis of the family's financial success. By the time the fourth volume is launched, Nelson is running the Toyota dealership. While, despite his ambivalence about an unrecognizable "America" Rabbit has admired the craftsmanship and marketing sagacity of the Toyota Company, Nelson sees the company as anachronistic: "They're still giving us cars that look like gas-misers when there's been a gas glut for ten years. Americans want to go back to fins and convertibles and the limo look and these Japs are still trying to sell these tidy little boxes."[69]

Of course, as is now well known, Toyota – and the rest of the Japanese auto industry – was more prescient than Updike's Nelson Angstrom. Detroit's failure to anticipate what consumers would want (and would be able to drive economically) resulted in a massive loss of their market share of auto sales – to the point of virtual bankruptcy. The subsequent government bailout of the American auto industry resulted in an exemplary "event" of moral economy. While many congressmen and senators have pushed a moral agenda – in which saving the auto industry was necessary both to protect workers in the industry, and in related occupations, to maintain America's pride in its auto industry – many editorial writers, and academic economists in editorials and blogs, have inveighed against "granting immortality to Detroit's big three."[70] As the moral economy–political economy encounter has proceeded, the different sides have weighed the immorality of supporting an industry that has grown "flat out lazy pursuing short-term profit" and "thus deserves to face the consequences"[71] against the moral urgency of protecting American jobs, inasmuch as "one in six American jobs are linked to the American automobile industry."[72] All the positions have been framed within a more general concern with the extent to which it is appropriate for the government to interfere in the economy, irrespective of who might suffer the

consequences of industry failure. However, rather than pursue the various positions of that extended event – the moralization of the auto industry segment of the
American economy – I want to return briefly to Dickens's ethical concerns elaborated in *Hard Times*. Then I shall consider a cinematic text that transcends the
capitalism–government relationship currently dominating the American scene in
order to provide a perspective on hard times that evinces a contemporary social
ethics of exchange, rather than a moralizing of economy.

Ethico-aesthetics and the economy in *Hard Times*

As I suggested, Dickens's *Hard Times* is a profoundly ethical text. However,
its ethical gloss on the industrial age works not through moral injunctions but
by virtue of the juxtapositions of its aesthetic subjects. In Dickens's novel, the
key aesthetic subjects are constituted as body–factory complexes (just as the
subjects of automobility are constituted as car–driver complexes). His text
delivers a "repetition of the factory structure in every aspect of Coketown's
life"[73] with an imagery that is so pervasive that Coketown's structure migrates
into its subjects. For example, the Coketown "of red brick," shows up in the
physiognomy of Mr. Gradgrind, whose face is represented as a "square wall
of forehead."[74] And throughout the novel, Dickens's figuration emphasizes the
factory as a machine of capture, entrapping the working class.[75] In suggesting
that such genre forms constitute ethical reflection rather than moralizing (what I
term an ethico-aesthetics), my distinction accords with Jill Bennett's treatment
of the empathic vision inherent in some aspects of the visual arts. Stating, "it is
always easy for art and for audiences of art to take the moral line," she credits the
artists Doris Salcedo and Willie Doherty (who develop oblique still and moving
violent images) with encouraging an "ethical imperative."[76] Their work thinks
beyond morally fixed roles. In the distinction that Bennett is suggesting, morality
is constituted as judgments based on fixed moral codes, while ethico-aesthetic
enactments seek to provide a frame for reflecting on the meaning and value of
events and arrangements in the face of either competing and incommensurate
value commitments and/or alternative perspectives. Ethico-aesthetic analytics
are oriented toward accessing the virtual as a space of "event potential" (i.e., a
space that contains alternative possibilities for actualization) rather than toward
judgment-making; they "overthrow ... the system of judgment."[77]

The ethico-aesthetic analysis I want to pursue here takes special heed of the
film form's advantages, which is well suited to offer alternative perspectives on
what is or could be the case. As Gilles Deleuze suggests, cinema can encourage
reflection on and negotiation of alternative perspectives because of the way it
functions without a dominant center. Its critical thinking capacity inheres in
its deprivileging of centered commanding perception, allowing the disorganized multiplicity that is the world to emerge. In his words: "Instead of going
from the acentered state of things to centered perception, [we] could go back
up towards the acentered state of things and get closer to it."[78] In addition to the
ethico-aesthetic effects of film form are the effects of the engagement between
the film's bundles of sensations – its affects and percepts – with concepts. When

philosophy encounters film, the encounter is one between a "practice of concepts" and "the other practices with which it interferes ... [cinema as] a new practice of images and signs."[79] The "interference" between the two practices encourages *thinking* rather than moralizing. Such interferences, according to Deleuze, are precisely the way philosophy (as opposed to moral judgment) renders cinema as critical thought.[80] To illustrate the difference, I want first to reengage briefly Cronenberg's film version of the Ballard novel *Crash*. One of the typical reactions to the film was moralistic condemnation in reaction to images of explicit sex and intentionally sought mutilation – most famously by the English film critic, Nigel Reynolds, whose review in the British paper, the *Daily Telegraph*, led to the film being banned in the UK: "The film is morally vacuous, nasty, violent and little more than an excuse to string together one scene after another of sexual intercourse."[81] An *analysis* (as opposed to a *moral* judgment) of *Crash* must heed the way the film effects a complex translation from a textual to a visual mode to treat the erotic entanglements between the flesh of bodies and the twisted and deformed metal surfaces of crashed automobiles. It would focus for example on Cronenberg's cinematic metonymies, which enact Ballard's concepts with images to convey what is unshowable, given the rating and censorship norms controlling film releases.[82]

Similarly, there are moralistic reactions to the film with which I end my analysis – Vachylav Krishtofovich's *Friend of the Deceased* (1997) – for example, one by a critic who complained about the aestheticized view of Kiev that Krishtofovich provides: "a place attractive to the foreign viewer ... a place of coffee loving people who sit around in cafés discussing literature and poetry or playing music ... the perfect tourist brochure of a city that is both historic and romantic."[83] That moralistic review belongs to what Jacques Rancière calls "the ethical regime of images," within which one renders judgments about what should be shown in relation to a particular ideal.[84] By contrast, a philosophical "interference" with the film would treat the way the film's images allow us to interpret the era of capitalism that deploys its forces through the experiences of its characters in relation to its governing concept, that of friendship, which is abrogated by the form of pirate capitalism dominating Kiev's economy. To philosophize rather than moralize the film is especially apropos because (as Deleuze and Guattari have pointed out) the "friend" is the persona that belongs to the Greek origin of "philo-sophy".[85] Thus, to conceptually juxtapose philosophy with capitalism is to examine the film's presentation of a Kiev whose characters struggle to extract friendship – or *Sittlichkeit* – in the midst of the chaos of a predatory economy.

Conclusion: the philosophized economy

Krishtofovich's *Friend of the Deceased* – based on Andrey Kurkov's novel *A Matter of Death and Life* (1996) – represents the city of Kiev during extremely hard times. Its historical period (as reported in an investigation by the United Nations Development Program) is "the transition to market economies in many post-communist societies of the former Soviet Union and other former eastern bloc countries in Europe."[86] At the time at which the novel and subsequently the film appeared, the society is experiencing a demographic collapse. Lives are radically unstable (life expectancy for men has fallen from 62 to 58), and the city – as represented by Kurkov and Krishtofovich – has a chaotic economy. People are experiencing an economic squeeze and lack of work opportunities, the local mafia runs the economy as a form of pirate capitalism, and rising animosities are yielding work for an array of contract killers. Although some automobiles are present, one of which symbolizes one of the city's primary fault-lines, Krishtofovich's Kiev is more a cityscape than a motorscape. And significantly, the transition that Kiev is experiencing is moral as well as ethical. The characters' reactions to events emerge from a variety of historical and contemporary sources of moral injunction – religious, Communist, and neo-liberal, among others. But none of them seems to inhibit the exploitation and violence surrounding systems of exchange.

Throughout the film, an absence of *Sittlichkeit* is in evidence as the economic chaos has rendered a situation in which "the normative relays between personal and collective ethics [had become] frayed and exposed."[87] The film's extreme version of predatory (and illicit) exchanges, which feature violent animosities and exploitive transactions, encourages reflection on what is absent – ethically based, enduring exchanges of sympathy. In short, (to use the film's main concept) genuine friendship – exchanges of affection and support – has been displaced by predatory forms of exchange. A few significant venues comprise the film's *mise en scène*. The first is an apartment where the viewer witnesses a deteriorating marriage. The husband, Anatoli (Andre Lazarev), is an intellectual with a linguistics degree. As the film opens he is an unemployed translator because the city (indeed the country as a whole) no longer has a need for his talents. His wife, Katia (Angelike Nevolina), has become a successful advertising executive with dwindling emotional largess for a depressed, apartment-bound Anatoli. She is having an affair with a co-worker, and the temporal rhythms and spatial uses of their apartment life keep her and Anatoli (Tolya for short) as separated as their small space allows.

As the film opens, the viewer sees what appears as the old Kiev – a skyline punctuated by traditional Russian architecture. The camera pulls back until we see that Kiev is being shown from the window of Tolya and Katia's cramped apartment. While Tolya is seated at a small desk, speaking on the phone about his inability to get decent fees for his translation work, Katia comes into view, asking to interrupt to make a call to her place of business. Then, as she leaves the apartment, Tolya watches her enter the street where we then see an expensive late model red car with a sunroof drive past with Katia as a passenger. She has been picked up by her co-worker/lover. Later in the film – after Katia has virtually moved out of the apartment – Tolya watches from a distance while she and her lover get in the car together (in an earlier conversation with Katia, he had referred to her lover as the man with the red car). The trajectory of image shots make it appear that Katia's desire for her lover renders him a car–driver complex. In the one scene in which he is visible outside the car we see a fashionably dressed young man – well coiffed and blow dried, in contrast with the continuously tousled and casually dressed Tolya. Katia's lover fits well with his fashionable automobile.

However, it is their habituses as a whole, rather than their modes of transportation, that locate the couple differentially within the local economy. As the film progresses, we witness two fractured contracts – the marriage and the social; fractures owed in large part to Kiev's chaotic economy. As I suggested, in such hard times some thrive while others fail. Accordingly, in the film narrative, Tolya's college education has gone for naught, largely because his government (we learn as he speaks on the phone) has been unable to pay for the services he has rendered thus far and has nothing else to offer. At the same time, his attempt to earn in the private sector yields very little as well. Throughout the film, shots of phone calls – emphasized when the camera moves in for close-ups of the phone on Tolya's desk – play an important role. In the early apartment scene – when Tolya's futile attempt to connect with a work opportunity on the phone is interrupted as Katia takes a call from her lover/colleague – we see that the phone's receiver is taped down. Voices from the outside enter the apartment as a whole through then phone's speaker rather than in the ear of the listener. However the couple's sharing of communication from the outside is soon to be abrogated. In a second apartment scene, Katia has acquired a cell phone, which allows her to exit from a shared experience of the exterior. Her connection with auto-mobility is seconded by her phone autonomy.

At one point, Katia's cell phone rings while she is in the bathroom and she shouts to Tolya to hand it to her (later explaining that it belongs to a colleague). When Tolya moves to hand Katia the phone, he murmurs that it is "a portable" – in contrast with his immobile, taped down phone. Their economic lives are thus symbolized by their phones. Katia is upwardly mobile in the economy (she is seen/heard on her cell phone arranging a transaction that involves billions in rubles), while Tolya's economic existence is on hold. Moreover – and crucially – Tolya and Katia have different socio-economic roles. Katia's vocation is attuned to the modern economy. As a rising executive in an advertising firm, she works on desire-provoking codes to stimulate consumption. By contrast, as a translator Tolya's vocation is one of bridging interpersonal socio-linguistic difference, of bringing people who are culturally separated into accord. The contrast between Katia's success and Tolya's marginal under-employed existence says much about the way an anarchic decentralized capitalism in the former eastern bloc has privileged alternative locations in the economy.

At the level of personal fates, the film narrative is complex. Depressed about his lack of employment and the imminent end of his marriage, Tolya recounts his bleak situation to an old acquaintance, Dima, who runs a black market store and also trades in killers for hire. "I know a man who makes a living with one finger," Dima says. He connects Tolya with the contract killer, Kostia, assuming that Tolya wants to have his wife's lover killed. However instead of giving the killer directions (in an unmarked mailbox) – a picture of the target and a place and time where he hangs out – Tolya includes his own picture and indicates the café *he* frequents. But unplanned events intervene. The café closes early on the day of the killing, and later that day, Tolya meets a young prostitute, Lena, who offers a romantic rather than a contractual relationship. Feeling that life is now worth living, Tolya tries to call off the hit. When Dima tells him that these things cannot

Figure 2.2
Anatoli

be changed, Tolya hires another contract killer (an unemployed former solider) to kill Kostia, the one hired to kill him. Once it's done, and Tolya discovers that Kostia was a young father and husband, he finds Kostia's wife, gives her the money he found in Kostia's wallet and some of the money he obtained by hiring himself out (thanks to Dima's recommendation) to falsely testify about having an affair so a husband can get off without paying alimony to his ex wife. By the end of the film, Tolya is involved with Kostia's widow who, when she asks his connection with her late husband, gets the answer, "I'm a friend of the deceased."

While the intricate narrative constitutes the film's drama, the way the film thinks is best derived from the way its dialogue and images reveal the tension between predatory forms of exchange and friendship. The second primary venue – the café where Tolya hangs out – is, by virtue of the film's cross-cutting moments, juxtaposed with Dima's black market shop. The proprietress of the café shows friendly concern for Tolya, giving him cake and free drinks to assuage his manifest melancholy. By contrast, Dima deals only in predatory exchanges and pointedly explains at one point, in response to Tolya's question about whether Kostia was Dima's friend, that there is "no such thing nowadays, just business relationships." It is undeniable that many in the film's version of Kiev are not suited for friendship – most notably Lena's pimp, who beats her up and tries to sell her to a Turk. As Jacques Derrida puts it in his treatment of the philosophy and politics of friendship, "the mean, the malevolent, the ill-intentioned" cannot be "good friends" because their focus is on possessing things.[88] But Dima's remark is belied by gestures that contradict it. The prostitute Lena – like the café's propri- etress – offers Tolya friendship and intimacy rather than a business relationship (noting that she is Lena for him, while as Vika – her professional name – he would have had to pay). And, finally, the last scene with the red car provides a telling contrast with the intimacy between Tolya and Lena. As Tolya watches, hidden behind a tree outside his apartment building, Katia's colleague/lover picks her up in his expensive red car. The couple look stylish as they hurriedly pack the car but there is no sign of warm intimacy between them. It would seem that each provides the other with sign function value; they make appropriate escorts, and the connection looks more like a symbolic exchange than a close bond. Their relationship, like many in the film, is a sign of the way exchange relations, in a dystopic Kiev, have displaced friendship and intimacy. Yet ultimately, despite how exotic Kiev (with its old Russian architecture and cobblestone streets) may appear to the viewer, the tensions between a predatory economy and friendship or intimacy that the film articulates, through the trajectories that its form creates for its aesthetic subjects, have broad significance. The film therefore lives up to one of philosophy's primary tasks – to think rather than to judge.

3 The blues subject

Counter-memory, genre, and space

Introduction: beyond mere "culture": Afro America's political aesthetics

In a critique of a social science perspective that renders African American artistic genres as politically benign cultural expressions – for example soul and blues as mere black urban cultural artifacts – Robin D. G. Kelley points to the onto-political significance of various historically situated black aesthetics. For example, he shows how soul, as a trans-genre aesthetic in the 1960s and 1970s, reflected a notable "transformation" – a "shedding of the old 'Negro' ways and an embracing of 'black' power and pride."[1] As Kelley illustrates, the typical social science interpretation of black culture has "collapsed a wide range of histori-cally specific cultural practices and forms," as it searched for a singular aggre-gating concept. As a result, it has been unable to comprehend "soul not as a thing but as a discourse through which African-Americans, at a particular historical moment, claimed ownership of the symbols and practices of their own imagined community."[2]

Ralph Ellison supplies another pertinent example, one with broader political significance. He points out that Jimmie Rushing's early twentieth-century blues shouts signified "more than aesthetic enjoyment"; they "embod[ied] an ideal that anyone oppressed or almost defeated might draw from."[3] As I note in the preface, although for those attuned to the familiar social research paradigms, the political register of blues is hard to discern, what may appear to some as mere enter-tainment, for example Bessie Smith's song "Crazy Blues" (1920), is experienced among much of the African American assemblage as "an insurrectionary social text ... contributing to an evolving discourse on black revolutionary violence in the broadest sense ... black violence as a way of resisting white violence and unsettling a repressive social order."[4]

How should that "social order" be understood? The twentieth century, during which the blues developed in various artistic genres (in the context of a "repres-sive social order"), was – among others (as I noted in Chapter 2) – "the color line century."[5] In the nineteenth century, the violence shaping the Euro American-dominated order exhibited a different carceral topology. In addition to the array of fixed plantation/gulags in the South was a violent, westward moving frontier, a dynamic partitioning that quickened once the Civil War was over and ultimately, both materially and symbolically, effaced the once-existing plurality of nations. However, by the twentieth century, the state-sponsored violence that took place on the U.S.'s western frontier in the nineteenth century had shifted to urban frontiers. It was a "transformation of the frontier from a moving western boundary into a relatively fixed partitioning of urban space ... a racial frontier."[6]

The juxtaposition between those two violent topological moments is musically figured in Spike Lee's film *He Got Game* (1998). The soundtrack alternates between the vernacular-inspired symphonic music of Aaron Copland and the rap sounds and lyrics of Public Enemy. Copland's music was inspired by the "Yankee musical mission," which began in New England in the nineteenth century, when Euro American composers were bent on crafting a uniquely American music, freed from its European aesthetic dependency.[7] His western symphonies move that musical "American" nationalism a step further; they are paeans to Euro America's "ethnogenesis," its whitening of the continent.[8] Beginning with his *Appalachian Spring* and moving on to the more far western themed pieces – *Rodeo* and *Billy the Kid*,

> Copland's western works are fundamental to his pre-eminence in American music because the West looms so large in the national consciousness ... It is well known that Copland's use of open intervals and wide spacing, clear orchestration, and plain folk-like materials has given Americans a powerful musical image of the frontier.[9]

The melodic landscapes of Copland's music articulate well with the scenes of the western landscapes they accompany in the film (former killing fields now looking and sounding serene). While large, well-funded basketball programs in universities in the subdued and settled West (musically framed in upbeat Copland tunes) are vigorously recruiting Jesus Shuttlesworth (Ray Allen), a high school basketball star who for them is potential human capital, another America, its urban venues inhabited by much of the African American population, is shown accompanied by the rap music of Public Enemy. Public Enemy's staccato rhythms and inner city-directed lyrics speak to and mimic the sensibilities of an economically deprived African American assemblage. While Copland's western symphonies reference a complacent Euro American narrative of the ethnic shaping of the continent, Public Enemy's raps provide a different spatial focus and a more strident political edge. They evince a commentary on a contemporary mode of oppression, a predatory capitalism visited on a sports enterprise that exploits young African Americans and more generally on the ever-present commerce that inflects the game. Note for example the lyrics of their "Politics of the Sneaker Pimps": "I see corporate hands up in foreign lands. With the man behind the man gettin' paid behind the man." And some of their other songs treat the pervasive inequalities that constitute the political economy of America's racial-spatial order, for example "white men in suits don't have to jump." In effect, Lee's soundtrack stages a contrapuntal encounter between the exemplary musical scores of two different Americas, which reference alternative ethnic experiences.

One of those ethnic Americas constitutes what Amiri Baraka has called the blues people, suggesting that rather than a mere musical idiom, the blues are integral to an African American ontology, a distinctive way of being.[10] And, as I noted in Chapter 1, Clyde Woods has emphasized the epistemological aspect of the blues, which he figures as a "tradition of explanation," a "longstanding African American tradition of explaining reality and change."[11] Distinguishing "blues epistemology" from "plantation block explanation" (a prominent feature of American social science), Woods identifies two "touchstones" of blues epistemology: "The first involves the constant reestablishment of collective sensibility in the face of constant attacks by the plantation block and its allies," and the second, "social relations in the plantation south" that constituted a "historic commitment to social and personal investigation, description, and criticism present in the blues."[12]

Earlier, Albert Murray had already distinguished the epistemic significance of the blues from the Euro American social science protocols by distinguishing the social science "hero" from the blues "hero." The social science hero is typically involved in a melodramatic success story, operating within a perspective that never acknowledges what the blues hero references: "the fundamental condition of human life as being a ceaseless struggle for form against chaos, of sense against nonsense."[13] Inspired in part by Murray's "blues hero," whom I refigure as an aesthetic-political subject, I turn to the ways in which that blues subject, always already present within the African American assemblage, emerges in events of encounter.

"Inharmonic harmony:" blues encounters

> America not as melting pot but mixing board, wedged between two turntables and a microphone, amalgamating tortured newness from the scraps of dying sonic dynasties …
>
> Adam Mansbach

The politics of aesthetics intrinsic to the blues has emerged in episodes of encounter. Two autobiographical moments narrated by notable African American writers reflect that fraught history. One involves John Edgar Wideman. He reports a conversation with a "white boy" during his freshman year at a college, where he had few African American classmates. When the "white boy," influenced by a stereotype of African Americans, asked him if he liked the blues, Wideman writes, "I figured [since] I *was* the blues, I answered yeah sure."[14] Another, more elaborate conversational encounter is described by Ralph Ellison. When he moved from Alabama to New York City, Ellison saw himself as a "pioneer in what was our most sophisticated and densely populated city."[15] As such, he was a prey to a variety of vexing encounters – for example one that occurred in a 59th Street bookstore, where he was shopping for one of T.S. Elliot's works. After striking up a conversation with a "young [white] City College student," he had what he calls "an incident of minor embarrassment." In the course of the conversation, he used "the old cliché … and was my face red." His interlocutor countered with the remark, "What do you mean by red ... what you *really* mean is ashes of roses."[16] Ellison continues:

> I didn't like it, but there it was – I had been hit in mid flight; and so, brought down to earth, I joined in his laughter. But while he laughed in bright major chords, I responded darkly in minor-sevenths and flatted fifths, and I doubted that he was attuned to the deeper source of our inharmonic harmony.[17]

Of course those familiar with the blues will recognize the blues form articulated in Ellison's musically figured lament. The use of minor chords and flattened notes reflects the blues' politically-oriented aesthetic as an implicit critical commentary on the structures of dominance articulated in the self-confident use of major chords and clear confident (unworried) notes. Thus for example, to become a blues man, B. B. King was inspired by Charlie Christian's use of "diminished chords."[18] And as he worked on "worrying" his notes, he became attracted to Hawaiian slack key guitar tuning practices, which makes the guitar sound closer to human voices, enabling it to echo emotions.[19] What is the "worry" or problematic to which the blues is addressed? It is nothing less than that of seeking to manage the difficult transition from being a people who began as possessions to being one that is self-possessed. Attuned to that problematic, Ellison, in his lyrically rendered treatment of the blues origins of Richard Wright's writing (in which the blues functions as "an autobiographical chronicle of personal catastrophe expressed lyrically"), sees "the blues [as] an impulse to keep the painful details and episodes of a brutal experience alive in one's aching consciousness, to finger its jagged grain, and to transcend it, not by the consolation of philosophy, but by squeezing from it a near-tragic, near-comic lyricism."[20]

In practice, musical realizations of the blues aesthetic, which take the form of worrying notes and shifting from major to minor chords, take on a different form in literary texts. In that genre, they refigure familiar Euro American texts in order to speak of and to a different assemblage. Ellison himself provides an exemplary instance of a literary blues aesthetic in his *Invisible Man*. In Chapter 5 his narrator tells the story of the founding of a "Negro" college in an unidentified southern state. The chapter's key moment is a eulogy to the college's Founder, which both mimics and re-inflects Walt Whitman's famous poem, "When Lilacs Last in the Dooryard Bloom'd," a eulogy Whitman wrote after the death of President Lincoln. As one commentator summarizes the reference, "All the Whitman symbols are there: the lilac, the star, the thrush – the bells and the funeral train."[21] But "Ellison employs them for almost entirely opposite reasons than did the bard of American poetry."[22]

While "Whitman was attempting to measure the potential of the poetic mind within the framework of the death of the great emancipator, Abraham Lincoln," Ellison "uses these same symbols ... to measure the great irony and bitter disillusion of racial betrayal brought about after the death of another great fighter for emancipation, the beloved Founder – Ellison's picture of a black and mythical Lincoln."[23] Lest there be lingering doubt about Ellison's contrapuntal homology between President Lincoln and the college's Founder, Ellison's eulogist has the

Founder confronting a "great struggle" which, rather than South versus North, is between "black folk and white folk … each fearful of the other [such that] A whole region is caught up in a terrible tension."[24] And the Founder is variously referred to as "great captain" (echoing one of Whitman's metaphors for Lincoln), and as a "President" whose significance loomed much larger than what one would expect of "just a president of a college;" instead "he was," claims the eulogist, "a leader, a – statesman – who carried our problems to those above us, even unto the White House."[25]

Two analytics apply to the political significance of Ellison's versioning/signifying of Whitman's eulogy. First, the style of his appropriation of Whitman's Lincoln eulogy falls within Houston A. Baker Jr.'s characterization of African American writing that evinces a "mastery of form," a strategy in which the black writer uses the genres and phrasings of established white writers but effects a displacement in context and tone that will engage effectively with white readers' modes of reception while at the same time addressing "the contours, necessities, and required programs of his own culture."[26] Second, Ellison's discursive gestures fall within Gilles Deleuze and Félix Guattari's concept of "minor literature," a literature [that] doesn't come from a minor language; it is rather that which a minority constructs within a major language.[27]

The minor literature concept applies to much African American bluesy writing – for example Alice Walker's blues idiom-inflected novel, *The Color Purple*, which "she wrote in a language both her own and not her own."[28] Writing in a style already made familiar by writers who participated in "the Harlem Renaissance," Walker uses both "a proper grammar" (i.e., that characteristic in the writing of the "white majority") and "a syntax of a modified African Americans [sic] dialect."[29] In what follows, I focus on the way that blues aesthetic-political subjects function in diverse literary enactments of blues ontology and epistemology, beginning with a treatment of the blues detective.

Blues subjects (1): the blues detective

> Fiction at its best may well be a more inclusive intellectual discipline than science or even philosophy.
>
> Albert Murray[30]

If one heeds the hardboiled detective genre, Walter Mosley's first Easy Rawlins detective novel, *Devil in a Blue Dress*, provides an exemplary instance of a blues literary refiguring. As the novel opens, it's 1948; a "white man," Dwight Albright, enters Joppy's bar in a black section of Los Angeles, where Easy Rawlins, having just lost his job at an aircraft plant (which had been run he says like a southern plantation), is reading the want ads in the paper. The novel's opening line, uttered by Easy, "I was surprised to see a white man walk into Joppy's Bar,"[30] is a riff on an early scene in Raymond Chandler's *Farewell My Lovely*, in which Chandler's detective, Philip Marlowe, accompanies another white man, a very large and fearsome Moose Molloy, making a surprise appearance in a black bar, looking for his former girlfriend, Velma (who had apparently worked there months before, when the bar had a mixed clientele).[31] In the case of *Devil*, the white man, Albright, is also looking for a (presumably) white woman, Daphne Monet, and is seeking to hire a black assistant who can unobtrusively investigate because, as he puts it, she has "a predilection for the company of Negroes."[32] Moreover, Mosley's description of Joppy, the bar owner, is a lot like Chandler's description of the black bouncer who ends up thrown against a wall by Moose Molloy. Both are described as having battle-worn faces.

As it turns out, Albright involves Easy in corrupt dealings associated with a mayoral election, which again has reference to an aspect of *Farewell My Lovely*, for Chandler's Marlowe is investigating a corrupt LA mayor, among others. However, while Chandler's detective is a typical white hardboiled sleuth – i.e., one whose codes apply to his vocation while he remains indifferent to the politics and morality of the milieu within which he does his sleuthing – Mosley's Easy functions as a "blues detective," one who is morally and politically attuned to the black urban experience and whose movements and voiced observations delineate the city's racial-spatial order. As Stephen Soitos points out, "Through their use of black detective personas, double-consciousness detection, black vernaculars, and hoodoo creations, African American detective writers signify on elements of the detective genre to their own ends."[33]

Moseley's aesthetico-political subject, Easy Rawlins, exemplifies the experiential basis that has historically given blues literary realizations their impetus. Mosley fashions Easy as one who, against the structures of racial oppression, has managed the transition that Baker ascribes as the condition for all African American creative genres:

> All African American creativity is conditioned by (and part of) a historical discourse that privileges certain economic terms. The creative individual (the *black subject*) must perforce come to terms with 'commercial deportation' and the 'economics of slavery.'[34]

Figure 3.1 Easy and Albright

As a result, Baker notes, African American writing invariably involves "an encounter with economic signs"[35] as their protagonists seek to effect the historical transition from having been, or having descended from, people who were commodities to being economically effective actors.

Mosley's Easy has a personal dilemma. He is afflicted by a complex identity paradox. In seeking economic independence – freedom from reliance on white structures of domination – he must negotiate an effective, economically situated self within the same white world that impedes that achievement. However, as an aesthetic subject, his political mission transcends the individual drama of the story; Easy solves the case, earns enough money to save his house, and – at least temporarily – gets the police, who were trying to pin a murder on him, off his back. But what is more politically telling: as a blues detective, Easy conveys a discovery other than the criminal wrong-doing of some of the novel's characters. He maps one of urban America's racial orders. As a "counter-reading to the hard-boiled detective's construction of the body politic,"[36] the novel turns attention away from the class emphasis of the crime novels of Dashiell Hammett and Raymond Chandler and towards delineation of the pervasiveness of the color line and all the political strategies enjoined by African Americans who must deal with it. It is a counter-text to various genres of Euro American expression – from minstrelsy through hardboiled detective fiction – that restage the boundaries of the "racial structure,"[37] and it "converts black communities from the exotic, marginal spaces of Dashiell Hammett's and Raymond Chandler's novels to the loci of competing political and social narratives."[38]

To effect that conversion, Mosley's Easy evinces the knowledge practices immanent in the African American community, one of which is the necessary reliance on networks of friendship. Easy enlists the assistance of his violent, sociopathic friend, Mouse, because he cannot rely on the institutionalized violence of white policing agencies; he also relies for advice on his more pacific friend, Odell, who supplies one of the novel's primary insights about the mid-twentieth century's racial-spatial order. At the end of the novel – while reflecting on the events of his sleuthing experience, especially his reliance on Mouse – Easy says to Odell, "If you know a man is wrong, I mean, if you know he did somethin' bad, but you don't turn him in to the law because he's your friend, do you think that's right?" Odell responds, "All you got is your friends Easy" – a simple response, pregnant with political implications.[39]

However, even though much of the blues aspect of Easy Rawlins's process of detection is manifest through the way his developing consciousness of his dilemma articulates a history of African American double consciousness – for example practices of masking, and trickster strategies – the political insights that the novel delivers are more available when Easy is seen as an aesthetic rather than a psychological subject. This is a conceptual shift I have already explicated in Chapter 1 with reference to Leo Bersani and Ulysse Dutoit's analysis of Jean-Luc Godard's film *Contempt* (1963), in which a couple become estranged as the wife becomes contemptuous of her husband. Although contempt is ordinarily understood as a psychological disposition, when the couple are rendered as aesthetic subjects, the film's focus is not on "the psychic origins of contempt" but on "its effects on the world," which the cinematic narrative articulates through "what contempt does to cinematic space ... how it affect[s] the visual field within which Godard works, and especially the range and kinds of movement allowed for in that space."[40] Similarly, *Devil*'s enactment of a blues epistemology is best appreciated less with attention to the drama associated with Easy's personal survival and more with attention to how the blues detective renders the racial topology and affective schisms of LA's mid-twentieth-century order.

Blues subjects (2): *RL's Dream*

While a blues aesthetic surfaces frequently in Mosley's Easy Rawlins detective novels, it is in his novel, *RL's Dream*, that the blues is the primary structuring aesthetic. The novel is at once about the blues and written in form that articulates a blues aesthetic. Mosley conceives it as "a prose ballad – a blues – of pain and redemption."[41] At the level of its narrative, the novel stages an encounter between two diasporic bodies from the South – Soupspoon, an elderly homeless African American blues man, and Kiki, a young alcoholic white woman who has undergone sexual abuse from her father. Kiki takes Soupspoon into her New York apartment after he is evicted from his in the same building. While they are living together, the old blues man sings the blues at a moment when he is awakened by Kiki's cries during a nightmare: "The blankets were kicked off her bed. Her naked behind was thrust up in the air because she was hunched over the pillow and some sheet," and Soupspoon reacts:

> A *white woman: skinny butt stuck out at me like a ripe peach in a low branch.* There was nobody left to understand how strange it was. How scary it was. Nobody to laugh and ask, "and then what you did?" *And then I died,* Soupspoon said to himself. There was nobody to hear him. And even if there was – so what? That was the blues.[42]

As the narrative progresses, Soupspoon attempts to revive his musical career; he has one last go at it in a back-alley gambling joint, only to come to the realization that he was never a real blues man, even though he had tried to emulate the legendary blues man, Robert (RL) Johnson:

> I never played the blues, not really. I run after it all these years. I scratched at its coattails and copied some notes. But the real blues is covered by mud and blood in the Mississippi Delta. The real blues is down that terrible passageway where RL traveled, sufferin' an singin' till he was dead. I followed him up to the gateway, but Satan scared me silly and left me back to cry.[43]

RL (Robert Johnson) enters the story both as actual historical person and as legend, actualized in his fictional playing companion/disciple's, Soupspoon's, account. For Soupspoon, "the memory of Robert Johnson was so strong in him that he sometimes felt that he could actually talk to the guitar man."[44] The historical Robert Johnson was a blues man from the Mississippi Delta. However, as a legend, his extraordinary virtuosity on the guitar has been alleged to stem from a pact he made with the devil. Soupspoon represents his virtuosity thus: "His hands were like angry spiders up and down them guitar strings. No man could play what R. Bob Leroy Robert Johnson could play."[45] However the actual Robert Johnson may have lived and played, his legend remains productive as "myth eclipses history."[46] Robert Johnson as legend migrates into diverse blues enactments. He serves as an icon of the emergence of the blues as it expresses the African American politico-aesthetic reaction to oppression.

Mosley animates the Robert Johnson blues subject to bring blues back to its experiential origins and thereby challenge more benign understandings – in which the blues is merely an object of musical reception. His Soupspoon expresses the difference:

> But the music they was hearin' was just a weak shadow, just like some echo of somethin' that happened a long time ago, They was feelin' something' but not what Robert Johnson made us feel in Arcola [Mississippi]. They can't get that naked. And they wouldn't want to even if they could, 'cause you know Robert Johnson's blues would rip the skin right off yo' back. Robert Johnson's blues get down to a nerve most people don't even have no more.[47]

Blues subjects (3): Robert Johnson's blues invests Indianness

> If blues songs do not explicitly protest social conditions, their accounts and declarations of heartbreak or of traveling urges resonate with the specific hardships of being black in America.
>
> Christine Levecq[48]

In Sherman Alexie's novel *Reservation Blues*, the legendary Robert Johnson visits a Spokane Indian reservation, lending his guitar to the Spokane, Thomas Builds-The-Fire, so he can express his tribe's "accounts and declarations of heartbreak [associated with being a Native American] in America."[49] That the blues is already part of the Spokane's historical experience is evidenced by the presence of a spiritual soothsayer, "Big Mom," who resides on a mountaintop and is doubtless a reference to the famous blues singer and composer, Big Mama Thornton. Thomas, a bluesy Native American storyteller who functions as a primary aesthetic subject in several of Alexie's novels, is edified and inspired in encounters with both Robert Johnson and Big Mom in this one. As he joins the Coyote Springs rock band, he infuses it with the African American blues tradition. However, reflecting the ways in which the Spokanes, like many Native American nations, had bought into an assimilative mentality (historically promoted by the Bureau of Indian Affairs, whose charge was to erase traditional forms of Indianness), few members of the tribe appreciate the blues-inflected turn of the band. Robert Johnson's arrival disturbs the Spokane's primary depoliticizing strategy, "forgetfulness." When Alexie has him perform "the worried blues," the Spokanes resist:

The music stopped. The reservation exhaled. Those blues created memories for the Spokanes, but they refused to claim them. The blues lit up a new road, but the Spokanes pulled out their old maps. Those blues churned up generations of anger and pain: car wrecks, suicides, murders. Those blues were ancient, aboriginal, indigenous.[50]

Certainly "Indian blues" emerges from an equally fraught history of Euro American domination. Their aesthetic initiatives, like those of African Americans, have required a response to a "degrading economy of signifiers."[51] However, the trajectories of their experiences – toward which their blues genres are directed – are different. Whereas the post-slavery experience of African Americans has involved segregation and other forms of violent exclusion, Native Americans have had to face various forms of forced assimilation as well. While African Americans have been spatially quarantined, Native Americans have been continually *re*spatialized in efforts – e.g., through violations of treaty agreements – to break up tribal (actually *national*) allegiances.

Confronting this historical experience, Alexie's *Reservation Blues* features the reality of a historically produced, Native American hybridity. His Coyote Springs band is a carrier of a hybrid blues idiom. While their lyrics treat the individual and collective catastrophes visited on Native American nations, their styles reflect an accumulation of diverse ethnic soundscapes. Moreover the group's composition references a diverse history of American popular culture genres (e.g., two of their singers are named Betty and Veronica, characters from the *Archie* comic strip). Here, as elsewhere in his writing, Alexie reaches not for authenticity – either of the blues or of Indiannness – but for a realization of the debts that identities owe to histories of encounter with otherness. As I have put it elsewhere, "Alexie's political point works not only for the Spokanes but also for all those engaged by a blues aesthetic: for the blues to be redemptive, a people must not only claim its past (its right to its history) but must also acknowledge its relationship with an estranged otherness."[52]

Blues subjects (4): Toni Morrison's blues fiction

Writing about music is like dancing about architecture.

Elvis Costello

The "about" to which Costello refers is not an appropriate grammatical account of the connection between writing and music in Toni Morrison's novels. Creating a blues aesthetic in her very first novel, *The Bluest Eye* (1970), as well as subsequently, Morrison refers to her writing as "speakerly, aural, colloquial."[53] *The Bluest Eye* is "the genesis of her effort,"[54] "to do," Morrison says, "what the music did for blacks, what we used to be able to do with each other in private and in that civilization that existed underneath the white civilization."[55] The novel is not *about* music; it *is* musical. For example, its main narrator, Claudia, and her mother are among the novel's "singing subjects."[56] Here is Claudia narrating her mother's singing, in a passage that captures the blues lyricism of both of them:

If my mother was in a singing mood ... She would sing about hard times, bad times, and somebody-done-gone-and-left-me times. But her voice was so melty I found myself longing for those hard times, yearning to be grown without "a thin di-i-ime to my name." I looked forward to the delicious time when "my man" would leave me, when I would "hate to see the evening sun go down" ... 'cause then I would know "my man has left this town." Misery colored by the greens and blues in my mother's voice took all the grief out of the words and left me with the conviction that pain was not only endurable, it was sweet.[57]

And one of three "whores" in the novel, Poland, is constantly singing the blues – for example:

I got blues in my mealbarrel
Blues up on the shelf
I got blues in my mealbarrel
Blues up on the shelf
'Cause I'm sleepin' by myself.[58]

Throughout the novel, Morrison's bluesy dialogue "is written ... but clearly chosen for how speakerly it is, how it bespeaks a particular world and its ambiance."[59] Her blues aesthetic presumes a "reliance for full comprehension on codes embedded in black culture," a language that is chosen, Morrison says, to "transfigure the wealth of Afro-American culture into a language worthy of the culture."[60] It is a culture of sounding, "the saying of words, holding them on the tongue, experimenting with them, playing with them."[61] Ralph Ellison would be especially appreciative of the way Morrison's novel articulates a blues aesthetic, for:

As a novelist, Ellison sees the tragicomic storyline in the music; as a former musician, he hears the blues sounding through fiction and other forms of repression. Most emphatically, he detects a blues-based jazz element at the core of twentieth century American culture.[62]

Much of the novel's lyricism is expressed by sung snippets from St. Louis Blues. However, its articulation of a blues understanding is only a part of the novel's political contribution. At the same time that it articulates a blues lyricism that captures aspects of African American cultural knowledge, the novel's theme serves as a counter-text to a history of racist thinking – particularly stereotypes about physical beauty. In effect, it counters such historical texts as Count Arthur Joseph de Gobineau's *Essay on the Inequality of the Human Races*. As one analyst puts it, "Morrison's novel, for all its eloquence and beauty of expression, engages in a sustained argument with modes of thought and belief [characterized by Gobineau's text] ... but perhaps more vividly presented in cultural icons portraying physical beauty: movies, billboards, magazines, books, newspapers, window signs, dolls, and drinking cups."[63] Morrison notes, "her purpose in writing the novel was to "'peck away at the gaze that condemns' Pecola's blackness as ugly."[64]

Nevertheless, while *The Bluest Eye*'s theme is politically powerful, addressed as it is to a historically virulent form of racism, its blues form is its major political vehicle. In particular, Morrison's use of "St. Louis Blues" – with its exemplary blues structure ("twelve-bar blues, augmented with an eight-bar bridge and an additional twelve-bar blues"[65]) projecting a theme that suggests ways out of troubled times – resonates with the much of the African American experience. While the lyrics and rhythmic motion of the "St. Louis Blues" convey situations and cultural positions that speak directly to the condition of the novel's main aesthetic subjects, Claudia and Pecola, it also references a life world of struggle that has to touch a broad cross-section of the African American assemblage.

Having effectively fashioned the blues novel at the very outset of her writing career, using singing subjects as her aesthetic vehicles – in her novel, *Jazz* (1992), written 22 years later – Morrison goes directly to the blues. Rather than mediating its expression through her characters, jazz itself "is the mysterious narrator of the novel."[66] As a result, the novel is a bluesy jazz performance: "The human stories play back-up to the dazzling improvisation rendered by the music itself."[67] Making use of the way novelistic form engenders political resonance by generating what M. M. Bakhtin calls "herteroglossia" – many contending voices that function centrifugally, pulling away from a verbal-ideological center[68] – Morrison renders those contending voices within African American linguistic practices. For example, there are "call and response" moments in the interactions between Malvonne, who functions as a knowledge agent, describing her neighborhood's singular cultural habitus; and Joe, a disgruntled husband, who knocks on her door, seeking to make use of one of her rooms as a romantic sanctuary to use with his paramours. Here's the opening banter in one of them:

JOE: "A favor you might say."
MALVONNE: "Or I might not say."
JOE: "You will. It's a favor to me but a little pocket change for you."
MALVONNE: "Out with it, Joe. This something Violet ain't in on?"[69]

Surrounding and contextualizing the narrative as a whole, jazz itself functions not only as one of the voices but also as the aesthetic force that stylizes the verbal interactions. Henry Louis Gates, Jr. captures its narrative functioning well:

What is compelling ... is not only the novel's plot, but how the story is *told*. A disembodied narrator slips easily and guilelessly from third-person all-knowingness to first-person lyricism, without ever relaxing its grip upon our imagination. It is a sensitive poetic narrator, in love with the language of fiction, enraptured with the finest and rarest of arts, the art of telling a good tale, reflecting as it goes along, upon its responsibilities as a composer and its obligation to the individual characters whose sole destiny is to make the composition come alive, to sing.[70]

That the jazz that narrates is a bluesy jazz becomes apparent in the novel's first two sentences, "Sh, I know that woman. She used to live with a flock of birds on Lenox Avenue,"[71] because Lenox Avenue is the venue in Langston Hughes's best known blues poem, "The Weary Blues", whose opening lines are:

> Droning a drowsy syncopated tune,
> Rocking back and forth to a mellow croon,
> I heard a Negro play.
> Down on Lenox Avenue the other night
> By the pale dull pallor of an old gas light
> He did a lazy sway ...
> He did a lazy sway ...
> To the tune of those weary blues ... [72]

Morrison's *Jazz* retains the blues origins of jazz: "She thematically [and lyrically] 'sings the blues' of black experience through the use of literary techniques that inventively borrow from blues patterns and the structure of jazz performance."[73] However, the bluesy jazz mode of the novel, as it stylistically shapes the movements and interactions of the characters, does not exhaust its political moments. Morrison constructs a spatio-temporal world that surrounds the destinies of the characters. While the novel's drama is initiated by the disintegration of Joe and Violet Trace's marriage, Joe's murder of his paramour, Dorcas, and Violet's attempt to attack the corpse in a jealous rage at the funeral, its treatment of the historical creation of the African American urban life world looms larger than the particular destinies of the characters. For example, Joe and Violet had joined "a steady stream of black people running from want and violence ... in 1906 ... like the others, they were country people, but how soon country people forget. When they fall in love with a city, it is forever, and it is like forever."[74] And like Joe, Violet and the other migrating African Americans moving to northern cities, the jazz narrator loves the city, rendering it at one point as an ode to Thursdays, a break "in the artificial rhythm of the week [when men] ... seem to achieve some sort of completion ... They make the women smile. The tunes whistled through perfect teeth are remembered, picked up later and repeated at the kitchen stove ... Up there in that part of the city [Harlem] – which is the part they came for – the right tune whistled in a doorway or lifting up from he circles and grooves of a record can change the weather. From freezing to hot to cool."[75]

Morrison thus locates the twentieth-century African American experience in the history of the twentieth-century's urban formation. And, in crafting her version of the urban scene, she sees the city itself as a critical actor. Perhaps the most apposite model of the way New York City life shaped the micropolitics of African American politico-aesthetics is articulated in Ash Amin and Nigel Thrift's dynamic model of the city as "a kind of force field of passions that associate and pulse bodies in particular ways."[76] Echoing this model of the city, but with a musical inflection, Morrison has her jazz narrator describing how the city, as a functioning phonograph, spins Joe like a record:

Take my word for it, he is bound to the track. It pulls him like a needle
through the groove of a Bluebird record, Round and round about the town,
That's the way the city spins you. Makes you do what it wants, go where laid-
out roads say to ... You can't get off the track a City lays for you.[77]

Yet the way the city "spins" the African American assemblage is singular.
In effect, for Morrison, the city "functions as the privileged site of a positive
construction of blackness, countering, as Morrison says, the white 'construction
of blackness and enslavement [in which] could be found not only the not-free but
also, with the dramatic polarity created by skin color, the projection of the not
me'."[78]

The right to the city, the right to history: the micropolitics of the blues

Black people's struggle has been the leaven in the democratic loaf. We look
at the catastrophe and like the Blues, we responded with a smile, not revenge
but justice, not hatred, but compassion.

Cornel West

Simply put, the macropolitics of race in America's twentieth century – as it has
affected black America – is articulated primarily in policy histories, especially
the histories of civil rights cases and legislation. As institutional history, the genealogy of rights granted to African Americans has been incorporated in a "story
of legal and moral ascent,"[79] and in "simplistic accounts of moral progress."[80] In
contrast, the micropolitics of race is articulated through the practices with which
African Americans have sought to manage their day-to-day life worlds in the face
of structures and policies of intolerance, exclusion, and violence, in "struggles
against racial hierarchy."[81] After the "Great Migration" of African Americans,
moving from the rural South to the urban North (mainly from 1900 to 1930)
– powerfully depicted in the painter, Jacob Lawrence's "Migration Series" (c.
1941) – much of that management has taken place in large metropolitan cities.
The migration itself was a powerful political gesture:

[Although] a difficult and sometimes bleak existence comes through in
Lawrence's images [for] the people portrayed are locked in a mighty struggle
against poverty, nature, spiritual degradation and physical violence [never-
theless, they] not only survive their condition; they strike back at it by
voting with their feet. Relocating was a conscious step to escape the system
of repression erected in the South, a quiet rebellion against a system the
migrants could not yet defeat but would not willingly or passively embrace.[82]

To appreciate the challenges of coping with the dangers and exclusions in
the large metropolises where the migration ended, we can turn again to Ralph
Ellison's commentary on the difference between living in Alabama and living in
New York City. He writes that, after his move, he had to learn a different set of

"thou shalt nots" governing the movements of differently raced bodies. He had to distinguish spaces of indifference, of disparagement, and of exclusion – in sum, to become alert to "the arcane rules of New York's racial arrangements."[83] In her *Jazz*, Morrison offers a similar observation about the micropolitics of managing the New York metropolis: "Hospitality is gold in this City; you have to be clever to figure out how to be welcoming and defensive at the same time, When to love something and when to quit. If you don't know how, you can end up out of control or controlled from some outside thing like the hard case last winter."[84] And in a passage that mobilizes one of her aesthetic subjects, Alice, she captures well what Ellison calls New York's early twentieth-century "racial arrangements":

> [Alice] had begun to feel safe nowhere south of 10th Street, and Fifth Avenue was for her the most fearful of all. That was where whitemen leaned out of motorcars with folded dollar bills peeping from their palms. It was where salesmen touched her and only her as though she was a part of the goods they had condescended to sell her; it was the tissue required if the management was generous enough to let you try on a blouse (but no hat) in a store, It was where she, a woman of fifty and independent means, had no surname. Where women who spoke English said, 'Don't sit there you never know what they have.' And women who knew no English at all and would never own a pair of silk stockings moved away from her if she sat next to them on the trolley.[85]

Although *Jazz* offers many such moments in which parts of the city are unwelcoming, some of her aesthetic subjects nevertheless claim a "right to the city." Henri Lefebvre famously addresses himself to that "right," noting that "The *right to the city* cannot be conceived of as a simple visiting right or as a return to traditional cities, It can only be formulated as a transformed and renewed *right to urban life*."[86] Lefebvre's injunction is on behalf of the working class: "only this class, as a class, can decisively contribute to the reconstruction of centrality destroyed by a strategy of segregation and found again in the menacing form of *centers of decision-making*."[87] In Morrison's case, the right to the city is enacted through challenges to its racial-spatial order, and it is her blues subject, Trace, who acts to reorder the sense of the city. Anne-Marie Paquet-Deyris's commentary captures his spatial practice:

> In Trace's city, space is reconfigured. It is willed into a fairy tale kingdom, some version of Eden complete with the characters to be featured in it. Suddenly urban destiny is no longer a collective phenomenon. Joe comes up with his own design: If the blues functions as a site of group membership, reclaiming the cityscape as his own allows him to come up with an alternative representation of reality. Space is transfigured.[88]

Through her aesthetic subjects – jazz and the other subjects' voices – Morrison's blues-oriented narration effects a right to the city with a reconfiguration of urban space. Her novel also articulates a right to history, which emerges in several ways: through the way the narration situates the lives of its characters in the experience of migration, through the way it characterizes the Harlem moment of the 1920s – when African Americans were involved in (re)fashioning themselves as city dwellers, through the way it evokes a history of musical technology – especially the phonograph and, most evidently, through the way the blues basis of jazz provides the frame for the characters' interactions. The musical voice "provides the historical background the narrative voice incompletely supplies ... It reconstitutes the complex journey of black migrants fleeing Southern oppression against the peculiar background of the Northern city."[89] And blues – as a genre of its own or articulated in bluesy forms of jazz – references a fraught African American history, not only the "themes of suffering and misery that had arisen from poverty and destitution, from disease and disaster, violence and brutality, from bad living conditions and aimless migration,"[90] but also the creative and redemptive moments of resistance, knowledge-building and collective self-fashioning. However, it would be misleading to see the Harlem of the 1920s as a historical moment of solely African American self-fashioning. For Morrison, it's necessary to recognize that the blues' contribution to the right to history is trans-ethnic. As she notes, during the post-WWI Harlem moment, "black culture, rather than American culture began to alter the whole country and eventually the western world."[91]

Conclusion: Duke Ellington's *Black, Brown and Beige*

Finally and importantly, Morrison's novels are only one among many of the blues genres with which African American artists have demanded a right to history. Perhaps the most notable is Duke Ellington's musical history of the African American experience, his *Black, Brown and Beige: A Tone Parallel to the History of the American Negro*. Ellington's composition was written for the concert hall, but rather than simply re-inflecting the "phonic legacies" of "conservatory trained musicians," whose music had dominated that venue, Ellington's working injunction was to write a piece "from the inside by a Negro."[92] The blues framing of the composition is immediately apparent. "Come Sunday, which inaugurates the "Black" segment, constructs the "Negro past" with a "Work Song" and a spiritual. "Come Sunday" straddles the two dimensions of the blues tradition famously distinguished by the classical and music scholar Albert Murray, the blues as feeling and the blues as music.[93] The former, he suggests, is a feeling of resignation and defeat, while the latter is a musical response to the ontological condition of African Americans. In this latter dimension, blues as music functions as "an experience-confrontation device that enables people to begin by accepting the difficult, disappointing, chaotic, absurd, which is to say the farcical or existential facts of life."[94] It moves beyond the negative facts of life to not only cope but also to triumph. The orchestration of blues through jazz then becomes "a fundamental device for confrontation, improvisation, and existential affirmation ... for improvising or riffing on the exigencies of the predicament."[95]

Thereafter, in the *Brown* segment, the rhythms and tonalities of the spiritual follow its historical and musical migration to the blues. In this register the music features the traditional twelve bar blues structure. Narratively, Ellington's aesthetic subject in the composition, Boola, experiences the blues in the last segment of *Brown* in which "Ellington's song 'The Blues,' is a masterpiece *about the blues,*" as Maurice Peress puts it.[96] And by the time the composition arrives at its *Beige* segment, the narrative moves from a "weary blues" mood to a hopeful one that is reflected in the intellectual contributions of the Harlem Renaissance and the patriotic contributions of black America's participation to the war effort.

The continuing and pervasive blues element in *Beige* contains reprises from the earlier segments, as emotional (and thus tonal) vicissitudes abound, and Ellington's piano "returns in medium stride to introduce the final shout chorus [incorporating] bits and pieces from 'Come Sunday' and 'Work Song'" from *Black*.[97] Among other things, Ellington's composition belies the misleading historical marker, "the jazz age," a marker that elides the historical trajectory of America's African American experience articulated in music. Ultimately, Ellington's *Black, Brown and Beige* effects an African American right to history by restoring what such simple historical markers efface. Ellington was well aware of that effect. As he puts it, "Negro music is America ... developed out of the life of the people here in this country."[98] But, at the same time, the African American sound world creates disjuncture as much as it blends because Ellington recognizes that "Negro music" must articulate dissonance with dissonant chords because, he famously notes, "dissonance is our way of life in America. We are something apart, yet an integral part."[99] Here Ellington's composition effects the "mastery of form" that characterizes much of African American literature (noted above) while showing how the historical trajectory of the blues is Afro America's primary contribution to a politics of aesthetics and of history.

4   Zones of justice

A philo-poetic engagement

Introduction: a justice *dispositif*

The initiating provocation for this chapter is a long passage in Mathias Énard's novel *Zone* (2010). The novel's protagonist, Francis Servain Mirković is a French Croatian who had enlisted to fight in the ethnic purification-driven Croatian independence war, motivated by the neo-Nazi ideology he had absorbed as a youth. As one line in the novel puts it, "the truth is that there were loads of neo-Nazis, hooked on the mythology of victory over the Serbs, on the mythology of the single 'independent' Croatian State scoured clean by the partisans."[1] The novel is structured as one sentence of reflections for 517 pages (there are no periods, only commas), narrated by Mirković while on a train trip from Milan to Rome to deliver an archive of the war crimes that had occurred in the "zone" (an area comprising Mediterranean nation-states) to the Vatican. The passage that inspires my analysis contains his recollection of the day he saw his former Croatian commander, Blaškić, at his war crimes trial, a "multilingual circus of the ICJ." Blaškić is:

> in his box at The Hague among the lawyers the interpreters the prosecutors the witnesses the journalists the onlookers the soldiers of the UNPROFOR who analyzed the maps for the judges commented on the possible prove-nance of bombs according to the size of the crater determined the range of the weaponry based on the caliber which gave rise to so many counter-argu-ments all of it translated into three languages recorded automatically tran-scribed ... everything had to be explained from the beginning, historians testified to the past of Bosnia, Croatia, and Serbia since the Neolithic era by showing how Yugoslavia was formed, then geographers commented on demographic statistics, censuses, land surveys, political scientists explained the differential political forces present in the 1990's ... Blaškić in his box is one single man and has to answer for all our crimes, according to the prin-ciple of individual criminal responsibility which links him to history, he's a body in a chair wearing a headset, he is on trial in place of all those who held a weapon.[2]

In this remarkable passage, Énard's protagonist, Mirković, provides a justice *dispositif,* where a *dispositif,* as Michel Foucault has famously elaborated it, is "a thoroughly heterogeneous ensemble consisting of discourses, institutions, architectural forms, regulatory decisions, laws, administrative measures, scientific statements, philosophical, moral and philanthropic propositions ... the said as much as the unsaid ... the elements of the apparatus."[3] Methodologically, to evoke a justice *dispositif,* rather than attempting to simply define justice, is to analyze a historical conjunction of emerging practices instead of treating an isolated concept (where the latter is empiricism's practice in which concepts are translated into measurement protocols to set up and test explanations of the causes of justice/injustice). Analyzing justice as a *dispositif* allows for a dense mapping of an emerging world of forces that justice – as part of an ensemble of knowledge practices and complex inter-agency relations – references. In short, "justice," as articulated in Mirković's recollection, is a complex historical event ("the concept speaks the event").[4] Mirković's recollection is a radical *interpretive* event in that it gestures toward an altered spatio-temporal world. In the analysis that follows, I draw on two genres of spatio-temporality – philosophical and literary – in order to pursue the insights that Mirković's recollection evokes. Adopting Énard's spatial trope, the "zone," I propose an approach to justice that emerges through a reading of Énard's novel by exposing the text's literary tropes to philosophical concepts.

A politically perspicuous philopoesis

With its emphasis on a particular zone of violence, the literary geography of Énard's novel provides an alternative "ideology of space."[5] It challenges both the state-centric map of European nation-states and the dominant narrative that locates European politics in a progressive story of negotiated economic and political integration. Rather than the traditional geopolitical cartography that features and legitimates centers of policy-making, the space of the novel is an axiologically-rendered map that both identifies and abjures spaces of violence. However, to grasp the ethico-political force of *Zone,* it's necessary to "interfere" with its literary content by engaging it with philosophical concepts – an interference that (as I note in Chapter 1) Cesare Casarino renders as philopoesis: "Philopoesis names a certain discontinuous and refractive interference between philosophy and literature."[6] Casarino's concept of "refractive interference" is predicated on Deleuze and Guattari's classification of the functioning of genres, in which philosophy is an "art of forming, inventing, and fabricating concepts," and artistic texts are "bloc[s] of sensations ... compound[s] of percepts and affects."[7] And it also draws inspiration from Deleuze's way of conceiving philosophy's interference with artistic texts: "Philosophical theory is itself a practice, just as much as its object. It is no more abstract than its object. It is a practice of concepts, and it must be judged in the light of the other practices with which it interferes."[8] In sum, for Casarino philopoesis-as-method is deployed by staging an encounter between philosophical concepts and literary texts. And, in attunement with the conceptual framing of this chapter, Casarino renders the topology of the interference between philosophy and literature as a conceptual *zone*. In his words, "a philopoetic discourse is one that produces the different zones of indiscernibility between philosophy and literature."⁹

The novel *Zone*'s governing spatial trope, the zone, provides a propitious opening to articulate philosophy with literature in this way because both have zones. In the case of philosophy, the zone becomes its main spatial trope when we heed Deleuze and Guattari's analysis of philosophy as a concept-creating practice; they treat concepts not in terms of their referents (through the use of "coordinating definitions," as is the case in empiricist modes of analysis) but in terms of the territoriality of their connections with other concepts. Concepts, they point out, have overlaps with other concepts, both temporarily: "every concept relates back to other concepts, not only to its history but in its becoming," and spatially: "each [concept] ... has a zone of neighborhood" (*zone de voisinage*).¹⁰ In the case of Énard's novel, its geographical setting – the zone – is the spatial imaginary that frames the dynamic shaping of the identity of the novel's protagonist or aesthetic subject, Mirković. However, that subject cannot emerge fully as political and ethical until he is brought into encounter with another zone: a set of philosophical concepts whose proximities constitute a conceptual zone. The interference between the genres (an inter-zonal engagement) provides for a political discernment of the contemporary justice *dispositif*, not only because that interference opens up "emergent potentialities that disrupt the status quo of the history of forms,"¹¹ but also because the philosophical concepts themselves challenge the already conceptually-invested political status quo. Here, I turn to a philosophical concept, plasticity – developed critically most recently by Catherine Malabou and earlier by M. M. Bakhtin – because its engagement with the novel facilitates the derivation of a critical politics of subjectivity.

Plasticities: chez Malabou and Bakhtin

Plasticity is a primary concept for both the philosopher, Catherine Malabou and the literary theorist, M. M. Bakhtin. However, although Malabou's primary genre is philosophical discourse and Bakhtin's is literary discourse, neither is a pure type. Literary tropes and examples are abundant in Malabou's texts and philosophemes abound in Bakhtin's. As Casarino suggests in his elaboration of philopoesis-as-method, political discernment derives from the mixing of idioms. He points out for example that both Marx and Melville inquire into the "political nature of being" precisely because the former "found it necessary to depart from the practice of philosophy" (as is the case for Malabou) and the latter "from the practice of literature in order to experiment with whole new worlds of writing and thought" (as is the case for Bakhtin).¹² And significantly, both Malabou and Bakhtin share a philosophical perspective on the writing subject. Malabou applies her concept of plasticity to herself, rendering her "conceptual portrait as a *transformational mask*,"¹³ as she rehearses her changing conceptual history throughout her various writings on philosophers. And Bakhtin (as I noted in Chapter 1) sees the writer as a mobile subject; his "authors" are open to themselves by seeing themselves as "unconsummated" – as subjects who are always becoming, who are, as he puts it, "axiologically yet-to-be." That mode of self-recognition articulates itself through how they fashion the "lived lives" of their protagonists as dynamics of accommodation to a complex, changing world.[14]

Spatially, Malabou's version of plasticity is constituted as a zone of concepts that exists in the interstices of the philosophical idioms of Hegel, Heidegger, and Derrida: dialectics, destruction, and deconstruction respectively. Drawn initially from Hegel's use of the concept and intended ultimately to replace Derrida's writing-predicated "motor scheme" (a tool or "image of thought" with which "the energy and information of the text of an epoch" is garnered),[15] plasticity for Malabou involves the self- and world-shaping work of "productive imagination."[16] Committed to a *"symbolic rupture between the plastic and the graphic components of thought,"*[17] she constructs a mode of subjectivity that emphasizes mutability rather than mimesis or representation, one that does not presume the traditional "I" subject: "plasticity ... by definition, doesn't need an 'I' to be deployed. "[18] The plasticity that Malabou derives while reading Hegel, is the "instance which *gives form* to the future and to time in Hegel's philosophy."[19] Subsequently, in a later text, as she connects philosophical and neuroscientific discourses, she notes that, "plasticity, far from producing a mirror image of the world, is the form of another possible world. To produce a consciousness of the brain thus demands that we defend a biological alter-globalism."[20] There Malabou articulates her plasticity model of philosophical consciousness with brain science, suggesting that we recognize the plasticity of the brain because thought is part of organic nature, not something separate, presiding over neurophysiology: "the mental is not the wise appendix of the neuronal." [21]

In contrast with Malabou, Bakhtin locates plasticity in the narratological structure of genre rather than in the dynamics of mentality. "The novel," he argues, "is plasticity itself" because "it is a genre that is ever questing, ever examining itself and subjecting its established forms to review."[22] In this sense, Bakhtin shares with Malabou a version of plasticity that privileges a future-oriented temporality, a commitment to the mutability of forms and to the ways in which changing forms attain greater proximity than fixed frameworks to the changing realities of the life world. Evoking the concept of the zone, Bakhtin notes that the novel as a genre "structures itself in a zone of direct contact with developing reality."[23] And crucially, for the purposes of my analysis, throughout his discussion of novelistic genres Bakhtin's analyses of space and temporality provide appropriate models for Énard's protagonist/aesthetic subject, Mirković's movements (both his traveling and his identity changes) which disclose aspects of his contemporary world. In particular, Bakhtin's analyses of some versions of the *"Bildungsroman"* apply very well to Énard's *Zone*, especially one type, the "travel novel": "[In] *The travel novel*: The hero is a point moving in space. He has no distinguishing characteristics, and he himself is not the center of the novelist's artistic intention. His movement in space – wanderings and occasional escapade-adventures ... enables the artist to develop and demonstrate the spatial and static social diversity of the world (country, city, culture, nationality, various social groups and the specific conditions of their lives)."[24] And in his treatment of another type, the "novel of emergence," Bakhtin captures the way the mutability of Énard's protagonist,

Mirković, reflects the historical changes in the world. In one version of this type, the changes in the character are not the sole focus. Rather,

> He emerges *along with the world* and he reflects the historical emergence of the world itself. He is no longer within an epoch, but on the border between two epochs, at the transition point from one to the other. The transition is accomplished in him and through him. He is forced to become a new, unprecedented type of human being. The organizing force of the future is therefore extremely great here – and this is not, of course, the private biographical future, but the historical future.[25]

Here, Bakhtin applies his concept of the chronotope to the way the text's temporal figuration orients his protagonist's changing character to reflect a reconfigured world. Similarly, in her conception of a future-oriented temporality, Malabou focuses on the way consciousness moves toward its future state as it is involved in dialectically-oriented transformative movement that is both form-giving and form-dissolving, as it shows "the capacity to differentiate itself from itself."[26] In what follows, I heed Malabou's approach to plasticity by conceiving Énard's Mirković philosophically as a changing "conceptual persona" – a figure in a philosophical text.[27] And I heed Bakhtin's approach to plasticity by conceiving Mirković as a "hero" (Bakhtin's term for his protagonists, or in my terms, an "aesthetic subject"[28]) in a literary genre, the novel, which privileges a process of self-fashioning that is responsive to changes in the socio-political arrangements of the life world. I thus conceive Mirković as both a conceptual and aesthetic figure in a novel that is both philosophically profound and lyrical, as it seems to mimic the genre of a prose poem. In effect, Mirković enacts two different "powers," where "the difference between conceptual personae and aesthetic figures consists first of all in this: the former are the powers of concepts, and the latter are the powers of affects and percepts."[29] So by combining the two "powers," we have a model to articulate a politics of literature. It's a model that is very much in accord with Jacques Rancière's version of the politics of literature, expressed in a passage that applies well to Énard's novel:

> Literature does not "do" politics by providing messages or framing representations. It "does" so by triggering passions, which means new forms of balance (or imbalance) between an occupation and the sensory "equipment" fitting it ... It is the politics of literature – that is, the politics of that art of writing – which has broken the rules that make definite forms of feeling and expression fit definite characters or subject matters. [30]

I turn then to offer a close reading of Énard's novel.

Zone

> Between the upsurge and explosion of form, subjectivity issues the plastic challenge.
>
> Catherine Malabou[31]

> Time itself abuses and praises, beats and decorates, kills and gives birth.
>
> M. M. Bakhtin[32]

> I'm changing my life my body my memories my future my past
>
> Mathias Énard's Mirković[33]

Much of the complexity of Énard's novel derives from one of the primary aspects of its form, its framing as an epic – Homer's *Iliad*. Like *The Iliad*, its 517 pages are broken up into 24 chapters, and as Énard attests, "I wanted to do a contemporary epic."[34] At times the other Homeric epic, *The Odyssey* is also evoked. The mixing of the two genres, the novel and epic (which Bakhtin sharply distinguishes, seeing the novel as "the sole genre that continues to develop" and the epic as a genre that "has not only long since completed its development, but one that is already antiquated"[35]), enhances *Zone's* critical effect for, as Bakhtin also suggests, "The novel parodies other genres (precisely in their role as genres); it exposes the conventionality of their forms and their language; it squeezes out some genres and incorporates others into its own peculiar structure, reformulating and re-accentuating them."[36]

Among the critical effects of the novel's epic framing is the juxtaposition of post-war fates that are afforded by the intermittent evocation of the adventures of Homer's heroes. Ulysses returns home to recover his domesticity, while Mirković is involved in radical transformation as he heads off toward a future that bears no resemblance to his origins. Accordingly, in its "reformulating" of the epic form, the novel lends philosophical weight to Mirković's type of journey. For example, at one point in the novel, one of Mirković's fellow soldiers, Antonio, is described as one who would avoid Ulysses' fate: "Antonio back from the Eastern Front runs through the countryside to escape the fate of Ulysses, his sewing wife, the good hunting dog who will sniff between his legs, he flees the future that he guesses at" (a return to mundane domesticity).[37] Malabou, as she involves herself in her philosophical journey, "deriving and arriving," also evokes Ulysses' path because of how freighted with significance his mythical journey is. Referring to "the paradigmatic value accorded in the West to a certain form of voyage: the Odyssey," she notes that, "In one way or another, the Western traveler always follows the steps of Ulysses."[38] It's a philosophical or symbolic voyage, which has for her (and Derrida, whom she accompanies), a "phenomenological motif," a type of symbolic drifting (a "*derived drift*").[39]

Énard's Mirković also summons the concept of drift, comparing the violent topology of his journey to Stratis Tsirkas's fictional trilogy, *Drifting Cities* (1974), a saga of the drift toward chaos of three cities – Jerusalem, Cairo and Alexandria – which are headed towards episodes of catastrophic antagonism as World War II recasts allegiances and enmities in the same "zone," the Middle East.[40] Like the subjectivity effect in Malabou's philosophical-territorial journey, Mirković's renders him as a plastic subject, as he purposively undergoes transformation while striving to reshape his world's self-understanding. To repeat the section's epigraph: "I'm changing my life my body my memories my future my past."[41] Like Malabou, who takes a territorial and philosophical journey with Derrida, Mirković combines the two modes; he is on both a territorial and symbolic journey.

To summarize: Mirković is a French Croatian, who joins the Croatian independence movement after being influenced by Yvan Deroy, his neo-Nazi childhood friend. Subsequently, he exits from his combat vocation and becomes a French secret agent whose zone is the Mediterranean area between Barcelona and Beirut. After being appalled by photos of the atrocities in the Westerbork concentration camp, he takes on a five-year task of compiling an archive of atrocities in the zone. Throughout the novel, his entire temporal trajectory is narrated as recollections while he is on a train from Milan to Rome, carrying his archive in a suitcase he plans to sell to the Vatican. His ultimate goal is to disappear after the sale with the woman, Sashka, with whom he wants to spend the rest of his life. Throughout the journey he reveals himself to be a quintessential plastic subject inasmuch as he is involved in erasing past selves, fashioning new ones, and creating a new form (in effect repartitioning the sense of the world he is and has been in). For example at one point he states, "Francis Sevain Mirković disintegrated in the same way Paul Ricken did [an SS man who assembled a secret photo archive of atrocities], maybe I too wanted to document the journey, disappear and be reborn with the features of Yvan Deroy."[42] And at another point he imagines himself dissolving into the archive in his suitcase: "I think little by little I left my identity behind in those pseudonyms, I split myself up, little by little Francis Servain Mirković dissolved into a single one."[43] Intimately related to his plastic subjectivity is Mirković's spatial isolation as he sits on a moving train. Enclosed in a train compartment, he is reminiscent of Joseph Conrad's Jim (in *Lord Jim*), who "is trapped in various kinds of space … in a 'womb like enclosure'," sitting on the steamer, the *Patna*, on which, like Mirković, "he flees from his past."[44] Thus for Énard, as for Conrad, identity and narrative space are radically entangled. The politics of the novel emerges from Mirković's spatial odyssey and the identity instabilities connected with it. However, crucially for purposes of appreciating a more elaborated perspective on the politics of the novel, while one narrative thread focuses on Mirković's transformations, another rearticulates the history of atrocities in the zone and speculates about the vagaries of bringing the perpetrators to justice in a world in which those who carried out the atrocities are minor players whose violence is aided and abetted by others – especially those who are involved in the exchange of commodities. Recalling Bakhtin's observations about how the hero or aesthetic subject in the travel novel "emerges *along with the world* and … reflects the historical emergence of the world itself. He is no longer within an epoch, but on the border between two epochs, at the transition point from one to the other. The transition is accomplished in him and through him,"[45] there is a telling moment as Mirković is observing some of his fellow passengers on the train. There are:

Egyptian, Lebanese, and Saudi businessmen all educated in the best British and American prep schools, discreetly elegant, far from the clichés of colorful, rowdy Levantines, they were neither fat nor dressed up as Bedouins, they spoke calmly of the security of their future investments, as they said, they spoke of our dealings, of the region they called "the area," the zone, and the word "oil" ... some had sold weapons to Croats in Bosnia, others to Muslims.[46]

Here Mirković's observations are not about himself but about a changing imaginative cartography of the zone. The map of cultural difference is being supplanted as persons from diverse national cultures become assimilated as predatory entrepreneurs in a world in which global capitalism is redrawing the map as it indulges its various clienteles, profiting for example from ethno-national enmities. As a result, warring bodies are treated not in terms of national and cultural allegiances but as human capital, as a clientele, and fates are determined by a network of initiatives in which violence is a consequence rather than an intention. As Mirković adds, "our businessmen from the Zone didn't see the threat behind the outstretched hand, the deadly games that would play out in the course of the years to come."[47] Achille Mbembe addresses succinctly the necropolitical consequences of the money flows that restructure perceptions of human capital in diverse zones of violence:

the controlled inflow and the fixing of movements of money around zones in which specific resources are extracted has made possible the formation of enclave economies and has shifted the old calculus between people and things. The concentration of activities connected with the extraction of valuable resources around these enclaves has in return, turned the enclaves into privileged spaces of war and death.[48]

How can we therefore render the novel's way of thinking about justice? At a minimum, in addition to such specific connections the novel provides – for example that between capital flows and violence – what it says about the atrocities and the issue of justice is radically entangled with the form of its expressions (i.e., how it works as a genre that affects how it is read). Its one sentence structure, which moves the reader through rapid juxtapositions of information and imagery, mimics Mirković's train ride, in which the rider witnesses rapid changes in the landscape. For example, jumping into one passage we join Mirković on his train while he narrates information about the forced train transfers of Jews from the zone to concentration camps in 1944:

the German administration [in Italy] went to the trouble of organizing convoys, transports for the partisans and the last Jews from Bologna or Milan, to Fossoli then Bolzano and finally to Birkenau ... Birkenau, where all the tracks join, from Thessalonica to Marseille, including Milan, Reggio, and Rome, before going up in smoke, my train has windows ... the Jews from Prague, the Greek Jews who even paid for their ticket to Poland, they sold them a ticket to death, and the community leaders negotiated bitterly over the price of the journey with the German authorities, strange cynicism of the Nazi bureaucrats, Eichmann, Höss, Stangl, calm men, quiet family men whose tranquility contrasted with the virile belligerent hysteria of Himmler or Heydrich, Franz Stangl loved flowers and well-ordered gardens, animals.[49]

Here, as elsewhere in the novel, rather than merely supplying information or offering an explanation, Énard creates ironic tropes and striking incongruities – in this case referring to the cynicism of "calm men" arranging the deaths of others – all located within a symbolic contrast between different kinds of train trips (the trains with blacked out windows that carried victims to concentration camps and Mirković's with windows that allow for observation as he carries the reader through a zone of atrocities, headed in the opposite direction). On the one hand, Énard's Mirković speculates conceptually about justice, agency, historical memory, and changes in the administration of justice – in this sense functioning as a conceptual persona. On the other hand, his observations – enacted within a genre that creates a clash of heterogeneous images – affect us with percepts and affects, as he also functions as an aesthetic subject, bringing us through the zone in a way that repartitions the political sense of European space. Simon O'Sullivan provides some appropriate language for how we are affected. Énard's Mirković challenges, in O'Sullivan's words, our "world of affects, this universe of forces [which is] our world seen without the spectacles of habitual subjectivity [and his dizzying ride through the zone, as he prepares to deliver a historical archive of horrors helps us] ... to remove these spectacles, which are not spectacles at all but the very condition of our subjectivity."[50]

The subjectivity to which O'Sullivan is referring is our traditional political subjectivity, our absorption into a world of separated sovereignties, on the basis of which we are located on the contemporary geopolitical map. Énard's passage thus disrupts the cartography of our traditional citizen subjectivity, moving us to reflect on our responsibility to a space and history of victimization. It shifts our focus from the archive of national consolidation ("the storing and ordering place of the collective memory of [a] nation or people")[51] to the archive of atrocities and injustice that contains the historical record of the violence in the zone. Ultimately, then, the "archive" emerges as an essential component of the justice *dispositif.*

Archives abound

It is not possible for us to describe our own archive, since it's from within these rules that we speak.

Michel Foucault

Nothing is less clear than the word archive.

Jacques Derrida

There are effectively three archives in Énard's *Zone*. The most explicit one is the archive of atrocities residing in Mirković's suitcase. Within the narrative of the train journey, Énard provides an oblique commentary on the politics of the archive. To secure that archive, Mirković handcuffs the suitcase to a bar on his seat. That gesture, along with the convenient symbols supplied by the train's destination – Rome's Termini station – and the suitcase's destination – the Vatican – implies that once they are situated in the archives of political or religious authorities, the records will be sealed, locked up, immune from modification, because those authorities (archons) administer "the law of what can be said."[52] However, as the novel's construction of its plastic aesthetic subject, Mirković (as he goes "backwards toward his destination")[53] shows, and its testimony to the fragility of historical recollections and allegiances to which his journey indicates, the archive is never finally secured. However much institutions, agencies, and bureaucracies may try to hold onto words and meanings (for example reifying them in the architectural sites and icons in the Vatican) they will ultimately be modified or supplanted. Despite Mirković's desire to terminate both the archive he carries and the selves he has embodied, they will continue to be part of an uncertain, continually modified future.

Apart from what is in Mirković's suitcase, the novel contains a literary archive: those who inspire the novel's unusual form – Apollinaire, Butor, Homer, Joyce, and Pynchon; the canonical fictional responses to war and atrocities by Joseph Conrad, Ernest Hemingway, Ezra Pound, and others who jostle for space in the narrative along with the perpetrators of the atrocities; and other literary figures, many of them writers who had personal connections with the zone and were personally affected by the violence that has transpired there. However, Énard does more than merely mention them. For some of them he retraces their journeys, both actually and symbolically. In this sense, his novel resonates with another recent literary trip aimed at disclosing a zone of atrocity, Sven Lindqvist's trip to Africa (reviewed in the Introduction), in which the author follows the route that inspired Joseph Conrad's fictional, anti-imperialist novel, *The Heart of Darkness*. To repeat the account: to tell the story of the extermination of much of Africa's native population by Europeans in the nineteenth century Lindqvist fashions *himself* as an aesthetic subject. He enacts a travel story as he visits the extermination sites to reflect on the violent nineteenth-century European–African encounters, while at the same time interspersing archival material to rehearse the rationales used to justify the slaughters. Rendering his investigation as a "story of a man [Lindqvist] traveling by bus through the Sahara desert while simultaneously traveling by computer through the history of the concept of extermination," he provides a view of Europe's violent encounter with Africa that is largely fugitive within traditional geo-political narratives. In small, sand-ridden desert hotels, his investigation is driven by one sentence in Joseph Conrad's *Heart of Darkness:* "Exterminate all the brutes". Textually, Conrad accompanies Lindqvist in his travels, through the many references Lindqvist provides from the story of Conrad's famous novel.[54] Conrad also accompanies Mirković, who recalls his "passion for reading" Conrad's *Nostromo* and *The Heart of Darkness,* among others, as a device to erase himself – "to forget myself," as he puts it.[55] Moreover, in his mentioning of those Conrad novels, the fictional Mirković – like the ethical traveler Lindqvist – summons a literary archive of violence.

The third archive enacted in *Zone* is the novel itself. Like Lindqvist's archive of the exterminism visited on Africa, which names perpetrators and the perverse thought models that legitimated their genocidal violence, Énard's novel provides a survey of the zone's atrocities, names the key perpetrators, and (also like Lindqvist) refers to those thinkers and activists who sought to either mitigate the violence or bring it to public attention. Both texts are in effect addressed to the justice of the historical archive. They refocus perceptions of the history of the territories whose violent encounters they narrate. Instead of such banal geopolitical concerns as "regime change" (a preoccupation of both politicians and political scientists), they focus on both the perpetuation of atrocities and the relatively anemic attempts of various agencies, national and international, to provide justice for the victims. With respect to this latter dimension, Énard plays with the trivia evinced in war crimes trials and speculates about the clashes of temporality involved in the contemporary justice *dispositif*:

> in the Great Trial organized by international lawyers immersed in precedents and the jurisprudence of horror, charged with putting some order into the law of murder, with knowing at one instant a bullet in the head was a legitimate *de jure* and at what instant it constituted a grave breach of the law and customs of war ... peppering their verdicts with flowery Latin expressions, devoted, yes, all these people to distinguishing the different modes of crimes against humanity before saying *gentlemen I think we'll all adjourn for lunch ... the Chamber requests the parties to postpone the hearings planned for this afternoon until a later date, let's say in two months*, the time of the law is like that of the church, you work for eternity.[56]

An alternative justice *dispositif*: the ethics and politics of the archive

All that one needs to moralize is to fail to understand.

Gilles Deleuze

In a treatment of the relationship between archives and justice from a South African perspective, Verne Harris narrates a version of the justice *dispositif* that contrasts with the one narrated in Mirković's observations about the trial of his former commander, Blaškić, which moves the justice process toward a judgment rather than an open-ended process of collective reflection. Committed, Harris writes, to "A World Whose Only Horizon Can Be Justice," he sees the justice *dispositif* as both contested and political:

> In this space archivists – together with the creators of records, and a host of other players – narrate the meanings and significance of "the record" in an open-ended and contested process. The record, then, is always in the process of being made. And all of us who narrate its meanings and significances, whether we do it in a togetherness of hospitality or in a separateness of insularity, are record makers ... The harsh reality is that the shape (and the shaping) of record making is determined by relations of power.[57]

Heeding the contestability of the South African archive of colonial violence, and recognizing that the past must be open to the future, Harris suggests that the archives that contain "the memory of the nation" should be rendered as a file open to new voices, new types of archivist vocations, and new technologies of inscription, so that "over time the file will be expanded or revised, and it will be made available in different ways and contexts … as it is migrated forward to new generations of technology." Structured in this way, the archive, as Derrida would have it "opens out of the future."[58]

Among the implications of Harris's transformative approach to the archives of violence and atrocity (he sees the archive as plastic, being shaped and in turn having a shaping effect) is an encouragement to consider "an ethics of time."[59] Considered within an ethics of temporality, the archives of atrocity might well evoke critique of what commentators of Walter Benjamin refer to as a "guilt history" – a history imagined in terms of "debt and payback" – contextualized within "the time of the law … in which the unavoidable incurring of guilt is atoned in an equivalent penance that is just as unavoidable."[60] Walter Benjamin's gloss on history provides the basis of that critique. Reacting against this model of history as guilt and atonement, which imposes a "uni-directionality [narrative] … of what occurs," Walter Benjamin famously juxtaposes "divine history" which resists such a uni-directional temporality (which he deems "a 'completely improper temporality'") and allows for "morally meaningful action" within a model of "genuinely historical time,"[61] which stands as an implicit critique of guilt history. From the poetry of Hölderlin, Benjamin derives what he calls a "plastic structure of thought"[62] – a "temporal plasticity"[63] or time "wholly without direction."[64] Jeffrey Skoller effectively summarizes this model of temporality (using a Benjaminian idiom): "The past and the present are not a progressive movement from one to another but coexist as a constellation of moments that together constitute the present."[65] Putting it another way, temporal plasticity accords well with Benjamin's view of a history that permits new beginnings instead of being seen as "a sequence of events like the beads of a rosary."[66]

Benjamin's "plastic temporality" model of history, which extricates ethical thinking from a uni-directional guilt history, is congenial with Harris's transformational model of the justice of the archive in which the archive is assembled within a complex and shifting *dispositif* – new technologies of inscription, increasingly different archival vocations, new forms of media exposure of the record-making process, and new contestations about relevant content.[67] And as Harris (edified by Derrida) points out, the temporal structure of the archive itself is plastic. Although aspects of the past shape the archive, the very form of its making – the technologies of record keeping – in turn reshape the way the past is understood.[68]

Ultimately, *Zone* articulates well with Harris's model of archival openness because it provides a counter-effectuation of a juridically-oriented justice *dispositif*. Although Énard's Mirković is headed toward Termini station (symbolically a termination of his task and thus an end to the assembling of his archive) to deliver his archive to an institution – the Vatican, not known for open-ended ethical negotiation – much of the novel's text suggests that what constitutes a just encoding of the atrocities in the zone is contestable. Although the form of the novel rushes the reader toward the termination of Mirković's journey, the passages reflecting on those whose pasts made them eligible for war crimes trials suggest alternative archival modes – for example the treatment of the self-archiving Paul Ricken, "Professor of art history" (and commander of the Mauthausen prison camp), who took "hundreds of self-portraits ... documenting his own moral collapse."[69] And, as many of the passages in the novel suggest, what has gone on at the ICJ in The Hague barely touches on the complex of forces that have created the conditions of possibility for atrocity. As noted in an earlier section, Mirković's former commander, Blaškić (an actual historical person, a Croatian commander who served eight years for war crimes), whom he sees on trial in The Hague "in his box [is] ... one single man [who] ... has to answer for all our crimes, according to the principle of individual criminal responsibility which links him to history."[70]

Here, as in other parts of the text, the implication is that a juridical model commands a very limited part of the ethical and political issues surrounding the zone's atrocities. To put it concisely, the juridical response must end in a judgment (for example the one that led to the actual Blaškić's prison sentence). However, the novel gestures toward a more critical analytic and a different ethos, one that accords with Deleuze's Spinoza-inspired approach to ethics, which "overthrows the system of Judgment" and substitutes an evaluation of alternative qualities of life for moral injunctions.[71] As I have put it elsewhere (heeding an application of Deleuzian ethics), "morality as traditionally understood is about deriving imperatives from fixed moral codes, while ethical imperatives are invitations to negotiate meaning and value, given situations of either competing and incommensurate value commitments and/or alternative perspectives on what is the case."[72]

To illustrate such alternative perspectives and thereby to offer a non-juridical justice of the archives, we can imagine an opening up of the U.S. National Archives to voices that, both at their inception and continuously, provide critical commentaries on the founding documents (the *archai* of the archives). Taking as an example the Declaration of Independence, we can imagine turning it from a sealed document to a Talmudic text – the exemplar of a text that is plastic, i.e. open to continuing commentary – whose history "is the history of its effacing ... a special effacing that is not necessarily the effacing of the text ... it takes place through the adding of ... additional texts ... there is effacing of the control of the discourse, of the violence perpetrated by the discourse."[73] For this purpose, I suggest three commentaries that could be affixed to the Declaration's margins in order to efface its discursive singularity by addition. One is David Walker's 1829 "Appeal" not only to "the Colored Citizens of the World" but also "and very Expressly to Those of the United States of America" (1965). Walker, an African American abolitionist did not achieve a substantial readership. Published privately in Boston and often confiscated and suppressed during its dissemination, Walker's "appeal" refers to the "disparity between the condition of people of African descent in the United States and the 'inalienable rights' and republican principles laid out in the Declaration of Independence."[74] Another is the nineteenth-century commentaries of the Pequot philosopher William Apess, who – in his autobiography, "Son the Forrest"[75] and his "Eulogy to King Philip"[76] – appropriates the language of white founders (often Thomas Jefferson) and urges Euro Americans to apply the principles in their founding documents equally to "Indians." For example, in the "Eulogy," Apess's "rhetorical strategy ... effectively seeks to disable white Americans' ready assumption of a seamlessly glorious and singular American story."[77]

For a more contemporary critical commentary, we could add Jamaica Kincaid's observations on the Declaration of Independence. Kincaid, an émigré from Antigua – a place whose ethnoscape was shaped by an enterprise, the sugar plantations, that brought in coerced labor – who was herself a bonded servant when she first came to the U.S., viewed the portrait of the signing of the Declaration of Independence (Jefferson *et al.*'s democratic initiative), differently from those who celebrate it as the inauguration of American's unimpeachable democratic experiment. Ignoring the lofty rhetoric of the document and instead heeding what she sees, Kincaid ponders the occupational infrastructure of the studied ease of the white men assembled in "Independence Hall" and speculates about those whose labor has provided the condition of possibility for the enactment of "freedom" by the signers and writes:

> America begins with the Declaration of Independence ... but who really needs this document ... There is a painting in Philadelphia of the men who signed it. These men looked relaxed; they are enjoying the activity of thinking, the luxury of it. They have time to examine this thing called their conscience and to act on it ... some keep their hair in an unkempt style (Jefferson, Washington), and others keep their hair well groomed (Franklin), their clothes pressed.[78]

She then refers to those who have worked to prepare the men for the occasion "the people who made their beds and made their clothes nicely pressed and their hair well groomed or in a state of studied dishevelment." (*Ibid.*). In effect, Kincaid's observations offer a political economy of the text, revealing the laboring infrastructure that served to create the conditions of possibility for the work that produced the text. (Similarly the work of commentary that created the Talmud, was enabled by among others, the domestic work of the daughters of Rashi, Rabbi Solomon ben Isaac (1040–1105), whose husbands (the Rabbi's disciple-sons-in-law) supplied much of the commentary on his commentaries.[79])

Ironically, in 2011 right-wing Republicans in the American Congress did their own effacing commentary on another founding document. Recognizing and wanting to conceal the founding violence of the U.S. Constitution, they skipped the "three-fifths" clause (referring to the enumeration of slaves) during a reading aloud of the text "on the House floor."[80] That gesture was not the critical one of effacing by addition; rather, the clause was subtracted in order to deny the darker side of America's founding and, in effect, to depoliticize the American archive by negating a violent event in African American history. This is not the place to rehearse the many ways in which African Americans have staged counter-effectuations of founding events – in effective, counter-hegemonic, archive-challenging modes of self-making in treatises and in a wide variety of artistic genres. However, one work stands out as an important and under-appreciated counter-archive to which I want to call attention – Duke Ellington's musical history of the African American experience: *Black, Brown, and Beige: A Tone Parallel to the History of the American Negro*, which I have already treated in Chapter 3.

Ellington's *Black, Brown and Beige* effects an African American right to participate in a dissonant way in the archive of American history by restoring what the dominant, Euro-American historical markers have tended to efface. It adds the experience of another America to the archive. Ellington was well aware of that effect. As he puts it, "Negro music is America ... developed out of the life of the people here in this country."[81] In Ellington's composition, as in many other parts of the African American sound world, what are articulated are the discordances in the American archive, the modes of separation in the midst of belonging that "founding violence" and "preserving violence" have wrought.[82] As a result, as Ellington puts it, "dissonance is our way of life in America. We are something apart, yet an integral part."[83] Ultimately, as Ellington's important composition shows, an effectively politicized and ethical archive is one that cannot be sealed; it operates within a "temporal plasticity," which, as I have noted, derives from a model of history that extricates ethical thinking from a uni-directional guilt history and promotes a transformational model of the justice of the archive. It is a model in which the archive is assembled within a complex and shifting *dispositif* that is hospitable to contestations about relevant content. Returning to the insights derived from Mirković's archival adventure, we can recognize that national archives, as textual zones of citizen subjectivity, are an essential part of the justice *dispositif*. To the extent that we unseal and continue to alter the archives of national consolidation ("the storing and ordering place of the collective memory of [a] nation or people"[84]), we provide an alternative to traditional citizen subjectivity, opening up participation in a transformative text that continually reflects on the violence of law-making and law preservation.

5   For an anti-fascist aesthetics

Introduction: the new fascism

Gilles Deleuze describes the pervasiveness of contemporary "micro-fascism" this way:

> The new fascism is not the politics and the economy of war. It is the global agreement on security, on the maintenance of peace – just as terrifying as war. All our petty fears will be organized in concert, all our petty anxieties will be harnessed to make micro-fascists of us; we will be called upon to stifle every little thing, every suspicious face, every dissonant voice, in our streets, in our neighborhoods, in our local theaters.[1]

Doubtless Deleuze's characterization of "the new fascism" is disturbing to those who are invested in their experience of the fascism associated with "the politics and economy of war." For example, Bruno Bettleheim's incessant attacks on anyone who tried to characterize the phenomenon reflect the hostility of many of fascism's war-time victims toward attempts at explaining, re-inflecting, or expanding its meaning.[2] That hostility toward people who poach on one's experientially cultivated, ideationally entrenched enmities is expressed by one of Don DeLillo's aesthetic subjects, Win Everett, a character in his *Libra* (1988) – a novelistic biography of Lee Harvey Oswald, the alleged Kennedy assassin. At one point in the narrative, Everett, the fictional commander of the abortive Bay of Pigs invasion, is listening to a radio announcer reporting on Cuba's role in "Marxist subversion in our hemisphere:"

> He didn't need announcers telling him what Cuba had become. This was a silent struggle. He carried a silent rage and determination. He didn't want company. The more people who believed as he did, the less pure his anger. The country was noisy with fools who demeaned his anger.[3]

Throughout his *Libra*, DeLillo gives Win Everett a psychological profile, both a paranoid security mentality and an obsessive compulsiveness. Among other things, Everett checks the door locks and the knobs on the gas stove more than once before retiring every night. However, given the genre within which DeLillo is writing, Everett and the rest of the novel's characters are better thought of as aesthetic rather than as psychological subjects. The fascist mentality enacted in DeLillo's *Libra* is expressed not as a psychodynamic development but in the way the novel's moving bodies – driven by their preoccupation with securing the imagined coherence of their identity-allegiance to "America" and to U.S. hemispheric dominance – reaffirm a cold war cartography. For example, as DeLillo recreates the historical characters Lee Harvey Oswald and David Ferrie and mobilizes them for an encounter in the novel at the historical moment just prior to the abortive Bay of Pigs invasion of Cuba, their different mentalities are animated in the ways they give Cuba alternative morphologies. Ferrie complains: "You can't invade an island that size with fifteen hundred men," to which Oswald replies, "Cuba is little." Ferrie responds, "Cuba is big," and Oswald once again says, "Cuba is little."[4] As I note elsewhere, the "polyvocal poetics of Cuba" that the encounter between the characters effects, maps much of the desire-shaped, geopolitically-focused, ideoscape of the America of the John F. Kennedy presidency.[5]

While *Libra*'s gloss on fascism is oblique, an earlier DeLillo novel, *White Noise* (1985), approaches the phenomenon more directly, albeit still from the point of view of invented characters. His main protagonist, Jack Gladney, who is the Chair of the Department of Hitler Studies at "the College on the Hill," has an academic calling that fits well with his preoccupation – a fascist-emulating obsession with death. (As Susan Sontag has famously observed, the fascist aesthetic includes a deep desire for intimacy with death.[6]) DeLillo's Gladney enacts another aspect of the fascist aesthetic. He screens a Nazi documentary that is reminiscent of Leni Riefenstahl's regime-sponsored documentary of Hitler's visit to Nuremburg, *The Triumph of the Will* (1934). His Hitler Studies department's documentary features mass, militarized rallies with

> close up shots of thousands of people outside a stadium after a Goebbels speech, people surging, massing, bursting through the traffic. Halls hung with swastika banners, with mortuary wreaths and death's-head insignia. Ranks of thousands of flagbearers arrayed before columns of frozen light, a hundred and thirty aircraft searchlights aimed straight up – a scene that resembled a geometric longing, the formal notation of some powerful mass desire.[7]

Appeals of fascism

The historic Nazi rally mimicked in *White Noise* conveys an aspect of the appeal of Hitler's party at the time it was assuming power. However, although much of the party's mass appeal was orchestrated by its visual displays (its public semiotics), it should also be noted that the party developed its following at a time of national economic deprivation. In a classic explanatory-oriented investigation of the rise of the Nazi party in Germany, Rudolph Heberle describes the economic and related status crises experienced by various social strata in Germany in the 1920s and 30s and surmises:

It should not be difficult to understand why, in such circumstances, a party led by fanatic patriots, which denounced radically all existing parties, which claimed to be independent of any particular economic interests, the only champion of the real people and the *avant-garde* of the awaking nation, would exert immense attraction for the uprooted middle class elements, for politically untrained youths, for political adventurers, and for counter-revolutionaries in general.[8]

Elaborating, Heberle writes:

When the terrible depression with its mass unemployment cast its shadow on the people's minds, when masses of young voters grew up who had never had a permanent job or any job at all, the Nazi party offered at least activity, an outlet from the doldrums, and also shelter, food, and uniforms, attractions which made it a bitter competitor of the Communists in certain proletarian areas of the metropolitan cities.[9]

Heberle conducts a data analysis to validate his economy-focused explanatory model. Analyzing public opinion and party voting patterns of diverse occupational groups in the rural, Schleswig-Holstein region of Germany from 1918 to 1932, he shows how the National Socialists were able to displace other radical parties, not only by playing on economic issues (all the parties were doing that) but also by promoting mass participation. However, there are hints of the other kind of appeal to which DeLillo gestures and to which Heberle refers as well – an aesthetic appeal that is evident in Heberle's remarks on uniforms and mass participation. The appeal of the National Socialists' elaborate and colorful uniforms and regalia was part of their aesthetic strategy. That strategy's effectiveness is registered in a statement attributed to Walter Henisch, a press photographer who served as Josef Goebbels's official war photographer. Henisch – a man wedded to his photographic art and not to the Nazi ideology – is described by his son Peter (in his novelistic biography of his father) as explaining the attraction of the National Socialist party when they marched into Austria: "Compared to the Socialists and even more to the conservatives, the Nazi's were remarkable. They did something for your senses, especially for your eyes, and therefore for the camera."[10] What Walter Henisch experiences is one small marker of a more pervasive aspect of the appeal of fascist aesthetics, which shows up in popular culture texts, especially films such as *The Night Porter, The Damned*, and *Scorpio Rising* in the form of "the eroticization of Nazi regalia in certain gay cultures."[11] Such contemporary aesthetic effects of Nazi – or more generally fascist – aesthetics points to what Kriss Ravetto has observed as the way "Fascism occupied the unique (if not contradictory) space of a historical past and a political present."[12]

Of course, as is well known, photography was only one dimension of the Nazi media strategy. Goebbels was particularly struck with the capacity of cinema to create mass appeal and was especially taken with Sergei Eisenstein's cinematic celebration of the Russian revolution. While Eisenstein rebuffed Goebbels after the latter wrote for advice about propaganda films, the very form of his cinematic art was also recalcitrant to Goebbels's propaganda plans.[13] As Jacques Rancière points out in a gloss on the film–propaganda relation in Eisenstein's films, they cannot function as propaganda because "a propaganda film must give us a sense of certainty about what we see, it must choose between the documentary that presents what we see as a palpable reality or the fiction that forwards it as a desirable end [and] ... Eisenstein systematically denies us this sense of certainty."[14]

While Rancière sees Eisenstein's films as recalcitrant to a fascist aesthetic, he construes Brechtian theater as positively anti-fascist:

> If Brecht remained as a kind of archetype of political art in the XXth century, it was due not so much to his enduring communist commitment as to the way he negotiated the relation between the opposites, blending the scholastic forms of political teaching with the enjoyments of the musical or the cabaret, having allegories of Nazi power discuss in verse about matters of cauliflowers, etc. The main procedure of political or critical art consists in setting out the encounter and possibly the clash of heterogeneous elements ... to provoke a break in our perception, to disclose some secret connection of things hidden behind the everyday reality.[15]

Rancière's gloss on Brechtian theater resonates with Walter Benjamin's discussion of the fascism–aesthetics relationship (in a Brecht-inspired essay). Although Benjamin famously noted the fascist tendency to aestheticize politics, he also saw cinema's potential as an anti-fascist genre because of the way it alerted (shocked) the spectator rather than – as was the case with the Nazi aestheticization – encourage mass allegiance through collective expression (as he put it in his "Work of Art ..." essay: Benjamin, 1968), or encourage the displacement of political sensibility through commoditization and mass consumption (as he implies throughout his incomplete *Arcades* project). What accords especially well with Rancière's reference to a "break in perception" is Benjamin's reference to the shock effect of film. As Benjamin puts it:

> The spectator's process of association in view of these images is indeed interrupted by their constant, sudden change. This constitutes the shock effect of the film, which, like all shocks, should be cushioned by heightened presence of mind. By means of its technical structure, the film has taken the physical shock effect out of the wrappers in which Dadaism had, as it were, kept it inside the moral shock effect.[16]

In his conclusion on fascist aesthetics as the aestheticizing of politics in "The Work of Art ... " essay, Benjamin writes, "All efforts to render politics aesthetic culminate in one thing: war."[17] However, here I want to focus on a cinematic aesthetic that supplies a critical response to what Deleuze calls the new fascism (to repeat part of the epigraph at the beginning of this essay), which is immanent in the current structure of "peace:" "All our petty fears will be organized in concert, all our petty anxieties will be harnessed to make micro-fascists of us;

we will be called upon to stifle every little thing, every suspicious face, every dissonant voice, in our streets, in our neighborhoods, in our local theaters."[18]

Heeding Benjamin's optimism that cinema can provide an anti-fascist aesthetic, while bearing in mind Deleuze's take on the manifestation of the contemporary micro-fascism, I turn to some artistic texts that produce a Deleuzian antidote to the micro-fascism to which he refers. To appreciate the Deleuzian conceptual riposte to micro-fascism, we have to understand the primary individual and collective identity fantasies (and their material implementations) that have animated the original fascist aesthetic. Among the most telling was the architectural projects that the Italian fascists undertook in the city of Arezzo. In order to overcome the contingencies associated with a complex, historically assembled ethnoscape that belied attempts to attribute racial homogeneity to an originary Italian nation, they decided to designate the Arentines as the original Italian race. And in order to backdate the Arentines' role in creating the basis of the nation, they altered Arezzo's buildings by medievalizing them.

The project "was simultaneously a tool for civic redefinition and a means for declaring Fascist allegiance."[19] Specifically, the fascists sought to "recover Arezzo's idealized medieval past" by changing the facades of buildings to turn back the architectural clock from what was a renaissance architecture to a medieval one.[20] The fascist project was aimed at turning the contingency of presence into fateful organic solidarity, at inventing a coherent and unitary historical people and individual identity coherences (racial among others) that accord with exclusionary membership in the collective. Architecture was one among several of the artistic genres that were pressed into the service of securing identity coherence. Festivals, exhibitions, theater, and film were also used. Like Goebbels, Mussolini saw film as "the regime's strongest weapon." Accordingly, the regime produced short documentaries which featured "shots of individuals outfitted in period costumes and panoramic views of medieval and Renaissance buildings decorated for the occasion with hanging tapestries, banners, and flags."[21]

Counter-aesthetics: Syberberg

Although cinema was central to the fascist aestheticization of politics, it also lends itself to a politics of aesthetics. While the aestheticization of politics encourages ritual allegiance, a cinematic text that enjoins a politics of aesthetics "suspends the ordinary coordinates of sensory experience and reframes the network of relationships between spaces and times, subjects and objects, the common and the singular."[22] Here I turn first to Hans Jürgen Syberberg's *Hitler: A Film from Germany* (1977) which resembles the anti-fascist aesthetic in DeLillo's *White Noise* as well as comporting with a Brechtian anti-fascist aesthetic (part of Syberberg's explicit intention). The aesthetic is Brechtian in the sense described by Benjamin (already noted), in that its shock effect creates a "heightened presence of mind" and in the sense described by Rancière in that it creates breaks in perception through its "clash of heterogeneous elements." *Hitler* is a seven hour film whose primary heterogeneity combines Brechtian and Wagnerian aesthetics to effect what Syberberg refers to as an "aesthetic scandal: combining Brecht's doctrine of epic theater with Richard Wagner's musical aesthetics, cinematically conjoining the epic system as anti-Aristotelian cinema with the laws of a new myth."[23] The "scandal" is heightened as well by Syberberg's combination of cinematic genres, a mixing of "documentation with subjective interpretation and imagination with historical fact."[24] In Susan Sontag's well wrought phrases, the film is a "medley of imaginary discourse" with a "complex sound track ... interspersed between and intermittently overlaid on the speeches of actors," and with "a varying stock of emblematic props and images."[25] Moreover, by focusing on minor characters – for example Himmler's masseur, Felix Kersten, and Hitler's valet, Karl-Wilhelm Kraus – the film encourages the viewer to discover "horror in the banal."[26]

One of the film's major analytic assumptions, which Syberberg shares with DeLillo, is that Hitler as a historical subject is fundamentally a cinematic character. In DeLillo's case, that assumption is enacted in his *Running Dog* (1978), a novel whose main drama is based on a search for rumored pornographic film of Hitler, created during the last days of the war. At the end of the novel, the film turns out to be something else. It shows Hitler as an aesthetic figure, imitating Charlie Chaplin for a bunch of children:

> The figure shuffles toward the camera, his cane swinging. Behind him, in a corner of the screen, one of the small girls looks on.
>
> Briefly the man is flooded in light – the bleached and toneless effect of overexposure. With the return of minimal detail and contrast, he is very close to the camera, and his lifeless eyes acquire a trace of flame, the smallest luster. A professional effect. It's as though the glint originated in a nearby catch light.
>
> He produces an expression finally – a sweet, epicene, guilty little smile, Charlie's smile, An accurate reproduction ...
>
> Three quarter view. At first he seems to be speaking to the smallest of the children, a girl about three years old. It is then evident he is only moving his lips – an allusion to silent movies. One of the women can be seen smiling.[27]

Syberberg also evokes Chaplin: Hitler's valet does "a burlesque of Chaplin's impersonation of Hitler in *The Great Dictator*."[28] In contrast to DeLillo's treatment, Hitler is a cinematic subject who does not command direct attention. Rather, Syberberg presents the Third Reich as a whole as a cinematic apparatus. Hitler appears through actors who "*re*enact the kitsch fantasies of the Third Reich."[29] Thomas Elsaesser puts it well: "Syberberg wants to rediscover art, this time imitating not the heroic self- and world-denying stances of German idealism, but one that builds on the kitsch-debris of history, the material consequences of such heroism."[30]

While a significant aspect of the anti-fascist aesthetic in Syberberg's *Hitler* is in the way the Hitler phenomenon is presented as a bad movie – a kitschy horror show that focuses on the banal and indirect aspects of Hitler's presence; for example, a commentary by Hitler's valet referring to underpants and night shirts and remembrances of breakfasts and film screenings – to appreciate the effects

we have to recall the heroic versions of Hitler and Germany that the film parodies. Thus, as Sontag points out, the film "uses, recycles, parodies of elements of
Wagner. Syberberg means his film to be an anti-*Parsifal*, and hostility to Wagner
is one of the leitmotifs: the spiritual filiation of Wagner and Hitler."[31]

To conceptualize the significance of such an aesthetic, we can turn to the
insights supplied by Deleuze in his analysis of the painting of Francis Bacon
(noted in Chapter 1). He suggests that Bacon does not begin to paint on a blank
canvas. Rather, "everything he has in his head or around him is already on the
canvas, more or less virtually, before he begins his work."[32] In order to resist
the "psychic clichés" and "*figurative givens*," the artists must "transform"
or "deform" what is "always-already on the canvas."[33] It is also the case for
Syberberg, for him, the Hitler phenomenon was always-already on screen with
its "psychic clichés and "figurative givens." Hence his *Hitler ...* deforms what is
on screen by deforming not only the heroic operatic epics of Wagner but also the
pious, hero-making Hitler documentary, Leni Riefenstahl's *Triumph of the Will*.
And ultimately Hitler's erasure as Syberberg's aesthetic subject is collective; it is
Germany's reception of the fascist spectacle: "There will be no other hero, only
us," as Syberberg puts it.[34] In effect, his film accomplishes an important shift,
one from Hitler as character to Germany as the domain of his reception. It is a
change, as Deleuze points out, "taking place inside cinema, against Hitler, but
also against Hollywood, against business ... A true psychodynamics will not be
found unless it is based on *new associations*, by reconstituting the great mental
automata that he enslaved."[35]

Philip Dick, another counter-fascist aesthetic

If the artistic mechanisms central to the fascist strategy for securing allegiance
were aimed at fixing originary and exclusionary national identity by among
other things creating a static, exemplary citizen body whose unity is organic,
what would constitute an anti-fascist aesthetic? Rather than a static historically
invested people with enduring and exclusionary characteristics, the anti-fascist
body is one – after Deleuze and Guattari's treatment of the body – that is a
turbulent assemblage of different rates of being, co-inhabiting a body whose
becoming involves radical contingency. Insofar as such a body achieves a
coherent order, it is not the homeostatic equilibrium of the well-run machine but
rather the dynamic coherence of Deleuze and Guattari's "abstract machine."[36]
Cinema is a medium that is doubtless best able to convey such a body, and no
film better exemplifies such a capacity than Richard Linklater's film version
of the Philip Dick novel, *A Scanner Darkly* (2006). Taking Benjamin's assertion that a politically progressive cinema can counter the fascist cooptation of
cinema to enact an aesthetics of war, but updating the "war" from the 30s and
40s geopolitical version to the contemporary ones involving wars on drugs and
"terror," I want to identify the way Linklater's film achieves a contemporary
anti-fascist politics of aesthetic.

At the level of its plot, *A Scanner Darkly* resonates well with the micro-fascism
problematic that Deleuze articulates. The main character/protagonist, Bob Arctor,

leads a double life. In one, he belongs to a household of drug users; in another he is Fred, an undercover police agent assigned to collect damaging evidence on the household's drug culture. The Dick scenario is as follows: the war on drugs has not gone well because a highly addictive, illegal drug – Substance D, which is made from a small blue flower – has spread all over the country. Bob Arctor is the undercover agent assigned to infiltrate the drug culture. In his undercover role, he moves in with drug-using housemates in a poor Anaheim, California neighborhood. When at his police station, he is code-named Fred, and he hides his identity from fellow officers by wearing a "scramble suit" that produces rapid changes in visible identity (in effect a visual realization of the Deleuzian turbulence as different ways and rates of being co-inhabit a single body). Moreover, the Dick story and Linklater film version add a grammatical twist to the Deleuzian version of micro-fascism. Rather than a general "we" who are invited to "stifle every little thing, every suspicious face, every dissonant voice, in our streets, in our neighborhoods, in our local theaters," Bob Arctor, as Fred, is called upon to stifle *himself*. As the story progresses, he becomes a divided subject who is both part of the surveillance team and one of its investigative targets. In order to maintain his cover after he becomes part of a drug-using household, Arctor uses substantial amounts of Substance D, which causes the two hemispheres of his brain to work independently and, ultimately, to compete ("Bob" has a dissonant voice within). Although one narrative thread of the film speaks to the damaging effects of drug use, Bob's schizoid condition constitutes an escape from normalized subjectivity. His schizoid body is nomadic in Deleuze and Guattari's sense, for its movements resist the modes of identification that bodies are captured by when they operate in terms of the usual organic functions.

Within the film, the surveillance regime, recognizing Bob's/Fred's growing dependence on and seeming disability from Substance D, treats Arctor's developing schizoid tendencies as a psychological issue. They see him as someone suffering from a neurocognitive deficit and rename him Bruce, seeking to create a subject they can treat. However, although the Bruce/Fred/Arctor body is psychologized by the police authorities, in the context of the film that body is better rendered as an aesthetic rather than a psychological subject. Two conceptual assets emerge from such a shift. First, the focus on the body as an aesthetic subject turns us away from psychological phenomena and toward a spatial analytic, as I noted in my earlier references to Bersani and Ulysse Dutoit's reading of a Jean-Luc Goddard film *Contempt*. As is the case in Godard's film about an increasingly estranged couple, a focus on aesthetic rather than psychological subjectivity illuminates cinematic space – in this case a space that mimes the micro-fascism of securitization – as the film inter-articulates the life world with the panoptics of drug surveillance. In that process, the scanner is a primary focal point. As a result, one of the film's (like the book's) primary questions, which Fred/Bob asks himself, is "What does the scanner see?"

I mean really see? Into the head? Down into the heart? Does a passive infrared scanner like they used to use or a cube-type holo-scanner like

Figures 5.1a and b Arctor in his scramble suit

they use these days see into myself. I see only murk outside, murk inside. I hope for everyone's sake the scanners do better. Because, he thought, if the scanner sees only darkly, the way I myself do, then we are cursed, cursed again and like we have been continually, and we'll wind up dead this way, knowing very little and getting that little fragment wrong too.

Second, while a primary narrative thread of the film is a story about the dangers of drug use, the Fred/Arctor body is recalcitrant to the narrative. Vincent Amiel's observations on the subversive cinematic body serve well here. Amiel analyzes those films (e.g., those of Robert Bresson, Buster Keaton and John Cassavetes) in which what he calls "the cinematographic body is no longer an object of film knowledge; rather it is a model of knowledge via editing … [It is] simultaneously that which is filmed and that which (re)organizes the film in the mind/body of the spectator … [becoming the] source rather than the object of cinema."[37] Referring to the subversive cinematic body of film, Amiel says that this kind of cinematographic body:

> is no longer an object of film or knowledge; rather it is a model of knowledge via editing … [it is] simultaneously that which is filmed and that which (re)organizes the film in the mind/body of the spectator … [becoming the] source rather than the object of cinema.[38]

While in what Amiel calls "classic cinema" the moving bodies were simply vehicles for a story; in his terms, the tendency was to "abandon the body's density for the exclusive profit of its functionality," so that it was merely "at the service of narrative articulations," in much of contemporary cinema "the idea is for the cinema to dis-organ-ize the body … by means of revealing its fragmented nature, by extracting from it the yoke of unity and consciousness, by giving it back the complexity of its own determinations."[39]

Certainly the protagonist in *Scanner* should be understood aesthetically, even though he develops a psychosis. "Bruce" (Arctor) discovers the blue flowers that are the source of the drug, Substance D. Inasmuch as the blue flower is a symbol of German romanticism, the psychosis-inducing flower is also an aesthetic icon. As such it assists in recruiting the film into a politics of aesthetics frame rather than moving it toward the simple policy problem of how to treat a drug-induced psychosis. Moreover, *à la* Benjamin, the blue flower motif suggests that the film evokes the pervasiveness of illusion (what Benjamin referred to as phantasmagoria) rather than psychic delusion (where illusion as phantasmagoria is Dick's emphasis in the novel). The cinema version of *Scanner* is ideally suited to such an aesthetic frame, especially in the way it situates the viewer *vis à vis* the couplet of reality versus illusion. As Benjamin suggests in his run up to the blue flower imagery, "the shooting of a film … presents a process in which it is impossible to assign to a spectator a viewpoint which would exclude from the scene being enacted such extraneous accessories as camera equipment, lighting machinery crew, etc. … Its illusory nature is a nature of the second degree, the result of editing." Benjamin adds, "The equipment-free aspect of reality here has become the height of artifice, the site of immediate reality has become the 'blue flower' in the land of technology."[40]

In interpreting Benjamin's meaning here, Miriam Hansen insists that the blue flower imagery helps Benjamin lend a political force to cinema-as-form. For Benjamin, she writes, "if film were to have a critical, [i.e., anti-fascist] cognitive function, it had to disrupt that chain [the 'mythical chain of mirrors'] and assume the task of all politicized art and [quoting Susan Buck-Morss] 'not to duplicate the illusion as real, but to interpret reality as itself illusion'."[41] The "metaphor of the blue flower – the unattainable object of the romantic quest," she adds, suggests the critical role of cinema's "distortion of distortion." And, most significantly, according to Benjamin, the actor who is able to maintain her/his "humanity in the face of the apparatus," frees the mass audience from myth as they "watch an actor take revenge in their place."[42]

To elaborate the critical anti-fascist aesthetic insights of Benjamin and others that *Scanner* delivers, we can consider the name of Dick's main protagonist, Arctor – likely a reference to the subject-as-actor – and follow his relationship to illusion. Arctor is under cover, acting an identity, performing in effect for the scanners. Moreover, his persona is deployed on both sides of the surveillance process; he is both a subject and object of surveillance and is therefore performing for himself as well. And the split in his focus of observation is doubled by the way Substance D has created a split between the hemispheres of his brain. These dual divisions encourage a model of historically fraught subjectivity that is decidedly anti-fascist in more or less the sense in which the Brechtian subject emerges from his theatrical practice. In Brechtian theater, what is in front of the audience, as it is acted out, is conveyed as something that might well be otherwise. The effect is a dualism that points to the possibilities of multiplicity, a sense of not simply what is being done "but what might just as well have not been done, what might have been something else altogether, or simply have been omitted."[43] As a result, what is presented is a challenge to the fascist desire to rein in contingency in order to establish historical necessity.

A cinematic Philip Dick's anti-fascism yet again, *Minority Report*

> "Everybody runs; everybody runs."
>
> John Anderton (Tom Cruise) in *Minority Report*

As Kriss Ravetto points out, "hundreds of films have been produced on the subject of fascism."[44] However, I want to emphasize that what makes a film anti-fascist is not necessarily a matter of the way it explicitly addresses the historically bounded phenomenon that produced a Hitler and Mussolini. Jacques Rancière makes the point well in his reference to the politics of the novel. For example, he suggests that Virginia Woolf's novels are more connected with democratic history than Emile Zola's, not because she wrote "good social novels but because her way of working on the contraction or distention of temporalities, on their contemporaneousness or their distance, or her way of situating events at a more minute level, all of this establishes a grid that makes it possible to think through the frames of political dissensuality more effectively than the social epic's various forms."[45] Accordingly, one might surmise that Dick's *Man in the High Castle* (1992), which explicitly addressed an America that is organized around the victory of fascism (Gemany and Japan have won World War II as the novel begins), is his most anti-fascist story. However, I want to suggest – in accord with Rancière's point – that, like his *Scanner*, Dick's *Minority Report*, especially in its cinematic realization, delivers a more effective anti-fascist aesthetic.

The film version of *Minority Report* articulates well the Deleuzian conception of micro-fascism and goes beyond *Scanner*'s anti-fascism because it displays a coercive society-wide securitization rather than the more focused assault on one of society's sub-cultures. That securitization is effectively an imposition of a "peace" that stifles all forms of dissonance. Although the society represented is not explicitly fascist – as it is in Dick's *Man in the High Castle* – it is nevertheless a society of totalizing control, run by a pre-crime unit that arrests and incarcerates anyone who is interpreted as planning a violent crime. The suborned interpreters are pre-cogs, psychic women who are connected to informational prostheses to form a person–technology assemblage. With its form as well as its content, Steven Spielberg's film version of the story provides the most notable representation of a contemporary politics of surveillance, well captured in Gilles Deleuze's conception of "societies of control." Whereas Foucault conceived the disciplinary society, based on enclosures – the school, the factory, the prison and so on – as historically supplanting the old societies of sovereignty, Deleuze argues that the society of control has displaced the disciplinary society. It is not a society of walls and containments but a system of domination that works through modulations and coding procedures: "In the control societies what are important are no longer numbers and names but codes, a password instead of a watchword."[46] They are codes that control movements from one function and setting to another and the coding mechanisms are located in dominant centers, centers of capitalism (global incorporations) but also articulated in the control measures of the state.

Although capitalism is disproportionately connected to "societies of control," there is also a micro-fascism that is state-oriented. With respect to this aspect, Deleuze and Guattari write, "The administration of a great organized molar security has as its correlate a whole micro-management of petty fears [amounting to] … a macropolitics of society by and for a micro-politics of insecurity."[47] Within this model of securitization, the social order has two opposing modalities: machines of capture in which bodies and spaces are coded, and lines of flight, which are the mechanisms and routes through which people elude the machines of capture. In effect, the lines of flight constitute micro-political reactions to the mechanisms of capture to resist the society's "normalizing individualization."[48]

Minority Report's enactment of a dynamic opposition between the machines of capture and the micro-politics of escape takes place in Washington DC in 2054, where the "pre-crime unit" – which has aspirations to become a national program – operates the policing mechanisms through which persons identified as future criminals are arrested and incarcerated. While the eventual escape and return to normal life of one of the pre-cogs – who has been held in a drugged state of suspended animation – is part of the film's drama, the most significant body (the primary aesthetic subject) in the film is that of John Anderton (Tom Cruise) who, when the film opens, is the head arresting officer of the pre-crime unit. Anderton's moving body, first as part of the mechanisms of capture and subsequently as a fugitive from the unit he formerly led, drives the film's primary narrative. At first he operates as a wholly suborned body: using gestures, he draws out the information on a future crime from his unit's media technology screen. Then, after he is set up and programmed by the unit as a future criminal, he moves to stymie the machine of capture.

Ultimately, Anderton's exoneration involves a recovery of the pre-crime unit's suppressed archive of minority reports (submitted by pre-cogs who see the future crime differently). As Philip Dick's version of the story puts it: "*The existence of a majority logically implies a corresponding minority.*"[49] In the film version, the minority reports have been suppressed (because the head of the program, eager to have it implemented nationally, has suppressed them in order to represent future criminal acts as certainties rather than probabilities). Anderton learns that his only hope is to find the one in his case – if it exists. Ultimately, although the narrative has a positive ending (John Anderton is exonerated, the head of the program is discredited, and the pre-crime program is eliminated), the film's most significant aspects are non-narrative, anti-fascist, and micro-political.

In the opening scenes, Anderton's body functions as a physical extension of the pre-crime surveillance and arrest functions, his body is filmed moving in a musically accompanied ballet in harmony with the machinery of prediction. His movements at this stage are wholly modulated and choreographed by the system. Specifically, his swinging arms are shown pulling up the relevant images on a large screen, and subsequently his moving body is shown closing in on the alleged perpetrator. Later, the images of his body and its movements are subversive. As his body challenges the totalizing pre-crime choreography he evinces a counter movement to those of the system's machines of capture.

To do so he has to modify his body to subvert the surveillance system – for example, by having his eyes replaced to subvert the coding system, which reads eyeball patterns.

As a result, Anderton is an exemplary Deleuzian fugitive: "Everybody runs," he says when the police first try to apprehend him. Thereafter, his running requires him to move in ways that allow him to escape from the coding apparatuses and exemplify Deleuze's suggestion that there are always forms of flow that elude the capturing, binary organizations. Notably, apart from Anderton's movements – which articulate Deleuzian lines of flight by exploiting the gaps in the apparatuses of capture – the subversiveness of his body is also a function of a film form that opposes the body to the narrative. As is the case with the aesthetic subject in *Scanner*, Bob Arctor, John Anderton's body performs as the kind of cinematic body analyzed by Amiel: "dis-organ-ized" and thus resistant to the functionality of the film narrative.[50] As a result, the film uses Anderton's body to realize the Deleuzian political inspiration – to resist the apparatuses of capture – and thus works not simply through its narrative drama but also through its imagery, as an exemplary anti-fascist aesthetic.

Conclusion: alternative methodological strategies

As I noted in Chapter 1, the experience of fascism has had a disproportionate shaping effect on the post-World War II development of the social sciences, especially political psychology. To repeat that observation: "In the case of political psychology what was enjoined was a search for the fascist personality, understood to be a deviant type susceptible to authoritarian impulses or appeals [and among the inquiries undertaken were] ... the authoritarian personalities studies of Theodor W. Adorno and his associates, Milton Rokeach's work on open versus closed minds, and H. G. Eysenck's addition of a tender minded versus tough minded axis of opinion to the study of political ideology."[51] In sum, for the social sciences in this period, to understand the emergent dangers of fascism, one must inquire into what Adorno *et al.* referred to as the "*potentially fascistic* individual."[52] Thus, for Adorno *et al.* – as was the case for Eysenck, and Rokeach – the problem of fascism emerges from susceptible mentalities. Those fascism-susceptible mentalities are treated by Eysenck as an ideological complex – a convergence of conservatism with tough-mindedness, articulated as a commitment to capital punishment and other harsh treatments for criminals, among other things.[53] Rokeach lumped fascist mentality with orthodox Marxism–Leninism and rendered both mentalities forms of dogmatic cognitive organization,[54] while fascism-susceptible mentalities are treated by Adorno *et al.* as an indication of "psychological ill-health."[55]

In contrast, when fascism is interpreted as a *dispositif* – a complex, coercive apparatus – rather than merely as a mentality, we are in a position to appreciate its insidious effects on the social order – its war against difference in the name of social peace – by turning to arts that mobilize aesthetic subjects who both mime and resist fascism's choreography. If we heed the familiar social psychology versions of fascism, we license a search for troubled psychodynamic stories and the identification of effective clinical interventions.

Figures 5.2a and b Two Andertons

If we focus on the fascist *dispositif* – where a *dispositif* (as I have noted in previous chapters, quoting Foucault) is "a thoroughly heterogeneous ensemble consisting of discourses, institutions, architectural forms, regulatory decisions, laws, administrative measures, scientific statements, philosophical, moral and philanthropic propositions ... the said as much as the unsaid ... the elements of the apparatus"[56] – we are encouraged to pursue inventive staging rather than psychological investigation. In short, we turn to the arts as they enact the fascist *dispositif* and thus, for example, let Hans-Jürgen Syberberg and Philip K. Dick's imaginations trump Adorno *et al.*'s recapitulation of the quest for dangerous mentalities.

6 The micro-politics of justice
Language, sense, and space

What might be called the intersentient plastic life of our sensory sociality goes unacknowledged, unplumbed, and unarticulated in its potential.

Christophe Wall-Romana

Justice does not exist only in words, but first of all it exists in words.

Carlos Fuentes

Introduction: the aesthetic subjects

In this chapter I pursue an inquiry into the micro-politics of justice. As is well known, the macropolitics of justice is deployed with the way states, through their decision-making bodies, promulgate, execute, and administer the law. Among the sub-disciplines in the social sciences involved macropolitical analysis has been the study of judicial decision-making. While legal scholars traditionally concerned themselves with doctrinal analysis, by the mid-twentieth century, social scientists had developed explanatory approaches that correlated judicial ideologies and/or the social backgrounds of judges with their decisions.[1] In contrast with the emphasis on explaining the behavior of those with judicial appointments, the micro-politics of justice references a process in which individuals and collectives, who are affected by legality/illegalities, participate in a culture of feelings or sensibilities and subsequently engage in discursive encounters about what is just. Because my concern is with the tension between formal legal justice and embodied senses of justice, and I turn to philosophical approaches to space, language, and embodied sensibility, I enact an "interference" between philosophy and two artistic texts. One text is cinematic and the other literary, and both stage discursive encounters between persons who embody incommensurate senses of justice – in order to derive political insights from them. More specifically, I conceptualize and illustrate with examples, interrelationships among law, space and cultures of feeling, especially in terms of the way justice-related encounters articulate the spatial bases – boundaries and cultural enclosures – separating alternative loci of enunciation. The vehicles for my analysis here, as in other chapters, are "aesthetic subjects," who function within the two texts that serve as the bookends of my investigation – a Romanian film (Cornelieu Porumboiu's *Police, Adjective*, 2009), and an Italian crime novel (Leonardo Sciascia's *The Day of the Owl*, 2003). In exploring the implications of locating justice in the critical interrelationships among law, bodies, discourse, and space, I aim once again to demonstrate the methodological advantages of turning to artistic texts whose characters serve as aesthetic subjects, embodying feelings and actions that deliver the critical insights central to my inquiry. My analysis begins with a focus on a cinematic protagonist whose feelings and action trajectory initiate the main concepts in my analysis.

In Porumboiu's film *Police, Adjective*, the detective, Cristi (Dragos Bucur), exhibits a tension between his official policing obligations and his conscience. He has been assigned to the surveillance of high school hashish smokers in his Romanian city, Brasov, and is ultimately ordered to set up a sting so that they can be arrested and prosecuted. Much of the film focuses on Cristi's physicality. The camera follows his movement about the city on foot, as he trails the suspects; it zooms in on his standing around for hours, trying to keep warm (by stuffing his hands in his pockets and drawing his sweater over his chin and mouth) as he watches them gather and smoke; and it frames tableaux of his proletarian eating practices (as he breaks up bread into his stew), his drinking until he's a bit tipsy (as he sits and ponders his dilemma in a bar), his attempts to connect with his wife (as he lounges and watches television while she listens to loud music on her computer next to him, and sits with her eating and conversing at the dining table), and his games of foot tennis (played in a foursome) in which he releases tension. In the film's narration, Cristi is a quintessential aesthetic subject, for – as I noted in Chapter 1 – *aisthitikos*, the ancient Greek word from which aesthetics is derived, refers to the pre-linguistic, embodied, or feeling-based aspect of perception.[2]

This sense of aesthetics is effectively enacted in Cristi's personal approach to justice, for it is based on his corporeal apprehension of crime and punishment. In two office scenes, one a conversation with a prosecutor and the other with his superior, the captain of his precinct, he attempts to resist the demand that he entrap and arrest the teenagers. While speaking with the prosecutor early in the film narrative, he reveals what has affected his reluctance to make the drug

Figure 6.1
Cristi and his wife

entrapment and arrest. He reports that, while on his honeymoon in the Czech Republic he saw people smoking hashish with impunity. It therefore strikes him as unfair to impose a law that will undoubtedly change once Romania catches up with other more progressive European states. At the end of the film, in an interview with his captain, he attempts to resist the demand that he set up the sting, saying that it would bother his conscience to bust "crazy kids" and subject them to a seven-year prison term for "smoking a joint." He adds that it would make him feel bad.

However, in the conversation with the captain Cristi is at a marked linguistic disadvantage – which the viewers can appreciate because they have been prepared by an earlier scene. The film therefore constitutes a double aesthetic: while its focus is on Cristi's bodily senses, it also considers the implications of his situation. It therefore *enacts* an aesthetic inasmuch as aesthetics has also come to refer to artistic texts. In a key scene, early in the film, both senses of the aesthetic are operating: Cristi's body displays his discomfort, and the discursive exchanges with his wife deliver an aesthetics of discourse. In the scene Cristi sits watching television while his wife is listening to a song loudly broadcast from her desktop computer. Initiating the conversation, Cristi says "the song doesn't make any sense." When his wife asks why he thinks that, he repeats a couple of lines: "what would the field be without the flower; what would the sea be without the sun" and says, "what else would it be? It would still be the field and the sea." His wife, who turns out to be a linguistic pedant and an advocate of the official Romanian grammar, points out that the lines are a figure of speech known as an *anaphora*. Cristi, who lacks an appreciation of figurative language, squirms and frowns as he asks why the song doesn't just say what it means directly. Subsequently, they converse about the report he is compiling about the hashish smokers. She says that she read it when he left it on the coat rack and that it contains a grammatical mistake; a particular construction has been changed by the Romanian Academy. Cristi responds passively, saying simply that he'll change it, although he thinks that official language policy is "crazy."

At the film's climax, Cristi again finds himself in a language confrontation. When summoned by his captain, who asks why he is not proceeding with the sting, he insists that he won't carry it out because if he did, his conscience would bother him. Cristi's refusal is reminiscent of a character I invoke in the Preface, Herman Melville's Bartleby in his "Bartleby, the Scrivener" who responds with increasing frequency to his attorney/employer's request for fulfilling tasks or explaining his recalcitrance with the phrases "I would prefer not to" and "I prefer not to."[3] As Gilles Deleuze points out, because the "prefer" construction is not an outright refusal, it does not effect Bartleby's transition from one employed, fulfilling his obligations as a law-copyist, to one shirking them.[4] Even when prompted by his employer: "Every copyist is bound to help examine his copy. Is that not so? Will you not speak," the response remains, "I prefer not to." Eventually, Bartleby's repetition of the phrase permeates the discourse of the office as a whole. The attorney and the other clerks find the word creeping into their statements unbidden. Ultimately, after Bartleby has deflected all attempts to get him to examine his and other copies, he gives up copying as well; the "formula annihilates 'copying'" and "erodes the attorney's reasonable organization of work and life."[5] For the purposes of comparison, Cristi and Bartleby both resist the sense-making that predicates the hierarchy of tasks within their respective vocations. However, Bartleby succeeds where Cristi fails. In Bartleby's case, he has an employer who lacks the phrases to contest his formula. The formula "stymies the speech acts that a boss uses to command."[6] Unable to engage in effective discursive contestation, the attorney "concocts a theory explaining how Bartleby's formula ravages language as a whole"[7] and leads to a logic that permits Bartleby to stop copying altogether. Bartleby has effectively "invented a new logic, *a logic of preference*, which is enough to undermine the presuppositions of language as a whole."[8] By contrast, Cristi lacks an effective formula. As a result, he is helpless in the face of the ones thrown at him by the police captain. While Bartleby has a formula that "severs language from all reference,"[9] Cristi's reference is confined to himself (his conscience and feelings). While Bartleby's formula casts him outside of all prescribed positioning, Cristi's attempt to step outside fails; he is repositioned by the captain's words within the extant policing roles.

After stating, "You're not making sense," the captain challenges Cristi by asking a colleague to write Cristi's reasons for his recalcitrance on a chalkboard and then asking his secretary to bring in a Romanian dictionary. The board's transcript reads, "Conscience is something within me that stops me from doing something bad that I'd afterwards regret" – to which the captain responds, "So you have a feeling, an intuition." In response to Cristi's statements – the kids are just "crazy" rather than serious criminals and thus it would not be moral to impose such a penalty (moreover, arresting them would make him feel bad) – the captain reads definitions of Cristi's oppositional concepts from the dictionary (conscience, morality, justice), all of which, when uttered without benefit of the alternative discursive contexts within which they might be understood, suggest that his position is based on idiosyncratic resistance to his official policing obligations. And ultimately, lacking linguistic facility, Cristi cannot find words adequate to his sensibilities (his reliance on the word "crazy" fails as much here as it did in the face of his wife's linguistic pedantry). What he needs are words that "exceed the function of rigid designation" in order to be able to translate what he senses into an intelligible discourse on crime and justice that opposes effectively "those who claim to speak correctly."[10]

Generalized beyond the particular confrontation in the film, the police captain's insistence on correct speech is anathema to a consideration of the politics of crime, punishment, and justice. Toni Morrison lyrically captures the depoliticizing aspects of the anachronistically rigid language of policing through the perspective of *her* conceptual persona (a blind woman) in her Nobel Prize acceptance speech:

> [I]t is unyielding language content to admire its own paralysis ... Ruthless in its policing duties, it has no desire or purpose other than maintaining the free range of its own narcotic narcissism, its own exclusivity and dominance ... Unreceptive to interrogation, it cannot form or tolerate new ideas, shape other

thoughts, tell another story, fill baffling silences. Official language smith-eryed to sanction ignorance and preserve privilege is a suit of armor polished to shocking glitter, a husk from which the knight departed long ago.[11]

Of course, Porumboiu's film as a whole is able to provide what his character, Cristi, cannot – a conceptual exploration of the relationships among sense, space, discourse and justice. Heeding the film's provocation on those relationships, I turn to an elaboration of the insights it provides.

The spaces of justice

The challenge that the linguistically limited Cristi mounts unsuccessfully is not just about language. He attempts as well to enlarge the spatio-temporality of justice. In his conversation with the prosecutor, he connects his small city, Brasov, to the rest of Europe and imagines a future in which Romanian drug penalties are abrogated as his country catches up with the more tolerant climate in other European states. Once Cristi reveals to the prosecutor that his reluc-tance to pursue young hashish smokers was reinforced while he was in Prague on his honeymoon, there ensues an exchange of seemingly idle talk that implicitly involves contestation about the spatial boundaries of the city's drug policing. After Cristi reports that some of Prague's buildings have gold roofs, that he saw a "theater with an entire ceiling of gold," and that Prague is known as the Golden City, the prosecutor brings the conversation's focus back to Brasov: "Did you know that the Black Church in Brasov once had a golden roof?" "Yes," says Cristi, "It burnt down." Undeterred, the prosecutor suggests that the government should renovate that roof, restoring its gold: "Then we could call Brasov The City of Gold; sounds great, yes?" When Cristi counters that "Prague is a much larger city," the prosecutor says, "Well then, we could call it the Little Prague ... We'd have Bucharest as 'Little Paris' and Brasov as 'Little Prague' ... Sounds great, doesn't it?"

Although verbally Cristi accedes, saying *Da* (yes), his body in this scene, as in other conversations in the film, is recalcitrant. While the prosecutor is leaning back in his chair and exhibiting a posture of self-satisfaction, Cristi's is troubled and resistant: hunched over and tense. Here, as throughout the film, Cristi is the kind of aesthetic subject that is not simply an instrument of the film narrative. Rather, he is the kind of subject – unlike those bodies in classic cinema whose "density" is abandoned as they function as "simply vehicles for a story [as they move about in] the service of narrative articulations" – who is found in some contemporary films that "dis-organ-ize the body ... by means of revealing its fragmented nature, [and] by extracting from it the 'yoke of unity' and conscious-ness, by giving it back the complexity of its own determinations."[12] Although unable discursively to oppose the policing structure, Cristi's body retains its "density" and "complexity," and in this scene's conversation is able to evoke what Paolo Virno calls a "spontaneous epistemology" embedded in seemingly idle talk. "Idle talk," Virno points out, reveals aspects of political opposition because it is often a form of "social communication" that breaks away from "every bond

Figure 6.2
Cristi and the prosecutor

or presupposition."[13] In this case, the spontaneous epistemology is an embodied knowledge, coming from within and reinforced by an experience of alternative legal spaces. It is enacted through Cristi's corporeally displayed resistance to capitulating to Brasov's parochial policing mentality. Nevertheless, by the end of the film, Cristi's resistance has broken, leaving him a suborned body as the outcome becomes an event of "linguistic domination."[14] However, although the politics of language is a primary frame within which the film cries out for analysis (and I do so below), much of the politics of the film can also be captured in an analysis of the relationship between justice and space toward which the encounters in the film point.

An effective conceptual rendering of such a spatial analysis is available by analogy in Michel Foucault's treatment of the spaces of disease. At the outset of his investigation of the history of the medical gaze, Foucault discerns three levels of spatialization. At the primary level, disease exists in medical language (in a classificatory system, expressed as "an area of homologies").[15] At a second level, it is located in "the space of the body." And finally, once medicine becomes a governmental task, it is located in a third space – an administrative structure where it is subject to an intensification of surveillance by a proliferating series of official agencies (including "a policing supplement").[16] To apply those levels of spatialization to the location of justice in Porumboiu's *Police, Adjective*, we can surmise that justice is located first of all in the languages of the law (specifically in the local codification of the law's narrow, dictionary-assisted languages of transgression and policing obligations), second in Cristi's body, and third in the law's administrative agencies: prosecutors, police officer hierarchies, and policing functionaries (forensic specialists, filing clerks, among others) – in effect a policing *dispositif*. Moreover, just as in the history of medicine – where a proliferation of agencies developed when medicine became a "task for the nation" – so in the case of the history of punishment, the state's monopolization of disputes has meant that proscribed forms of drug use also evoke a policing supplement, which includes an "intensification of surveillance" that requires complex intra- and inter-agency cooperation.[17] However, while Foucault's spatial analysis of medicine provides an apt analogy for understanding the specific case that the film addresses, we need a more historically situated perspective to grasp more generally what the film implies, with its image and narrative provocations. In what follows I give the primary conceptual contributions of the film some historical depth.

Bodies, discourse, spaces: achieving historical distance

In order to gain a politically perspicuous view of the way Porumboiu's film mobilizes the tensions between Cristi's sense of justice and its location within the extra-corporeal spaces he cannot control or effectively address, we need to defamiliarize contemporary justice–space relationships. As Foucault has noted, when referring to his "method" (here I repeat a passage from Chapter 1), to be able to grasp "the history of successive forms" and appreciate how peculiar the contemporary form is, he had "to stand detached from it, bracket its familiarity, in order to analyze the theoretical and practical context with which it has been associated" (hence his analysis of the way sexuality was problematized in ancient Greece).[18] In a similar methodological gesture, the classical historian, Paul Veyne, writes that he is interested in analyzing Roman history because of the way it allows him to see the present: "Rome ... takes us out of ourselves and forces us to make explicit the differences separating us from it."[19]

Where can we go historically to bracket the familiarity of the problematic in Porumboiu's fictional (yet very realistic) Brasov, recognizing that the contemporary spatial strategy for responding to crimes is dominated by agencies whose ultimate horizon involves mechanisms of confinement (hence the seven-year term facing the young hashish smokers)? While there are many historical venues and periods that would serve as effective defamiliarizing contrasts, the system of law and justice in medieval Iceland is perhaps the best historical moment we can use to "take us out of ourselves" – it had no institutions of confinement and no centralized state to administer punishment. As the writers of Icelandic sagas teach us, medieval Iceland had a singular way of identifying political affiliation and allocating legal protection. A person's affiliational identity was not that of the modern citizen subject. It was primarily bio-political, rather than territorial, inasmuch as it was tied to family and clan heredity. Nevertheless, one's legal identity could migrate into a spatial mode because the movement from inside the law to outside of it (being outlawed) was juridically determined at a yearly meeting of the clans at the Icelandic *Althing*. For example, if a person was charged with murder and thereby ordered to pay compensation to a victim's family or clan, failure to come up with the payment would outlaw the perpetrator. Once outlawed, a person could be killed with impunity. In Giorgio Agamben's terms, the perpetrator would become "bare life," one without legal or political standing, and thus without the protections of community qualification; he (always "he") could be killed without there being a murder.[20]

Although pieces of literature – and thus imaginative reenactments of Icelandic events in general and juridical history in particular – the sagas yield a significant analytic. Their characters serve as aesthetic subjects whose varying relationships to juridical space – being either inside or outside of it – reflect a relatively unfamiliar model of the administration of justice. Unlike the mechanism of confinement, which has characterized centuries of the European and American justice systems, medieval Iceland allocated justice by making the penalty a very precarious form of exclusion. For example, in *Njal's Saga*, both a well-intentioned character – the noble warrior Gunnar, who killed to protect himself – and an ill-intentioned character – the notorious Killer Hraap, who killed arbitrarily – end up outside the law and are killed by their enemies. At a minimum, the part-time administration of justice at the medieval Icelandic *Althing* (comprised as a yearly gathering of the clans) functioned to allocate bodies to a space "devoid of law" (to invoke another of Agamben's concepts).[21]

By looking back at the juridico-political system of medieval Iceland from the present, we are able to reflect on the historical trajectory of relationships between bodies and legal spaces and defamiliarize the current relationship. The outlawing practice in medieval Iceland was not predicated on the kind of security issues that preoccupy the contemporary state. Outlawing was designed to disconnect wealth and violence and to regulate inter-clan violence. The almost certain consequence of being placed outside the law was death at the hands of one's enemies. Because there was no centralized system of revenge, retaliation for the alleged crime was strictly freelance; it was in the hands of the aggrieved parties and their allies. The result could be catastrophic because it was common for cycles of retaliation to develop and engulf the entire social order. Indeed, the justice system of the modern state was designed in part to avoid the escalating cycles of violence that have occurred in pre-state political systems. By monopolizing retaliation, the state monopolizes and depersonalizes revenge.

However, as Fernand Braudel has pointed out, the history of forms is conjunctural rather than linear. As new forms develop, some of the older ones persist rather than being wholly surpassed.[22] Thus, although the administration of confinement within a comprehensive array of "enclosure milieus"[23] for those citizen subjects "brought to justice" remains the ultimate horizon of contemporary justice systems, the strategy of outlawing remains; it is invoked when a citizen (someone presumptively inside the law) is, by executive order, translated into an enemy status (for example the current U.S. practice of designating some Americans as "enemy combatants"). Such translations are increasingly the case. For example, once the "war on terror" reached its current level of expansion, it began functioning within the tripartite spatiality that Foucault ascribed to modern medicine; its locations included a nomenclature (a list of terrorist acts), interpreted bodies (e.g., those inscribed by psycho-biological discourses on the terrorist), and a proliferating set of surveilling and policing agencies. Some of those agencies lack killing power – for example, the public health services that are now enjoined to heed the dangers of biological terrorism. However, after the 11 September 2001 attacks on the World Trade Center, President Bush authorized the CIA – an agency *with* killing power – "to kill U.S. citizens abroad if strong evidence existed that an American was involved in organizing or carrying out terrorist actions against the United States or U.S. interests," a policy subsequently extended by the administration of President Obama.[24] But as one analyst points out, in some cases "combat is not what we're talking about." Some people on the CIA's "'hit list' are likely to be killed while at home, sleeping in their bed, driving in a car with friends or family, or engaged in a whole array of other activities."[25] In effect, the post-9/11 space–justice inter-articulation has increasingly involved a mix of strategies, supplementing confinement with outlawing. But, unlike the Icelandic practice of outlawing, it is the state's executive power that launches the killing. "Enemies" are enemies of the state rather than the unredeemed antagonists of individuals and groups with uncompensated grievances.

Nevertheless, the increasing use of such a supplement – or "state of exception" – has invited reaction in the form of counter discourses that contest the discursive practices that are complicit in outlawing citizens (for example the discourse on enemy combatants) and used to warrant extra-judicial killing. As a result, the post-9/11 contentions over justice are expressed through what J.-F. Lyotard calls a clash of "phrase regimes" (a conception to which I return below).[26] However, in the case of the altered spatialization of justice after 9/11, a mere cataloguing of the different positions on the states of exception to juridical protections would not achieve a rendering of the micro-political implications of clashes over juridical and/or extra-juridical deployments of punishment. Because – as Porumboiu's *Police, Adjective* shows – the tensions between senses of justice and the application of official legal or extra-legal authority are best appreciated when the subjects involved are mobilized into encounters that reveal the complexities of those tensions. It is aesthetic modes of apprehension, articulated in artistic texts – films and novels for example – that often provide the most effective analytic. In what follows, I turn to the Italian writer Leonardo Sciascia's first crime novel, *The Day of the Owl* (Italian edition, 1961). The novel mobilizes aesthetic subjects whose encounters create the moments needed to map the tensions between the administration of justice and senses of justice, as they unfold within a realistic scenario. It therefore effectively articulates and contextualizes the conceptual basis of my analysis of the micro-politics of justice.

A policeman who needs no adjectives

> Political art … means creating those forms of collision or dissensus that put together not only heterogeneous elements but also two politics of sensoryness. The heterogeneous elements are put together in order to provoke a clash.
>
> Jacques Rancière

Like all nation-states, Italy contains politically centrifugal regions which embody diverse "structures of feeling" – a concept invented and developed by Raymond Williams to refer to "affective elements of consciousness and relationships: not feeling against thought, but thought as felt and feeling as thoughts: practical consciousness of a present kind in a living and inter-relating continuity."[27] In understanding the epistemic implications of the encounters that Sciascia's crime novel stages across two of Italy's diverse regions, Williams's observation that a structure of feeling is not universally shared and is often not "fully understood by living people in close contact with it" is especially apropos.[28] The novel features an encounter between an investigator from Parma in the north of Italy – Police Captain Bellodi, whose sense of justice in based on a commitment to the law as codified and applied to the country as a whole – and a Sicilian sub-culture in which justice functions wholly outside of such a commitment. It is a regional sense of justice based on a historically deep structure of feeling rather than on an allegiance to Italy's centralized codifications of the law. As Captain Belodi ultimately recognizes as he struggles to consummate his case:

> The only institution in the Sicilian conscience that really counts, is the family; counts that is to say, more as a juridical contract or bond than as a natural association based on affection. The family is the Sicilian's State. The State, as it is for us, is extraneous to them, merely a *de facto* entity based on force; an entity imposing taxes, military service, war, police.[29]

Thus, as is the case with the justice systems in other nation-states, where centralized power has failed to impose completely a unitary legal culture, Italian justice deploys itself differently in different, culturally incommensurate spaces of application. The differences in the law's reception – realized as a mosaic of justice sub-cultures across the regional spaces in Italy – is in evidence in other places that display complex cartographies of justice.

Although there are doubtless several examples, Thailand is notable in retaining a markedly hybrid cartography of justice. There, the traditional justice system was based on "principles of control over people rather than the administration of geographically bounded units."[30] Because "space was defined in terms of hierarchical relationships between people and groups" that "enjoined acts of ritual obligation,"[31] the system of justice functioned within a political culture that was based on "ceremonial acts of fealty." However, by the twentieth century the old royal legal structure – in which juridical subjects were defined by their hierarchically structured, ritual obligations – gave way to generalized legal obligations, based on a centralized order administered from the capital.[32] While the old decentralized system – in which there was a mosaic of different localities, each with its own justice norms and enforcement procedures – was forced into a system of equivalence, the new system never completely displaced the traditional one. As a result, Thai justice has emerged as an "interplay of multiple systems of dispute resolution," where one can observe competing normative systems based on heterogeneous (spiritually invested) social spaces.[33]

Modern Italy manifests a similarly heterogeneous legal cartography. The implications of the resulting centrifugal application of justice become evident once Sciascia's characters (his aesthetic subjects) encounter each other in dialogues. As in Porumboiu's film, contentious conversations are featured in the novel. And although the genre of the novel lacks cinema's image supplements – which (as I noted) are additional vehicles for representing corporeal and discursive dissensus with respect to justice – *The Day of the Owl*'s literary geography plays a role that is similar to *Police, Adjective*'s cinematic cartography. And what the novel lacks by way of images, it compensates for with characterizations of the passions and ideological commitment of its characters. The novel's grammatical style frequently makes psychological moments concrete. For example, a verb form noting that Belodi thought X becomes Belodi's observation of X.[34] The cinematic grammar of Porumboiu's film juxtaposes the capitulating words elicited from Cristi with shots of his body's resistance (based in part on the way his travels confirm his bodily sense of what is just). By comparison, the novel's primary vehicles are grammatical shifts that render the psychological subject as aesthetic subjects whose remarks and actions articulate disjunctions between codified and cultural-spatial perspectives on justice. Ultimately both texts, using their respective genre forms, articulate the effects of culturally incommensurate legal spaces, senses of justice, and discursive styles.

Briefly, the novel, like most of those in the crime story genre, begins with a murder. But unlike many crime stories, the immediate post-murder scene is culturally elaborated. The victim, a building contractor named Salvatore Colasberna, is shot dead as he runs to catch a bus. Because it was known throughout the area that he had refused the mafia's demands for protection payments, the bus conductor's remark, "They've killed him,"[35] represents the general consensus of everyone on the scene who witnessed the killing – the bus driver, the passengers, and nearby vendors. Yet once the *carabinieri* arrive and try to obtain the details of the killing from the witnesses, no one is willing to admit to having seen anything. George Scialabba effectively captures the cultural significance of this passivity in the face of such events. Referring to the witnesses who, as the novel describes them, "sat mute, their faces as if disinterested from the silence of centuries,"[36] he suggests that it points to the "immemorial inertia of the local culture."[37] In short, as is the case of Thailand's cultural dispersion, some regions in Italy manifest a historically dense, cultural inertia that militates against being drawn into Italy's centralized system of justice.

Captain Belodi's arrival at the venue of the killing constitutes a disturbance to the region's "immemorial inertia."[38] But Belodi is also disturbed: on the one hand he has unalloyed respect for Italy's centralized justice system; on the other (like Sciascia himself) he has "affection for the region's landscape and literature" and thus its structure of feeling.[39] As a result, Belodi is a complex aesthetic subject, one with divided loyalties that generate ambivalence as he attempts to bring the perpetrators to "justice." At the same time, however, his knowledge of the region allows him to recognize the spaces and genres of relevant evidence. While potential informants will not speak reliably about the events surrounding a crime, they often write (anonymously) about what they know or think: "'It's odd,' said the captain ... 'how people in this part of the world let themselves go in anonymous letters. No one talks, but luckily for us ... everyone writes'."[40] Nevertheless, once Belodi's investigation gets underway, he extracts oral reports (mostly unreliable) from a variety of local informants. And as the process unfolds, it becomes evident what the tension is between the codified system of justice that Belodi represents and the local *senses* of justice. At a minimum, there is no *sensus communis*, as Immanuel Kant presents it: a shared "moral law within."[41]

To provide a critical philosophical framework for what is involved in the novel's encounter – incommensurate modes of justice and conversations that articulate tensions – we do well to heed Lyotard's neo-Kantian version of critical philosophy. In place of Kant's figuration of philosophy as a "tribunal," where "critical philosophy is in the position of a juridical authority," Lyotard substitutes the battlefield.[42] Arguing that Kant's model cannot comprehend the negative events that engender "the exploding of language into families of heteronomous language games," Lyotard insists that "we need a philosophy of phrases rather than one of the faculties of the subject."[43] As he puts it in his extended treatment of a philosophy of language, *The Differend*:

> As distinguished from a litigation, a differend would be the case of conflict between (at least) two parties, that cannot be equitably resolved for lack of a rule of judgment applicable to both arguments. One side's legitimacy does not imply the other's lack of legitimacy.[44]

The "incommensurability" or "heterogeneity of phrase regimes" that Lyotard posits as the fundamental basis of social encounter is especially congenial with the novel form of Sciascia's crime story.[45] As M. M. Bakhtin has famously put it, the novel is fundamentally "heteroglossic," consisting of many contending voices that pull against the verbal-ideological center of the nation.[46]

One of the most telling discursive encounters in the novel, which articulates the discursive contention it features, is between Captain Belodi and a mafia associate of the alleged mafia head – Don Mariano Arena – who is suspected of soliciting the murder. This local interlocutor challenges Belodi's model of the mafia's role in politics and crime by juxtaposing to the discourse of "justice," as it emerges from centralized state authority, "a sense of justice," as it operates within his Sicilian city:

> 'The Sicilian that I am and the reasonable man I claim to be rebel against this injustice ... D'you know him [the alleged mafia head]? I do. A good man, an exemplary father, an untiring worker ... Certain men inspire respect: for their qualities, their savoir-faire, their frankness, their flair for cordial relations, for friendship ... . "These are heads of the mafia?" Now here's something you don't know: these men, the men whom public opinion calls the heads of the mafia, have one quality in common, a quality I would like to find in every man, one which is enough to redeem anyone in the eyes of God – a sense of justice ... naturally, instinctively ... And it's this sense of justice which makes them inspire respect.'[47]

When Belodi responds, "That's just the point. The administration of justice is the prerogative of the state; one cannot allow ..." his interlocutor interrupts, "I am speaking of the sense of justice, not the administration of justice."[48]

To appreciate the local understanding of the "administration of justice" (by Italy's central government-sanctioned crime enforcement agents), against which Belodi's interlocutor is juxtaposing "this sense of justice," we must heed another exemplary encounter – one between Belodi and a quasi-professional "informant," Calogero Dibella (nicknamed *Parrinieddu*, "Little Priest ... due to the easy eloquence and hypocrisy he exuded").[49] Dibella – who, like others in his city is forced to balance mafia demands with those of the crime-fighting establishment – has the typical local perspective on the law:

> To the informer the law was not a rational thing born of reason, but something depending on a man, on the thoughts and the mood of the man here

> [Belodi] ... To him the law was utterly irrational, created on the spot by
> those in command ... The informer had never, could never have, believed
> that the law was definitely codified and the same for all; for him between
> rich and poor, between wise and ignorant, stood the guardians of the law
> who only used the strong arm on the poor; the rich they protected and
> defended.[50]

Dibella's view of law enforcement reflects a politics of justice that transcends
local structures of feeling. For example, Foucault's broadly applicable, critical
perspective on the politics of juridical penalties is wholly in accord with Dibella's
sentiments about the differential application of officially sanctioned justice:

> Penalty would then appear to be a way of handling illegalities, of laying
> down the limits of tolerance, of giving free rein to some, of putting pressure
> on others, of excluding a particular section, of making another useful, or
> neutralizing certain individuals and of profiting from others, In short, penalty
> does not simply 'check' illegalities; it 'differentiates' them, it provides them
> with a general 'economy'. And, if one can speak of justice, it is not only
> because the law itself or the way of applying it serves the interests of a class,
> it is also because the differential administration of illegalities through the
> mediation of penalty forms part of the mechanisms of domination.[51]

However, although Dibella's perspective represents a politics of justice that
transcends the particular encounter, the clash of phrases involved in the conversation between him and Captain Belodi is also framed by the historical forces
shaping the novel's aesthetic subjects. Captain Belodi "was by family tradition
and personal conviction a republican, a soldier who followed what used to be
called 'the career of arms' in a police force, with the dedication of a man who
has played his part in a revolution and has seen law created by it."[52] Given his
background and experiences, Belodi's affective connection with justice is one of
righteousness; he sees himself as one with a sacred task of safeguarding liberty
and justice. In contrast, Dibella's primary affective connection with the law
is fear (figured as a "dog inside him" that "bit, growled, and bit again"). And
Sciascia renders Dibella as an aesthetic subject with an aesthetic strategy (he is
figured as a painter). An informer by vocation, Dibella must survive by balancing
the mafia demand that he "inform" in a duplicitious way that keeps law enforcement from imperiling the mafia's power structure and keeps him from being
returned to prison (where he has already done time). He must "perform like a
painter ... feverishly adding and retouching," creating a canvas that will satisfy
the prosecutor, not betray the mafia, and – ultimately and most importantly – not
destroy its creator.[53]

Sciascia's Dibella gestures toward historical forces that have shaped the
dilemmas of other types, informers among others. Indeed much of the novel's
meditation on the problem of culturally and nationally divided senses of justice
harks back to the fascist and immediately post-fascist periods. As Dibella
contemplates the informer's dilemma – a vocation that risks death daily – "he

thought of other informers buried under a thin layer of soil and dried leaves high in the folds of the Apennines [nearby mountains]. Wretched dregs, soaked in fear and vice; yet they had gambled with death, staking their lives on the razor's edge of a lie between partisans and fascists."[54] Here is the historical basis, not only of Sciascia's crime story but of other contemporary ones set in the fraught period of dramatic political change in post-fascist Italy.

As the history of the period reveals, the frantic political positioning of informers during the events of political change is of a piece with that of law enforcement types. Carlo Lucarelli, who began as a scholar of the history of the police during the fascist period and ended up as a crime novelist, points to the perils of political choices at the point at which Italy is "split in two":

> as the German army occupies that part of the country not yet liberated by the advance of the Anglo-American forces and puts Benito Mussolini in charge of a collaborationist government. This is one of the hardest and most ferocious moments in Italy's history. There is the war stalled on the North Italian front, where there is fierce fighting for a least a year. There is the dread of the *Brigate Nere*, the Black Brigades, and the formations of the new fascists political police who, together with the German SS, repress sabotage activities and resistance by partisan formations. There is, above all, enormous moral and political confusion that mixes together the desperation of those who know they are losing, the opportunism of those ready to change sides, the guilelessness of those who haven't understood anything, and even the desire for revenge in those who are about to arrive.[55]

Lucarelli ultimately found that the best way to capture that moral and political confusion was to focus on a man who had spent "forty years of his life in the Italian police force, during which with every change of government he found himself having to tail, to spy on, and to arrest those who had previously been his bosses." And, in response to Lucarelli's query about his seemingly opportunistic political choices, responded, "What does that have to do with it? I'm a policeman." From this historical figure, Lucarelli invented Comissario De Luca, the protagonist of a trilogy of crime novels: *Carte Blanche*, *The Damned Season* and *Via Delle Oche*. And as he puts it, "[I] lost myself in his adventures. And I never did write my thesis."[56] The combination of political identity- and regional-partitioning, to which Lucarelli's trilogy is addressed, surfaces in Sciascia's *Day of the Owl* as well. For example, it is revealed that the murder victim, Colasberna, has a "criminal record," but that fact is immediately dismissed – in a discussion between Belodi and local police functionaries – as irrelevant. The "record" had been acquired during the war, when he was reported for making a contemptuous remark about a patriotic statement by a fascist Blackshirt, who had overheard him.[57] Yet, as becomes evident through the testimony of other characters in the novel, having a fascist past in Sicily does not attract the level of moral obloquy that it would in other parts of Italy because Sicily was less oppressed under Mussolini. It was "the only region given liberty during the fascist dictatorship, the liberty of safety of life and property."[58] Ultimately, as the novel shows, in addition to the diverse structures of feeling, it is political history that constitutes much of the basis for regional fault-lines.

It is a fraught history of political change that has yielded diverse political choices during the radical transitions in both centralized and local levels of control. As a result, a historically invested identity matrix has emerged. Although Belodi's background is republican and partisan, he understands the special circumstances in which some of his interlocutors embraced fascism. By the end of the novel – despite his disparate political background and the dissension between his legal vocation and the local sense of justice – Belodi finds a small window of consensus with his prime suspect, Don Mariano Arena, the alleged mafia head. As his interrogation of Arena proceeds, Belodi discovers – by dint of a corporeal moment of perception – that they share at least one dimension of a structure of feeling: a trans-regional sentiment about the importance of being a "man."

The novel's final interrogation pits Belodi's intellectual and experiential attachment to justice against a man who has lived a life of violence and conducted it unapologetically:

> Beyond the pale of morality and law, incapable of pity, an unredeemed mass of human energy and of loneliness, of instinctive, tragic will. As a blind man pictures in his mind, dark and formless, the world outside, so Don Mariano pictured the world of sentiment, legality and normal human relations. What other notion could he have of the world, if around him, the word 'right' had always been suffocated by violence and the wind of the world had merely changed the word into a stagnant, putrid reality?[59]

Although the Belodi–Arena encounter is primarily antagonistic – with accusations coming from the former and denials from the latter – a degree of mutual respect arises when Arena, who feels that those who are less than men do not deserve justice, accords the quality of manhood to Belodi. Thus, although Arena's sense of justice is accorded on the basis of character, not territory, while Belodi's represents a territorialized version – based on the state's codification of justice – their encounter ends with a degree of harmony, for Belodi is pleased to be among those whom Arena calls men. When asked by a journalist to clarify what he, Arena, means when he refers to Belodi as a "man" – does he mean that like all men Belodi is fallible or "whether … there was an adjective missing," Arena replies, "Adjective be damned! A man doesn't need adjectives."[60] In referring to Belodi as a "man" at that moment rather than as a representative of a national or regional justice bureaucracy, Arena is evoking a different assemblage (a masculinity assemblage) that transcends geopolitical space and thus refigures the warrants involved in claims about justice. Ultimately then – as is the case with Porumboiu's *Police, Adjective* – Sciascia's *The Day of the Owl* raises onto-political questions about whose experiences, perspectives, and positions (vocational or regional) can entitle one to make claims about justice, while at the same time providing nuanced episodes of linguistic exchange.

Conclusion: "Italy is incredible" (and so is Romania): micro-politics and method

Jacques Rancière poses succinctly the questions that the two texts I have explored raise about the politics of justice. After stating the obvious, "Politics is the public discussion on matters of justice among speaking people who are able to do it," he adds that there is a vexing "preliminary matter of justice: How do you recognize that the person who is mouthing a voice in front of you is discussing matters of justice rather than expressing his or her private pain?"[61] In the case of *Police, Adjective*, what could have been recognized as a political event – an encounter between incompatible senses of justice – became a matter of policing. Because he was unable to legitimate his sentiments about the injustice of arresting and prosecuting young hashish smokers within the narrow language of the policing vocation's obligations, Cristi's words were ascribed to the expression of "private pain." He was repositioned from one seeking to be able to speak about justice to one unwilling to carry out his policing obligations correctly.

If the clashes in both Porumboiu's film and Sciascia's novel are to be heeded as realistic encounters articulating fault-lines in the structures of feeling within Romania and Italy, a turn to Kantian shared moral sensibility has been impeached because it is evident that such sensibilities exist in a cultural dispersion. Rather than searching for a transcendent model of justice, I have turned to the post-Kantian models offered by Lyotard and Rancière, which resonate well with encounters staged in both texts: Lyotard displaces the Kantian tribunal and shared moral sense with a fight of phrases; Rancière displaces the Kantian aesthetic comprehension – predicated on a *sensus communis* – with a politics of aesthetics based on events of dissensus. Politics, for both Lyotard and Rancière, is not the exercise of power or authority within territorial assemblages. Rather, for both politics emerges in events of encounter – whenever a differend occurs for Lyotard or whenever an act of subjectification takes place (when the unheard demand that their words be regarded as political statements) for Rancière. However, instead of elaborating the frames that Lyotard and Rancière provide, I want to conclude by dwelling briefly on the problem of method by contrasting my turn to cinema and literature with the more familiar approaches in the social sciences, which turn to attitude surveys.

My reflections on method are inspired by a remark of Sciascia's Captain Belodi, near the end of *The Day of the Owl*. After brooding because he sees his case dissolve when the confessions he has extracted are withdrawn (new witnesses invent alibis for the accused, police operatives are reassigned, and the inquiry into the murder is reopened) Belodi remarks that "Sicily is incredible" and adds, "Italy is incredible, too."[62] Although given Belodi's understandable frustration, the ready-to-hand inference one might make about his remark is that Italy defies normal expectations about the administration of justice. However, I want to interpret the remark differently. I take it to mean that there is no such thing as "Italy," if it is meant to refer to a unitary national culture. What is credible, in Sciascia's imaginative yet very realistic account, is that there is no unitary ideational, justice-implemented Italy. To assay what Fredric Jameson refers to as "the existence of Italy" is to inquire into the extent to which it achieves a reality, which is necessarily always already mediated (as the complex and paradoxical phrase, "the representation of the real" implies).[63]

The methodological issue I want to pose involves a contrast among alternative methods: the social science attitude investigation, within which psychological subjects are constructed through interviews, with the aesthetic subjects invented and animated in film and literature. As an example of the former, I offer a brief gloss on Robert Putnam's investigation of "civic traditions" in Italy, in which he focuses on what he calls "civic engagement." With elaborate interview protocols (applied to seven hundred interviewees – regional councilors, "community leaders," bankers and farm leaders, mayors and journalists, labor leaders and business representatives, as well as voters), Putnam investigates attitudes toward political institutions in a wide variety of Italian cities and regions and offers inferences about the attitudinal and participatory bases of regional democratic institutions.[64]

In contrast with Sciascia's novel, the mafia plays no role in Putnam's survey; it is dismissed as an irrelevant criminal organization with no connection to civic life. However, the gaps in types of actors evident in Putnam's investigation is less significant than what his approach effaces more generally. Conceived within typical social science methodological conceits, Putnam refers to the importance of "careful counting," stating that "quantitative techniques" can correct misleading impressions derived from "a single striking case or two."[65] Putnam's statistical rendering of civic attitudes (he adds up his subjects to produce a view of the aggregate support for institutions) makes Italy incredible. It effectively negates the ideational fault-lines that become evident when subjects are located within the densities of their regional and city locales and are mobilized into encounters in which they have to defend their positions against alternative perspectives.

Putnam's investigation is thus insensitive to the politics of disparity that Sciascia's novelistic approach, with its mobilized aesthetic subjects reveals. Literature's (and film's) aesthetic subjects cannot be arithmetically assembled. They aim less at reflecting individual attitudes than at rendering the complex political and cultural cartography within which the actors strive to manage responsibilities, and at manifesting the consequences of encounters with incommensurate perspectives as the characters strive to flourish – or at least to merely survive. While Putnam's Italy is incredible, Sciascia's (Belodi's remark to the contrary notwithstanding) is credible. Ultimately, Sciascia's crime story shows the multiplicity of structures of feeling that renders Italian justice an encounter-ready dispersion by enacting a fight of phrases. Porumboiu's police procedural film achieves a similar account of dispersion in a Romanian city by rendering its aesthetic subjects through interrelated image frames, as an exemplary body resists the closed language of policing. As regards a unitary approach to justice, "Romania," like "Italy," is incredible.

7 A continuing violent cartography

From Guadalupe Hidalgo to contemporary border crossings

Here beyond men's judgments covenants were brittle.

Cormac McCarthy

Introduction: Spanish America and the violent borderscape

There is a curious omission in Alexis de Tocqueville's nineteenth-century observations about America's racial-spatial order. When he treats what he calls the
"three races that inhabit the territory of the United States" (Black, Red, and
White), he excludes a sizable "Brown" population – the Hispanic people. As I put
it elsewhere, "while apparently uninformed about the Hispanic-Anglo struggles
in California, [de Tocqueville] was at least aware that Texas was a contested territory. But he read the conflict geopolitically rather than culturally, foreseeing the
outcome as militarily definitive. After stating that 'the province of Texas is still
part of the Mexican dominions,' he added that this 'province' will soon contain
no Mexicans."[1]

Coincident with de Tocqueville's American visit there was a substantial
Mexican presence in the American Southwest. And contrary to de Tocqueville's
biopolitical imaginary (his notions about the relative presences in American
ethnoscape), the U.S.–Mexican inhabitants in California (the *Californios*) were
the area's major cultural and political presence. As for the developing inter-
cultural future, Mariano Vallejo, the commandant of the San Francisco Presidio
and subsequently the military governor of Sonoma, wrote extensively, imaging
ultimately a bi-cultural American with a shared sovereignty, even though he
envisioned a U.S. annexation of his territory. Here is his projection:

> When we join our fortunes to hers [the U.S.], we shall not become subjects,
> but fellow citizens possessing all the rights of the people of the United States
> and choosing our own federal and local leaders.[2]

However, Vallejo's fantasy was not to be realized. His hold over his territory
ended with the Anglo American conquest led by Captain John Charles Fremont.
And very shortly thereafter, the Anglo conquerors established control over
California, Texas, and the rest of Spanish America, creating a dramatic identity

change for the *Californios*: "Those who had been Mexican suddenly found themselves inside the United States [as] foreigners on their own land."[3]

Vallejo's hoped-for equal citizens became instead national and cultural exiles,
subjected to economic and political discrimination. Suddenly the Spanish territories were remapped, eventually turning the primary cultural and political
nodes of Hispanic California – missions, presidios and pueblos – into anachronistic cultural curiosities and the Mexican nationals into an "ethnic minority."
Although Anglo American history texts have scarcely registered the fate of the
Californios since the 1848 Treaty of Guadalupe Hidalgo, vestiges of it can be
recovered in Spanish American literature. For example, in *The Squatter and the
Don* (1885) – a romantic novel by Maria Amparo Ruiz de Burton – there is a
significant historico-political register: Ruiz de Burton "writes against the grain of
dominant U.S. historiography and represents the cultures of U.S. imperialism not
only as territorial and economic fact but also inevitably as a subject-constituting
project."[4] Although much of the novel narrates a romantic quest, it also follows a
track in which it is "marked by its historicity." The novel's *Californio* characters
are first displaced by squatters, whose takeover is sponsored by governmental
acts. They are then victimized by powerful economic monopolies.[5] The central
drama – featuring the rancher Don Mariano Alamar – is embedded within a
commentary on a history of encounter in the Southwest. Don Mariano refers to
himself and the other *Californios* as "the conquered people" and complains, "We
have no one to speak for us. By the Treaty of Guadalupe Hidalgo the American
Nation pledged its honor to respect our land titles."[6]

Although "the conquered people" expression would seem to validate de
Tocqueville's observation about a future of Anglo dominance, the Anglo
conquest is now being attenuated by a process that one writer aptly describes as
a "reLatinization"[7] of much of the American Southwest – a result of what Carlos
Fuentes refers to as "Mexico's chromosomal imperialism" – and reconquest with
"the most Mexican of weapons, linguistic, racial, and culinary"[8] (much to the
dismay of those who lament the diminution of Anglo American supremacy –
most famously articulated in the academic writings of Samuel Huntington).[9] The
reLatinization process is also drawing intense popular and official attention to
border traffic between Mexico and the U.S., as the issues of illegal immigration
and illicit trafficking in both directions across the U.S.–Mexican border increasingly occupy policy-making at federal and state levels. It is also attracting a
sizable and violent vigilante movement, which adds a new dimension to a border
area that has already been a space of violent encounter between policing authorities and migrants (among others).[10] The early decades of the twenty-first century
are therefore an especially propitious period to heed the way that border transgressions and policing initiatives reflect the violent cartography that has existed
within a contentious history in the borderscapes of the Southwestern U.S. for
centuries.

To preview briefly that history, I want to recall two border scenes – one actual
and one fictional (although the latter is based on historical archives). The first is a
historical episode described in John Cremony's nineteenth-century account of his
life as an army Major assigned to the territory of the Comanche nation. Cremony

reports a tense conversation that he had with a Comanche chief, Janamata (Red Buffalo), in 1847, shortly before the Treaty of Guadalupe Hidalgo. Janamata had led his warriors in a raid from U.S. territory across the Rio Grande to attack a Mexican village. Cremony – who with his troop of cavalry had ridden out to intercept Janamata and his warriors in order to dissuade them from cross-border attacks – tells Janamata that he must leave the Mexicans in peace as now the U.S. and Mexico are no longer at war. Janamata, who operated within a wholly different political imaginary – not one that observed the rhythms of state-oriented geopolitical hostilities and peace treaties – replied, "I hear your words and they are not pleasant. These Mexicans are our natural enemies" and adds that he is surprised at Cremony's insistence inasmuch as, given what he knows about the U.S. (Mexican wars), "they are also your enemies." Although Janamata agrees to retreat for the time being, rather than go to war with his "American brothers," he asserts that he will not promise to refrain from future attacks.[11]

The small window into the violent interactions rendered in Cremony's account – which involved Anglos, Native Americans, and Mexicans in the border areas – has a long legacy, only slightly altered by official treaties from Guadalupe Hidalgo to NAFTA. One of the most interesting reflections on the legacy is the second (fictional) episode to which I referred. It is a scene in John Sayles' feature film, *Lone Star* (1996). Sayles describes his film as a "story about borders" and adds that "within the movie there are lines between people that they choose either to honor or not to honor. It may be this enforced border between Mexico and the United States, it may be one between class, race, ethnicity, or even military rank." As for Sayles's political perspective, which gets articulated in the film: "I wanted to erase that border and show that these people are still reacting to things in the past. There is a preoccupation with history in the film, whether it's Sam Deeds [the Sheriff] wanting to find out the personal history of his father, or the grandfather Otis, the bartender of an African American bar that caters to black soldiers from a nearby military installation "looking back into the roots of the black Seminoles."[12]

It is Otis (aka O), who is involved in the episode I want to highlight from the film. He takes his grandson, Chet, on a tour of a small personal history museum in a side room of his establishment that features a Black–Seminole exhibit. This is how the screenplay describes the scene:

> On the walls there are photo-blowups, some artifacts, hand-lettered information on cardboard. Chet stops to look up at a picture of a bare-chested Black man with a couple of feathers stuck in his headband.

Otis tells Chet that the Seminoles were led by Juan Caballo (John Horse), who is a family relative. He and his warriors were mercenaries attacking people on both sides of the border, "Indians" included," and were the "best trackers either side of the border. Bandits, rustlers, Texas rednecks, Kiowa, Comanche ..." The grandson, Chet, registers surprise that he must therefore be "part Indian," to which Otis (doubtless representing an aspect of Sayles's theme) responds, "By blood you are. But blood only means what you let it." To the extent that the history of the border areas involved many who let blood mean a lot (and consequently shed some), those areas have been the scenes of bio- as well as territorial politics. The two politics are intimately connected, for attempts to control or exploit the territories have involved the production of modes of identity/difference in which diverse assemblages have been alternatively nations and "races."

The two episodes – Cremony's historical one and Sayles's fictional (but history-based) one – attest to a space of violence that has failed to achieve significant recognition in the familiar nation-building narrative that has reported the process of Anglo American conquest of much of the North American continent. Although Sayles's film is fiction – a cinematic intervention into the history of the border region – its mobilization of aesthetic subjects and the encounters among them give the viewer a sense of the experiential implications of the border history. Moreover, as a set of sensory effects with shock value, the film has a powerful aesthetic effect in the neo-Kantian sense articulated by Rancière; it disrupts the prior "community of sense,"[13] forcing the viewer to think rather than (as is the case with abstract histories) merely acquire information.

What is there to think about? The southwest border area has been among other things what Cormac McCarthy calls a "blood meridian." His novel by that title constitutes at once a counter-history to the dominant nation-building narrative and a stark reenactment of an aspect of the violence visited on that domain in the nineteenth century. Like many films, it provokes thinking by enacting shocking encounters that disturb prevailing sensibilities. In this chapter, much of the analysis involves a juxtaposition between McCarthy's novel and the space-pacifying, nation-building perspective that has been made familiar in traditional American history texts, as dramatized in John Ford's version of the West through his Western films. After contrasting McCarthy's and Ford's Wests, I return to the contemporary scene, which bids to replicate the level of violence reenacted in McCarthy's historically attuned novel. By engaging the powerful affects and percepts in the novel with conceptual analytics that "interfere" with the text, my

Figure 7.1 Otis's grandson in the bar's museum

aim is to evoke a rethinking of a cartography that has been historically pacified in most familiar accounts of the American Southwest.

Cormac McCarthy's deformation of John Ford's West

There's a striking moment of ambiguity in a scene in John Ford's film *My Darling Clementine* (1946). It's time for the famous showdown at the O.K. Corral. As the scene opens the viewer is looking down the street toward the Corral. It's dark, and as the dawn sky begins to lighten, a shape that looks like one of the large buttes in Monument Valley (where eight of Ford's Westerns have been shot) begins to emerge. However, as it becomes light enough to discern the figure with that shape, it turns out to be the hat worn by the patriarch of the Clanton gang, Old Man Clanton (Walter Brennan). Lest the viewer has forgotten how that shape has been impressed in her/his memory bank, as the camera cuts to Wyatt Earp (Henry Fonda), Doc Holiday (Victor Mature), and Wyatt's brother, Morgan (Ward Bond) – approaching for the decisive gun battle – the butte whose shape the hat replicates precisely can be seen in the background, over Wyatt's left shoulder. The homology between a synecdoche of the human (the hat) and the landscape is central to the Ford effect, which Gilles Deleuze captures in his remark about Ford's Western milieu as an "encompasser." In his words, Ford's West is a place where "the milieu encompasses the people."[14]

Cormac McCarthy's novel *Blood Meridian* (1992) – which offers a darker, more violent West than is created in John Ford's cinematic corpus – also provides a radical entanglement between peoplescapes and landscapes. Ford's landscapes, mixed with ultimately hopeful collective becomings, are softened by an idealized transition that is spoken by another character in *My Darling Clementine* – the eponymous Clementine (Cathy Downs), who refers to the changing of a wilderness into a garden. Although McCarthy's *Blood Meridian* contains numerous wilderness references, his wilderness is not softened with agricultural tropes and the prospect of "civilized" settlement. Rather than a space of expanding settlement, McCarthy's Western landscape is a killing field, a "nature," which as Nietzsche famously put it, "has no opinion of us." It is without sponsorship, divine or otherwise – "anti-Edenic" as Susan Kollin puts it.[15] And in McCarthy's rendering it has Gothic overtones, in contrast with the pastoral yearnings that Ford's landscapes attract.

As is well known, the Gothic genre "abandons the rational individualist desire to draw strong boundaries between self and world."[16] However, unlike Ford's inter-articulations between territory and character, McCarthy's Gothic mood leaves no person or thing benefitting from the person–space encounters. Rather than a paean to Euro American nation-building, *Blood Meridian* provides a critical counter-memory to the narrative of modern political development, which represses violent encounter and dispossession. The Gothic overtones of McCarthy's novel resonate with Orson Welles' treatment of the U.S.–Mexican border in his film noir-oriented *A Touch of Evil* (1958), whose Gothic mood is articulated in the darkened scenes of rooms – police vaults and other cramped and threatening spaces (e.g., darkened motel rooms) – and by the way threatening characters are filmed – for example, the low-angled shots that make the evil character, Hank Quinlan (Orson Welles) loom – in very much the way McCarthy fashions his massive judge.

While Ford's cowboys, nomadic and unsettled though they are, function primarily as vehicles for legitimating (white) settlement, McCarthy's characters function as vehicles for disclosing a history of cynical violence and exploitation. Unlike the ideals, expressed by Ford's characters, which provide the political imaginaries through which the West-as-becoming part of "white" America shape his cinematic narratives, McCarthy's "writing" as Robert Penn Warren puts it, "has, line by line, the stab of actuality."[17] That "stab of actuality" has a historical basis. While most of Ford's characters are invented idealizations (even the historical Wyatt Earp bore little comparison with Ford's version), many of McCarthy's are based on actual historical personages, whose character and actions closely resemble McCarthy's novelistic reproductions.[18]

In what follows, I pursue the Ford–McCarthy contrast, focusing on the critical political insights and ethical injunctions that McCarthy's *Blood Meridian* provides, as alternatives to the more familiar Ford versions. While Ford's films, which also have their dark sides, ultimately deliver regulative ideals that affirm and even celebrate a Euro American "ethnogenesis"[19] – a whitening of the North American continent – McCarthy's novel offers critical versions of the violence attending the euphemistic trope of "nation-building," while at the same time offering a philosophical meta-commentary on America's inter-ethnic Western experience – especially in the contested border areas where Spanish, Native and Euro Americans conducted geo- and biopolitical struggles. Among other things, *Blood Meridian* offers both another powerful version of Melville's "The Metaphysics of Indian Hating" (in his *The Confidence Man*), and a glimpse of another form of violent enmity – a metaphysics of Mexican or Hispanic hating (which is also well conveyed in Welles' *A Touch of Evil*). Two characters in *Blood Meridian* are the primary vehicles for McCarthy's deformation of Ford's West: "the kid," whom I will designate as the primary "aesthetic subject," and "the judge," who functions as the primary philosophical subject, or "conceptual persona."

John Ford's cinematic Western dramas became the most familiar popular cultural narrative and set of images of Euro America's expanding possession of the North American continent. But genres generated earlier – paintings, stories and histories – had held favored places in the public imagination of the "taming of the West." Land- and people-scape canvases collaborated with a variety of other genres in legitimating the completion of the Euro American control of continental United States in the nineteenth and early twentieth centuries. For example, the novels of James Fenimore Cooper and the juridical discourse issued by Chief Justice John Marshall both addressed the problem of translating "American claims in the face of the nation's Revolutionary origins and the Indians' prior claims."[20] They mobilized the categories of race and patrimony to locate the English and the Indians in "a narrative of kinship and inheritance as ancestors willingly bestowing their authority and property on their rightful American heirs."[21] And Euro American novelists collaborated in the appropriation of Native American provenances by relocating the Indian as an anachronistic presence. As Teresa Goddu points out, nineteenth-century American novelists, lacking the Gothic props of the English tradition (gloomy castles, antiquities, hoary mysteries), gothicized the Indian. That aesthetic gesture solved two problems: "The translation of the Indian into a Gothic form solved the problem of how to create a uniquely American literature and also provided a discourse that justified the nation's expansion."[22] Thereafter, various writers and artists collaborated in the process of symbolically clearing the continent of a Native American presence, while infectious diseases, the destruction of buffalo herds, and the U.S. army were largely effacing their physical presence. Three textual productions – a historical epic by Theodore Roosevelt, a series of cowboy stories by Owen Wister, and the paintings of Frederick Remington – collaborated in constructing a deserved Anglo presence in the West. Their texts constituted much of what the U.S.'s Euro American population came to know about their continental acquisition.

As I have noted elsewhere, in his epic, *The Winning of the West*, Roosevelt:

> alternatively depopulates and repopulates the West. He justifies the expansion of white America in some places by claiming that they are occupying 'waste' spaces visited only 'a week or two every year' and in others by having 'savage and formidable foes' fighting heroic settlers with 'fierce and dogged resistance,' virtually every step of the way. Adding a biopolitical corollary to his romantic *soldatesque* and reproducing the anti-Spanish sentiment that was integral to English imperialism, Roosevelt praises 'the English race' for maintaining its ethnic integrity by exterminating or driving off the Native Americans rather than, like the Spanish in their colonial venues, 'sitting down in their midst' and becoming a 'mixed race'.[23]

Roosevelt's friend, the writer Owen Wister, helped to popularize Roosevelt's view of the superiority of the English "race" in much of his fiction. For example, in his story, "The Evolution of the Cowpuncher," he features an English nobleman who, after ending up in Texas, "adapts rapidly because of his superior horsemanship and marksmanship."[24] The painter, Frederick Remington – a friend of both Roosevelt and Wister – supported their biopolitical conceits by depicting their invention of the cowboy as a legacy of the English aristocracy. Among the paintings with which he lent visual support to their narrative of the Anglo legacy is his *Last Cavalier* (1895), which shows a cowboy in the foreground against a background that consists of "a faded panorama of historical horsemen, of which the most prominent are generations of English knights."[25] In addition, Remington did the illustrations for many of Wister's stories in *Colliers* magazine, which represented the West as an evolving (and whitening) social order.

By the mid-twentieth century, the role of the art historical paintings of Remington and others in the legitimating of Euro America's Western expansion was being rapidly displaced by cinema – especially the films of John Ford. His first notable Western was *Stagecoach* (1943), a film in which the narrative suggests that the white occupants of a Westward traveling stagecoach demonstrate the level of superior moral worthiness that suits them to displace a menacing Indian presence and a capricious Hispanic one in the West. In that film, as in subsequent ones, Euro America's continental ethnogenesis is figured as the locating of the (white) family on the land. *Stagecoach* (1939) – Ford's first film starring John Wayne (as the Ringo Kid) – is among his less critical versions of an increasingly Anglo-dominated West. As a legitimating cinematic narrative, what is central is a sorting process, a selection of character types that are to become part of the dominant national culture. In *Stagecoach*, the West is presented as an evolving social order that is to become assimilated into the Euro American geopolitical and social space. The occupants of the stagecoach journey, which supplies the primary narrative and image spaces of the film – a disparate and often feuding group of types – are a microcosm of that evolving social order. While a tribute to the historic expansion of a tolerant social democracy, the film's Anglo characters – a southern gentleman gambler, a prostitute, a soldier's pregnant wife, an outlaw, an alcoholic doctor, a liquor salesman, and a banker – are, despite their lack of social cohesion, a group of types represented, for all their flaws, as part of a Euro American-dominated future. They are destined to displace unreliable Hispanics and dangerous "savages," who are depicted, during the stagecoach's various stops, as of unfit character to negotiate a shared political order.

While the romantic part of the story – in which the Ringo Kid and the ex-prostitute, Dallas, become a couple – is one aspect of the film's resolution, its more general historical resolution involves the successful incursion of white society into Indian country. Nevertheless, the film conveys some ambivalence about that success, primarily through its use of irony: for example, the exaggeratedly frightened reactions of the travelers when they encounter an Indian woman, the wife of a Mexican managing one of the stagecoach stations. For the most part, however, the Indians are simply a menace in the Western landscape. Their attack on the stagecoach is repulsed, thanks to the heroics of the Ringo Kid and the last-minute arrival of the cavalry, which is depicted as an effective arm of the reach of white governance.

The Searchers (1956), arguably Ford's most significant Western (also shot in Monument Valley), rearticulates the Ford trope of the family on the land. The opening scene is both cinematically powerful and narratively expansive. It is shot from inside the cabin of Ethan Edwards's (John Wayne) brother's cabin, providing a view of a vast expanse of prairie, from which Edwards is approaching. Edwards, a loner who is headed west after having fought on the Confederate side in the Civil War, is part of a historical migration. He represents one type among the many kinds of bodies that flowed Westward after Euro America emerged from the fratricidal conflict of the Civil War and was then free to turn its attention to another venue of violence – the one involved in the forced displacement of indigenous America. Edwards's approach is observed by his sister-in-law from her front porch, which, architecturally, plays a role in designating the house as a refuge from outer threats. In a lyrical soliloquy by a character in an Alessandro Baricco novel, the porch is aptly described as being:

> inside and outside at the same time ... it represents an extended threshold ...
> It's a no man's land where the idea of protected place – which every house,

by its very existence, bears witness to, in fact embodies – expands beyond its own definition and rises up again, undefended, as if to posthumously resist the claims of the open ... One could even say that the porch ceases to be a frail echo of the house it is attached to and becomes the confirmation of what the house just hints at: the ultimate sanction of the protected place, the solution of the theorem that the house merely states.[26]

Shortly after the opening shot, we are taken inside the cabin of the resident Edwards family. They are part of an earlier movement Westward that established what Virginia Wexman identifies as part of an American "nationalist ideology," the Anglo couple or "family on the land."[27] The couple (Edwards's brother and his wife) and their children are participants in the romantic ideal of the adventurous white family, seeking to spread Euro America's form of laboring domesticity Westward in order to settle and civilize what was viewed from the East as a violent untamed territory, containing peoples/nations unworthy of participating in an American future. By the end of the film – after the five-year-long search for Debbie, who has been abducted by Comanches – the relationship between the searchers, Ethan Edwards (John Wayne) and his nephew Martin, has softened. Early in the film, Ethan expresses contempt for Martin's part Indian heritage (at their first meeting he says, "Fellow could mistake you for a half-breed," even though Martin is, by his account, only one-eighth Cherokee). However, by the time they are sequestered in a cave being attacked by Comanches, Ethan has come ambivalently to accept his family bond with Martin, even though he continues to insist that Martin is not his kin. Given Ethan's change in attitude, the scene in the cave becomes an instance of family solidarity. The implication seems to be that Native America can be part of Euro America if it is significantly assimilated and domesticated. Ethan effectively supports that domestication by ultimately bequeathing Martin his wealth. He has apparently discovered that part of himself that craves a family bond, a part that has been continuously in contention with his violent ethnic policing. And on his side, Martin fulfills all of the requirements of a family-oriented, assimilated Indian. He becomes affianced to the very white daughter of Swedish Americans after he has rejected an Indian spouse he had inadvertently acquired while trading goods with Comanches.

By becoming part of a white family, Martin is involved in a double movement. He is participating in one of Euro America's primary dimensions of self-fashioning – its presumption that a Christian marriage is the most significant social unit (that such "legal monogamy benefitted the social order")[28] – and he is distancing himself from Native American practices in which the nuclear family was often not a primary psychological, economic, or social unit (and was often viewed by settlers as a form of "promiscuity.")[29] Ford's West continued to be domesticated as his cinematic corpus developed. Because at least one of his other films – *The Man Who Shot Liberty Valance* (1962) – is exemplary in this respect, I visit that film briefly below in what follows, in connection with my reading of Cormac McCarthy's West.

McCarthy's *Blood Meridian*

While Ford's West becomes increasingly striated – with new boundaries, coercively and administratively imposed, as the Euro American ethnogenesis moves toward consummation – McCarthy's is relatively smooth. It remains a place of violent contact or encounter in which moving bodies are involved in contingent encounters in a West that cannot be easily assimilated into a grid of institutionalized, proprietary relations. It is a West that is perhaps best conceived in Neil Campbell's term "rhizomatic"[30] – a West that (after Deleuze and Guattari's famous distinction) defies the rooted tree-like structures applied to institutionalized hierarchies and is more grass- or rhizome-like. In Campbell's terms the West is "a hybrid, performative space, a staging place for myriad intersecting and constantly changing identities."[31]

In keeping with this more open and contingent model of the development of Western space, McCarthy's *Blood Meridian* mobilizes subjects and stages encounters to supply a radically different geo-history than the one that emerges in Ford's Westerns. Two analytics shape my reading of the novel. The first is the concept of deformation, which is central to Gilles Deleuze's study of the painter, Francis Bacon. As I noted in Chapter 1, in his analysis of Bacon's canvases, Deleuze suggests it is wrong to assume that the artist "works on a white surface." Rather, "everything he has in his head, or around him is already on the canvas, more or less virtually, before he begins his work."[32] To resist what Deleuze calls "psychic clichés" and *"figurative givens,"* the artist must "transform" or "deform" what is "always-already on the canvas."[33] Elsewhere I have noted the way Robert Altman's film *McCabe and Mrs. Miller* effects a deformation of Ford's West. As I put it, inasmuch as the familiar West was John Ford's vast open prairies,

> Altman needed to find a different kind of landscape, filled with characters other than the heroic types, in order both to deform the classic western and to achieve a different, more complicated and politically perspicuous West in his *McCabe and Mrs. Miller* … Altman's film is not a story about the importance of establishing a stable, Euro American domesticity in the West. The contrast between McCabe's opening ride and Ethan Edwards's overturns the Ford clichés in various modalities. First, as John McCabe (Warren Beatty) rides toward the town of Presbyterian Church in the opening scene, the soundtrack begins with a ballad, in this case Leonard Cohen's *Stranger Song*. While the ballads by The Sons of the Pioneers in *The Searchers* and Leonard Cohen's in *McCabe* manifest the typical ballad style – they are both narrative poems with repeated refrains – Cohen's portrays a very different kind of character. Rather than a heroic wanderer, Cohen's "stranger" is a anti hero, a hustler looking for shelter rather than a tough loner, the typical western hero who is unfit for domesticity, even though he helps those who are weaker achieve it.[34]

Certainly, Samuel Peckinpah's Western films – which are intended as critical commentaries (in the form of parodies) on the classic versions – effect deformations of John Ford's West. Richard Slotkin provides an effective summary of the Peckinpah aesthetic:

> *Deadly Companions* was a dark and ironic reworking of Ford's *Stagecoach*; *Ride the High Country* was as much a homage to old Westerns as to the Old West; *Major Dundee* is in continual dialogue with Ford's cavalry films.[35]

The second analytic is the concept of the aesthetic (as opposed to the psychological) subject, which is drawn from Bersani and Dutoit's analysis of a Godard film that I have already detailed in previous chapters. Adapting the Bersani–Dutoit analytic, I am suggesting that, rather than seek to interpret the psychologies of *Blood Meridian*'s characters, we are best served by noting what their drives and interests do to novelistic space – in short, how they render *Blood Meridian*'s critically mapped Western landscape.

With these two analytics in mind, we can appreciate the primary aesthetic subject that we meet in *Blood Meridian*: "the kid," whose mother is dead and whose father "never speaks her name."[36] Unlettered and with "a taste for mindless violence," he runs away from his Tennessee home, as his initial wandering renders him as "a solitary migrant upon that flat and pastoral landscape."[37] Certainly (at least initially) "the kid," whose "origins are become as remote as is his destiny,"[38] bears a resemblance to Western heroes who – as Will Wright has famously noted – are loners and outsiders who briefly enter society to right wrongs and then leave because they are not suited to domestication within a social order.[39] However "the kid" deforms the model of the heroic outsider in two respects. Rather than righting wrongs, he participates in them; his "taste for mindless violence" suits him well when he at first joins Captain White's marauders – who hunt and kill Mexicans – and then joins the Glanton gang – a group of violent scalpers who are paid for Indian scalps by the governments of Mexican towns (and often just harvest Mexican scalps and sell them as Indian ones). Moreover, and even more significantly, "the kid" is illiterate. As a result, he functions as an effective anti-type to Ford's Ransom Stoddard (James Stewart) – the reluctant hero in *The Man Who Shot Liberty Valance,* the man who (in the words journalist Dutton Peabody speaks to an election commission) "came to us not packing a gun but a bag of law books ... a lawyer and a teacher" and who, early in the film, teaches literacy to a generational mix of the white citizens.

Stoddard's heroic identity is undermined because the reverence for words and books, for which he is an avatar, is undermined by the moral ambiguities afflicting his identity (he is falsely credited as the "man who shot Liberty Valance"). His heroic status is ultimately ironic because, as Alan Nadel puts it, of his "chronic inability to give authority to his assertions until be becomes the man who shot Liberty Valance ... until he becomes the person he's not."[40] Nevertheless, Ford privileges the word over the gun in his cinematic narratives of the winning of the West. The issue of words and the West arises again in what is Ford's most sympathetic treatment of Native Americans, his *Cheyenne Autumn* (1964), based on a historic, futile trek by what was left of a branch of the Cheyenne nation, as they attempted to defy the U.S. government and leave their arid southwestern reservation to return to their homeland in the Dakotas. In his earlier *Fort Apache* (1948) Ford had also dealt with white injustice toward Indians, but there – as Tag Gallagher points out – the *dramatis personae* are white, never red; Ford's focus is on "the traditions and community values that render otherwise decent individuals into willing agents of imperialism and genocide."[41] But in treating the Indian with more ethnographic depth in *Cheyenne Autumn*, Ford emphasizes the Cheyenne's inability to have their words count and includes scenes in which they have decisive, withinnation conversations about their options. The film foregrounds the disjuncture between white and red systems of intelligibility, and ultimately represents the Euro American victory as not simply an example of superior firepower but also a discursive one. As it is put in the film, "it is white words, white language that have been our potent weapon against Indians."

McCarthy's *Blood Meridian* contrasts sharply with Ford's reliance on the discursive aspect of the inter-nation struggles in the West. "The kid" is not the only aesthetic subject that undermines the significance of words. Throughout the novel there is a disjuncture between words and reality. Judge Holden, a massive, violent yet learned character, who also becomes part of the Glanton gang, first appears bearing false witness. He speaks up in a revival tent, claiming intimacy with the sexual transgressions of the evangelist and subsequently admitting to an assemblage in a bar that he had never met the man. Thereafter, "the Judge" uses words not to alter the structures of racial dominance in the West but to personally take charge of the world. Writing ceaselessly in a ledger, he responds to the inquiring witnesses of his task that "whatever exists. ... Whatever in creation exists without my knowledge exists without my consent"[42] and adds shortly thereafter, "that man who sets himself the task of singling out the thread of order from the tapestry will by the decision alone have taken charge of the world and it is only by such taking charge that he will effect a way to dictate the terms of his own fate."[43] Ultimately, the Judge regards words as unreliable. They are presented not as windows into a shared, consensual world but as weapons of appropriation. In this respect he, like "the kid," is an anti-type of Ford's Ransom Stoddard, who brings law books to the West to have the printed word displace an anarchic culture of the gun with lawfulness. "Books lie," the Judge says and goes on to suggest that God doesn't: "He speaks in stones and trees, the bones of things." However, once he has turned his listeners into "proselytes," "he laughed at them for fools."[44]

At times, the judge seems to be McCarthy's alter ego because McCarthy also "speaks [or in his case writes] in stones and trees, the bones of things." McCarthy, like the judge, implies (in his various meta-commentaries) that whatever may be the human conceits about proprietary investments in the landscape, nature has a voice that endures irrespective of the ways it is screened by interest-based human voices. What McCarthy offers throughout the novel is a poetics of landscape that, like Ford's, encompasses the characters. Thus at one point "the kid" and another character, Sproule, "moved very slowly in the immensity of the landscape,"[45] but, unlike Ford's landscape, McCarthy's has an awe-inspiring aesthetic impact (akin to Kant's sublime):

That night they rode through a region electric and wild where strange shapes and soft blue fire ran over the metal of the horses; trappings and the wagonwheels rolled in hoops of fire and little shapes of pale blue light came to perch in the ears of the horses and the beards of the men. All night sheet-lightning quaked sourceless to the west beyond the midnight thunderheads, making a bluish day of the distant desert, the mountains on the sudden skyline stark and black and livid like a land of some other order out there whose true geology was not stone but fear.[46]

Rather than a place of invitation for the Euro American expansion, McCarthy's landscape is a deathscape: "Bone palings rules the small and dusty purlieus here and death seemed the most prevalent feature of the landscape."[47] And he often lends the land/deathscape theological overtones, for example describing it in one place as a "purgatorial waste" (63). Ultimately, McCarthy does not allow the landscape to privilege anyone's history. It is a space of encounter in which many of the events of encounter never find there way into "history." For example, at one point Glanton, on horseback, looks out over a scene: "Sparse on the mesa the dry weeds lashed in the wind like the earth's long echo of lance and spear in old encounters forever unrecorded" (105).

What is ultimately afoot (or mounted) in McCarthy's West cannot be incorporated in a narrative that privileges particular destinies, Euro American or otherwise. For example in this rich passage, describing the movement of the Glanton gang, McCarthy likens optical illusions to the illusions that a people's destinies are transcendently sponsored:

> They ate and moved on, leaving the fire on the ground behind them, and as they rode up into the mountains this fire seemed to become altered of its location, now here, now there, drawing away or shifting unaccountably along the flank of their movement. Like some ignis fatuus belated upon the road behind them which all could see and of which none spoke. For this will to deceive that is in things luminous may manifest itself likewise in retrospect and so by sleight of some fixed part of a journey already accomplished may also post men to fraudulent destinies. (120)[48]

The judge as a counter-Ford, philosophical subject

As I have suggested, the judge serves throughout the novel as a philosophical subject. He is seemingly attentive to Nietzsche's gloss, in *The Birth of Tragedy*, on the self as an inter-animation of the Apollonian and Dionysian energies – the former being detached and form-giving and the latter being both creative and destructive. In Nietzsche's view that productive tension was lost when philosophy became inflected by Plato's Socrates, whose mission was to suppress the tension in order to make existence appear rationally intelligible and thereby self-justifying. What a Nietzschean ontology offers – as articulated throughout *Blood Meridian* – is a frame that resists legitimating ontologies that offer conciliation. Ford's West ultimately becomes pacified as wildernesses are turned into gardens and the landscape-as-deathscape is displaced by one of cultivation. McCarthy effectively restores the tensions and enigmas to a landscape that contains a history of encounters that are exorbitant to the ones chronicling Euro American triumphalism.

One trope in particular serves to demonstrate the sharp contrast between Ford's and McCarthy's Wests – the dance. To return to the film with which my analysis began – Ford's *My Darling Clementine* – I refer to a dance whose significance in the film looms much larger than the famous gunfight at the O.K. Corral. Toward the end of the film narrative, there is a celebration of the building of a church. In the scene, it is only partly built; it has wooden beams and an open framework with a wooden platform as its base. Onto that platform step the two key characters, Wyatt Earp and his intended, Clementine, to begin a dance whose significance is underscored by a musical soundtrack that conveys the promise of a happy conjugal/familial future. The effect of the scene – as is the case in so many of Ford's familial bonding scenes – is to moralize a West that is being incorporated into Euro America, to positively sanction the "white" expansion rather than, for example, pondering the costs of the violence associated with that expansion (as he does in *Cheyenne Autumn*).

McCarthy's *Blood Meridian* is a thoroughgoing riposte to that moralizing. McCarthy's primary aesthetic subject, "the kid" – a feral character rather than an innocent youth on his way to becoming enlightened – begins his Western life by joining a rogue army band that is out to kill Mexicans. And in a passage reminiscent of Melville's gloss on "the metaphysics of Indian hating" (displaced onto Mexicans), *Blood Meridian*'s Captain White, the leader of that rogue army says, "What we are dealing with, he said, is a race of degenerates. A mongrel race, little better than niggers. And maybe no better. There is no government in Mexico. Hell, there is no God in Mexico, never will be."[49] And in contrast to the illusion that the U.S. version of "America" is constituted through peace-fostering treaties, *Blood Meridian*'s treatment of treaties emphasizes how they are ignored. At one point "the kid" asks about "the treaty" (referring obviously to Guadalupe Hidalgo) only to learn that his troop's killing spree is unaffected by it.

Figure 7.2
Wyatt and Clementine

Apart from giving us a West as a deathscape that endorses no-one's hating or self-serving legitimations, McCarthy's *Blood Meridian* also enlists the trope of the dance, but with a very different valence from Ford's. His character, Judge Holden, is figured as a dancer when at one point, as the Glanton gang is seated around a fire, one character – the "expriest" – says, "God, the man is a dancer." [50] Just as Nietzsche, in many places, affirms the value of the dance – e.g., "I would believe only in a god who could dance" [51] – the judge himself valorizes the dance: "What man would not be a dancer if he could, said the judge. It's a great thing, the dance." [52] Subsequently, in a soliloquy, the judge has more to say about the dance, as he ponders the rationale for the orchestration of events:

> This is an orchestration for an event. The participants will be apprised of their roles at the proper time ... As the dance is the thing with which we are concerned and contains complete within itself its own arrangement and history and finale there is no necessity that the dancers contain these things within themselves as well. In any event the history of all is not the history of each nor indeed the sum of those histories. [53]

The point of this passage – as Nietzsche would have appreciated – is that subjectivity is epiphenomenal to creative action. To invent a preexisting subject is to moralize by inventing and privileging a subject behind the action. However distasteful the judge's violent actions may be, his point articulates with McCarthy's: there is no privileged historical agency. The landscape has witnessed violent encounters, driven by enmities. It contains numerous unrecorded histories and privileges none. Contrary to Ford's embrace of legitimating legends, McCarthy offers "reality." In place of fraudulent destinies, he offers the contingencies of encounter. In place of moralizing what has already been institutionalized, his novel invites ethical reflection, where "ethics" is opposed to morals. As I have put it elsewhere, "morality, as traditionally understood, is about deriving imperatives from fixed moral codes, while ethical imperatives are invitations to negotiate meaning and value, given situations of either competing and incommensurate value commitments and/or alternative perspectives on what is the case." [54] To extend that suggestion, I want to note that McCarthy's art – his aesthetic version of the West – articulates well with ethical reflection. This chimes well with Rancière's version of the politics of aesthetics, in which the problem of the aesthetic is compatible with ethical and political judgment – even when it is focused on "beautiful objects" (or horrifying ones) – because the politics of aesthetics involves reconfiguring the way the sensible is partitioned, revealing new objects and subjects and rendering visible that which has not hitherto been visible. [55] Certainly that is what McCarthy's *Blood Meridian* does.

The contemporary "Blood Meridian"

The various U.S. policy initiatives aimed at controlling the traffic across the Mexico–U.S. border are accompanied by several unofficial actions that render the area a renewed "blood meridian." Here's one report that features the deadly consequences of the increasing vigilantism in the border area:

PAUSING INTERMITTENTLY under the merciless sun, Cesareo Dominguez desperately scanned the desert near the Arizona border for twenty-one consecutive days. In a well-known migrant corridor, just south of Pima County, his search came to a tragic end when he discovered what he hoped he wouldn't, the lifeless body of his daughter, Lucresia. She had made a desperate attempt to cross from Mexico without papers, in order to reunite with her husband now living in the United States. On the other side of the same stretch of desert, right-wing vigilante squads calling themselves the Minutemen have begun patrols along the U.S.-Mexico border. Sporting fatigues, a small arsenal, and paramilitary bravado, their migrant hunting expeditions are designed to open a new front of the "war on terrorism" by portraying the "porous border" as a threat to national security and "American culture."[56]

The Minutemen project is merely a harder version of the policing/surveillance practices all along the U.S.–Mexican border, which reach northward into large metropolises such as Los Angeles as well as much farther north. In the case of Los Angeles, as Lawrence Herzog puts it, the Los Angeles–Mexico interface is part of a set of U.S, border relations that constitutes a "transfrontier Metropolis."[57] Increasingly, the controls over the moving Mexican bodies crossing the border are spreading from the border territory inward, both within the U.S. and in Mexico, an expanding "interior enforcement."[58] As a result, the spatial practices of the U.S.'s immigration control policy process has made Mexico's border "as deep as it is wide."[59] And now there are other governmental players involved – "small town governments" that have "in recent years, posted the most aggressive challenge to national immigration policy, primarily through municipal ordinances that preempt federal policy,"[60] and the state of Arizona, which is challenging federal policy with draconian surveillance procedures.

Temporal rhythms, which operate outside of territorial enforcement, weigh as heavily as spatial controls on the fates of Mexican immigrants – rhythms that belong as much to economic as to political forces. For example, along with policy time, a changing set of laws and extra-juridical enforcement mechanisms designed to inhibit illegal immigration, is capital time and labor union time. "Capital time," which is a function of money flows "tends to escape the juridical frame of political territoriality."[61] Not surprisingly, therefore, entrepreneurs who find illegal immigrants useful employ capture and control rather than prevention and inhibition policies. As I point out elsewhere, for illegal immigrants the political threats of punishment and deportation that operate within the political domain effectively support the coercive controls operating within the economic sector.[62] They create the conditions of possibility for turning immigrants into vulnerable, suborned bodies. Thus although a political temporality manifests itself as an increasing securitizing that seeks to inhibit the flow of immigrant bodies, a globalizing economic temporality, which includes "urban development policies [that] favor state deregulation and privatization of services," encourages immigration and thereby places the increasing number of foreign born residents under political threat while at the same time pushing them into a condition of "economic or social marginalization."[63] Among the kinds of vulnerable lives in various global venues of late are "deportable lives."[64] In particular undocumented people living in the vicinity of the U.S.–Mexico border – who live with the reality of imminent deportation – are often too fearful to make use of health services or contest harassment from neighbors, lest they invite police scrutiny.[65] The anxiety with which they must live constitutes a softer version of the violence in "the blood meridian."

However, much of the violence in the border area is enacted by the landscape itself. While two contending forces are operating to both encourage the flow of bodies and to inhibit it – the enticement of entrepreneurs willing to hire undocumented cheap labor and the policing forces seeking to inhibit it – the casualty rate is growing dramatically. "The landscapes of the desert southwest" are so perilous that thousands die of dehydration while making the trek. As a result, the landscapes play an increasingly "key role in the biopower of U.S. border enforcement policy."[66] The death-producing practices of deterrence, ranging from "Operation Hold the Line" in Texas to "Gatekeeper" in San Diego and "Safeguard" in Tucson and Nogales constitute "a micropolitics of the body based on its need for water."[67] Although the deterrence practices are not the kind of direct killing practiced by marauders from the nineteenth century to the present, their body count exceeds those produced by the armed gangs, who have robbed and murdered for profit. Nevertheless, while deterrence policies claim bodies indirectly, the more direct killing by marauders continues. On the Mexican side of the border, a twenty-first-century equivalent of the Glanton gang – armed narco-traffickers who have expanded their operations to include demanding money from Mexicans headed for the border, add another level of violence. At times aided and abetted by U.S. law enforcement agencies (interested more in their arrest records than in Mexican lives)[68] it recalls the version treated in McCarthy's novel. In 2010, one of the most powerful narco-trafficking gangs, the Zetas, murdered 72 laborers, apparently because they either refused or could not pay a fee for a safe crossing.

Conclusion

As is well known, the flow of bodies across the U.S.–Mexican divide is both enticed and abhorred. At the same time that a variety of policy initiatives, public and private, seek to discover and deport undocumented Mexican laborers, diverse enterprises desire their work and exploit their vulnerability. Yet despite the grim picture that their vulnerability creates, there have been counter-forces operating. For example, there is the case of Los Angeles, where changes in "capital time" have turned the downtown area – one of the spaces most affected by trans-border movements – into more of a service than a manufacturing economy. Thanks to the activity of the service unions, entrepreneurial controls over and exploitation of service economy workspaces have been diminished. A new "service unionism" has been involved in continuous organizing to keep up with the flows of immigrant, undocumented workers.[69] At the same time, the arts (cinema in particular) have been a parallel counter force challenging the forces of neo-liberalism with images of valued and disvalued bodies and compositional forms that offer a different political model from neo-liberalism's abstract economic spaces, regulated by legal, bureaucratic, and entrepreneurial codes. Along with union initiatives, cinema has constituted a form of political activism that challenges such abstractions through the way it provides concrete images of the vulnerable undocumented workers and the lived spaces within which they dwell.

Here I turn briefly to the Laverty/Loach film version of a "Justice for Janitors" movement begun in 1985 in many U.S. and Canadian cities: their *Bread and Roses* (2000), which deals with an episode in the labor struggles of undocumented workers in Los Angeles.[70] From the point of view of traditional geopolitical discourse, the issue of cross-border migration involves the governance of state-controlled sovereign space. By contrast the film explores the micropolitical spaces of households and enterprises as it provides close-up views of a clash in which marginalized and exploited Mexican workers achieved a measure of justice. Showing the micro-level forces operating within the historical frame of the more familiar macro-political level of policy concerns about the illegal immigrant workforce, the film recreates the drama and images associated with the "Justice for Janitors" initiative. It therefore effects again what the original struggle did. It mounts a challenge to legal and bureaucratic abstract space, and it shows – contrary to the more familiar civic discourse, recycled in mainstream American politics texts – that U.S. citizenship continues to be an unstable result of diasporic and migrant flows.

Indeed, ever since cinema turned from treating Mexico as an illusory refuge destination for those in the U.S. seeking to escape their problems (for example the killer, Walter Neff in Billy Wilder's *Double Indemnity* 1944) and focused on fraught, cross-border relations (for example, Anthony Mann's *Border Incident* (1949) and Orson Welles' above-mentioned *A Touch of Evil* (1958)), it has shown the micropolitical consequences of border policing – for example, the structures of geopolitical enmity and the vulnerabilities of migrating bodies. Mann's *Border Incident* is especially noteworthy here, for like *Bread and Roses* it treats the vulnerabilities of the illegal Mexican workforce, and it offers a contrast to the Laverty/Loach film. While *Bread and Roses* is primarily located in the cityscape of downtown LA, with its tall buildings in which the exploited undocumented Mexicans are working, in *Border Incident*, it is the California farms that employ them, a "great agricultural empire" (as the documentary style voice-over puts it). In both films, however, the Mexican "migrants occupy a twilight zone while in the United States, remaining Mexicans by nationality but suffering from a radical geopolitical dislocation and estrangement."[71]

The primary aesthetic subject in *Bread and Roses* is Maya (Pilar Padia), whose trans-border journey – managed by violent coyotes (types also featured in *Border Incident*) – to LA from Mexico, initiates the film's drama. Once she crosses the U.S.–Mexican border and escapes a pervasive aspect of the violence in the border area, the exploitation of border crossers by the coyotes (one of whom demands sexual favors in exchange for releasing her), her movements back and forth between her sister Rosa's (Elpidia Carillo) domestic situation (young children and a seriously ill husband for whom her low wages and absence of benefits cannot provide medical help) and the Century Building, map the concrete spaces of Los Angeles's exploited Latino workforce. Downtown Los Angeles, which appears benign in city panoramas that render it an abstract urban space (for example, an area zoned for high rise buildings), becomes a place of menacing injustice when framed from the point of view of Maya's first approach to the Century Building. A shot that looks down on Maya from a vantage point near the top of the building emphasizes her vulnerability as the built-up environment containing downtown commerce is shown looming over her. A subsequent shot – looking upward from Maya's street-level vantage point at the Century Building and others nearby – gives the viewer a sense of Maya's initial disempowerment, which has already been underscored in her encounter outside, when an African American security guard forces her to leave the front of the building: "You can't hang here," he tells her.

Once Rosa gets Maya a position in the janitorial crew, the viewer enters a building in which security within is as pervasive as it is on the building's perimeter. The violence associated with border crossing is reproduced within the building: on the one hand, one sees oppressed service workers (often harassed and exploited by the janitorial superintendent, who demands payoffs for their initial employment) in the cramped basement of the building; on the other, professional staff are shown to occupy spacious offices on the higher floors. While the professional staff enjoy a comfortable non-threatening work environment, the Latino cleaners are regimented, exploited and continually threatened with the loss of their livelihood. Ultimately, however, with the help of a union organizer, Sam Shapiro (Adrien Brody), Maya and her co-workers turn both the inside of the building and the street into spaces of political resistance and negotiation.

Rather than cover all details of a plot in which, among other things, Maya and her sister Rosa become temporarily estranged, I want to note how the film thinks about temporal and spatial repartitioning – the tactics through which a marginalized group of Los Angeles Latinos succeed in reshaping their working environment. In accord with one of Henri Lefebvre's key political concepts in his *The Production of Space* – "appropriation" – the janitors appropriate their work space, changing it from a space of domination to one of solidarity and joint action.[72] At a key moment, they use their access to the building to allow a large group of janitors to enter and stage a protest during a corporate merger celebration. In addition, staging a rally and parade, they appropriate the streets and bridges of downtown Los Angeles to change a space of vehicular circulation into a spectacle of protest and resistance.

The political dynamic in Laverty and Loach's *Bread and Roses* reflects one of the most pervasive and contentious aspects of global politics that unfolds within a wide variety of contemporary global cities and implicates diverse bodies. Contentious urban politics reflects a shift in the political problematic to which Lefebvre famously addressed himself: a shift from the traditional forms of domination belonging to the state form, when the center of economic activity was within agrarian formations, to the exploitation of the urban labor force.[73] The victims of the exploitation to which Lefebvre was referring were primarily citizen industrial workers, whose many gains throughout the twentieth century are now being effaced by the dynamic of de-industrialization. Those focusing on contemporary global or "international" politics would do well to address the new – and doubtless more cynical – form of violence that is visited on foreign workers, who arrive precariously as they cross the Mexico–U.S. border and then live precariously in the cities where they work. There is thus a new violent "bio-cartography" in evidence,[74] a series of contentious "contact zones" one finds in contemporary global cities.[75]

8   The presence of war[1]
"Here and Elsewhere"

The contemporary is he who firmly holds his gaze on his own time so as to perceive not its light, but rather its darkness.

Giorgio Agamben

Introduction: changing political topologies

How can we make sense of the contemporary topology of U.S. warfare, especially in light of the complications attending the post-cold war era, reoriented global antagonisms and the disappearance of the traditional battlefront? In what sense is war present, now that remote targeting occurs, the information war displaces the industrialized warfare of the past and lethality is frequently delivered from the home front? To answer such questions, we must follow Nietzsche's suggestion and be "untimely," recognizing that one belongs to the present while at the same time keeping a distance from it.[2] I begin my untimely investigation by collecting these issues under the rubric of "the presence of war," turning first to the conceptual problems associated with presence: topologies of the political, grammar, and technologies of perception, treated initially through an encounter I stage between the politics-space perspectives of Hannah Arendt and Jacques Rancière.

Many assumed that the end of the cold war would lead, as Rancière puts it, to "a more peaceful post-historical world where global democracy would match the global market of liberal economy."[3] With Rancière, we have to observe that given "new outbursts of ethnic conflicts and slaughter, religious fundamentalisms, or racial and xenophobic movements [and, we should add, the new pax Americana involving a global and domestic "war on terror"], ... the territory of 'post-historical' and peaceful humanity proved to be the territory of new figures of the inhuman."[4] As a result, the end of the cold war, then the emergence of the current war on terror, has had the kind of shattering effect that Hannah Arendt addressed in the face of the totalitarian horrors of the twentieth century, which, she noted at the time, "have clearly exploded our categories of political thought and our standards for moral judgment."[5]

A recent series of events, which can be addressed from both Arendt's and Rancière's angles of vision, articulate the challenges to political thinking that have resulted from reoriented modes of political action and the reconfiguration of political spaces they have created. They are an example of a unique kind of *vita activa* (to use an Arendt expression) that confounds the topography of political action, as it has been historically understood, in a trajectory of treatises stretching from Aristotle to the modern period. In the canonical political theory tradition, the domestic sphere has been radically separated from the public sphere (at least until the emergence of critically oriented feminist approaches to political theory). Arendt suggests that the separation is effectively ancient history. As she puts it in her treatment of "The *Polis* and the Household," "The distinction between a private and a public sphere of life corresponds to the household and the political realms, which have existed as distinct, separate entities at least since the rise of the ancient city state."[6] Arendt goes on to point out that the emergence of society and of a nation-state managed economy has blurred the lines between the two spheres. By the mid-twentieth century, she observes, "all matters pertaining formerly to the private sphere of the family have become a 'collective' concern. [Hence] In the modern world, the two realms indeed constantly flow into each other like waves in the never-resting stream of the life process itself."[7] As Arendt summarizes that boundary transgression more extensively:

> The emergence of society – the rise of housekeeping, its activities, problems, and organizational devices – from the shadowy interior of the household into the light of the public sphere, has not only blurred the old border line between private and political, it has also changed almost beyond recognition the meaning of the two terms and their significance for the life of the individual and citizen.[8]

Arendt's observations about the blurring of the boundaries between the two spheres were prompted by her understanding of the role of the state in political economy. The "state form," she writes, increasingly involves "a nation-wide administration of house-keeping." So to analyze the new relationships, it is "no longer political science [to which one must turn] but 'national economy' or 'social economy' or *Volkswirtschaft*, all of which indicate a kind of 'collective house-keeping'."[9] However, the topographical drama I have in mind is provoked from within the household rather than from the historical dynamic of the governmentalization of the economy to which Arendt referred. It involves political engagements, initiated by Cindy Sheehan, the mother of an American casualty in the Iraq war.

In 2005, while grieving over the loss of a son in a war she regards as illegitimate, Sheehan first camped outside the White House in Washington D.C. and then in the town of Crawford in the vicinity of President Bush's Texas ranch, at a site she named "Camp Casey," after her son Casey Sheehan. Seeking a conversation with the president about the domestic costs of the war, she made several public appearances and rallied a group of mothers who have also lost sons. At one rally she said:

> The president says he feels compassion for me, but the best way to show that compassion is by meeting with me and the other mothers and families who

are here. Our sons made the ultimate sacrifice and we want answers. All we're asking is that he sacrifice an hour out of his five-week vacation to talk to us, before the next mother loses her son in Iraq.[10]

Certainly, by identifying herself as the mother of a war casualty, Sheehan moved from "the shadowy interior of the household into the light of the public sphere." After having been treated as a trespasser and denied access to the vicinity of the Bush ranch, Sheehan took a dramatic step. She purchased "five acres in Crawford with some of the insurance money she received after her son was killed in Iraq."[11] Whereas Arendt had noted that, given the state's management of the economy, "the two realms [the household and the public sphere] indeed constantly flow into each other,"[12] here is a case in which the household has effectively migrated outside of its expected boundaries and into a zone that had not heretofore been politicized – the private space of a governmental leader. The compelling questions raised by Sheehan's actions are specifically about the spaces in which war is to be understood as present and generally about the conceptualization of politics. She has disrupted traditional understandings of the inter-articulation of action and space by altering the familiar, largely depoliticized identity of a mother.[13] She has changed her status from an object of official compassion to a political subject – someone with a voice that articulates political dissensus. As a result, her gesture can be better interpreted within Rancière's conception of politics than within Arendt's, because Rancière's approach to politics provides an apt interpretation of the shift that Sheehan has produced:

> Politics itself is not the exercise of power or struggle for power. Politics is first of all the configuration of a space as political, the framing of a specific sphere of experience, the setting of objects posed as "common" and of subjects to whom the capacity is recognized to designate these objects and discuss about them. Politics first is the conflict about the very existence of that sphere of experience, the reality of those common objects and the capacity of those subjects.[14]

We therefore have two accounts of the ways in which events impinge on the relationship between space and political action – Arendt's and Rancière's – which diverge sharply. What distinguishes Arendt's political imaginary from Rancière's is her understanding of the relationship between events and action. The *polis* for Arendt is not a hierarchical structure of governance or ruling, "it is the organization of the people as it arises out of acting and speaking together, and its true space lies between people living together for this purpose no matter where they happen to be."[15] For Arendt, acting and speaking together result from reactions to world events. Thus, in the face of twentieth-century totalitarianism, which "has brought to light the ruin of our categories of thought and standards of judgment,"[16] a political response is called for – one that may not necessarily involve pervasive public policy adjustment but rather acts of the imagination that reconfigure understandings of the history of the present. By contrast, Rancière does not assume that there exists a bounded political space that people enter once provoked by events. What many regard as the sphere of politics – the spaces from which policy is implemented – Rancière regards as mere policing. For Rancière, politics – as opposed to policing – is itself an event. The domain of "the political" is not a pre-existing space; it emerges through action that is addressed to a wrong. There are no political parties with an existence prior to "the declaration of a wrong." Thus, to take one of Rancière's examples: "Before the wrong that its name exposes, the proletariat has no existence as a real part of society."[17] Instead of seeing the political as emerging from collective responses to events, Rancière sees the political *as* an event, an event of dissensus. And, instead of mapping a world of political and non-political spaces, Rancière identifies acts that reorder spaces and reconstitute identities, rendering persons as political subjects.

My preference for Rancière's perspective therefore stems from my concern with analyzing events and spaces of contemporary warfare in general and, more specifically, the reordered relationships between the domestic space and the spaces of war. While Arendt's approach to political topography registers the ways in which the state has crossed (and thus attenuated) the public–private boundary, she nevertheless maintains a strict separation between private and public realms when she addresses the issue of political action. For Arendt, to be a politically engaged citizen-subject, one must exit the domestic space. As a result, her conception of politics is uncongenial to a recognition of the micro-politics of the household, as it operates within a world of outside forces that inflect its motivations and outcomes and to moments when it asserts itself as a political voice. Cindy Sheehan's initiative is but one among many episodes that have altered the ways in which war is connected with domesticity. In what follows, I turn to critical philosophical and artistic perspectives that illuminate the ways in which contemporary warfare's presence or actuality registers itself in space–body relationships and to the relevance of Arendt's observation that events "have clearly exploded our categories of political thought and our standards for moral judgment." However, I want to add a corollary. Rather than a need for merely new categories, we have to reassess our grammar as well.

Jean Baudrillard and grammar

As the U.S.'s twenty-first-century wars proceeded in Afghanistan and Iraq, their impacts were experienced very differently in the diverse life worlds of the participants/observers. Some were at the war front, exposed to the actual "theaters" of war, where all in close proximity are in mortal danger; some were at the home front, attending cinematic theaters, where their participation involved consuming images and narratives from a safe distance; and some experienced the wars vicariously, playing video games that interpolate them as warriors with the same level of actuality as those "service personnel" who operate lethal weapons from computer consoles at a great distance from the war theater. In what sense then is contemporary war present (and for whom)? Among those who have raised those questions is the French philosopher/culture and media theorist, Jean Baudrillard. Reflecting on the information war's mediation between warriors and their targets,

Baudrillard pointed out – in his epigrammatic meditations on the first Gulf War: *The Gulf War Will Not Take Place, The Gulf War is it Really Taking Place, The Gulf War Did Not Take Place* – that the Iraqi targets in that war were observed and targeted on various screens from remote (and safe) distances. As a result, for much of that war, the war and cinematic theaters (and small-screen games) were effectively equivalent. Because some "warriors" were able to deliver lethal force at the war front from the home front, we have to radically rethink the spaces of war, the roles and skill sets of subject/antagonists, and our political language as it applies to war.[18]

In terms of subjects/antagonists: while the GI Joe doll was once the appropriate avatar of the warrior – a battlefield soldier skilled in hand-to-hand combat – it is now more appropriate to fashion an avatar of a video game-playing teenager: for example, the one described by Peter Singer, a nineteen-year-old high school dropout who wanted to join the army to be a helicopter mechanic. Although he turned out to be unqualified for that role, once the army recognized his video game prowess, he was recruited as a "drone pilot" instead. He joined a group of warriors who go to war at their computer consoles – often in their own homes – from which they guide weaponized drones (pilotless aircraft) and, once authorized, fire missiles at suspected antagonists. Singer describes a scenario in which a video warrior is helping his children with their homework at the dining table in a city in Arizona, shortly after firing lethal weapons at targets in Afghanistan. Effectively, what Singer refers to as the "wired war" has radically changed how one can speak about the spaces of war and thus the extent to which it is present to those involved.[19]

The trend to which Singer addresses himself was already famously evoked by Paul Virilio in his analysis of the Vietnam War, in which for the first time the battlefield was "a cinema location."[20] And it was also evoked by Baudrillard in response to the technologies used in the first Gulf War, which did not "take place," he asserted, because there was virtually no direct contact between combatants. According to Baudrillard, because of the technological prostheses intervening between U.S. forces and their targets, the prosecution of the war for the American forces and their allies was a "bellicose equivalent of safe sex."[21] As the grammatical shifts from future to present to past proceed through Baudrillard's three texts on the war, it becomes apparent that, in the era of information war, the question of the actuality or presence of war presents grammatical challenges.

The fundamental intimacy between presence and grammar was famously articulated centuries ago by St. Augustine, when he tried to become present to himself by reconciling the non-presence of past and future states with the supposed unity of one's existence in time. How, he wondered, can "these two kinds of time, the past and the future, be, when the past no longer is and the future as yet does not be?"[22] In Augustine's case his concern with one's presence to the self through time led him to a grammatical exercise in which his self was "distended into memory" (to re-collect his past), and extended into the future (through the operation of "expectation").[23] In Baudrillard's case, as he runs through a grammatical trajectory while speculating about the war's presence – as it was anticipated, as it is conducted, and as it will have been (its future anterior) – he concludes that the war fails to achieve a unity or coherent actuality because it fails to live up to what "war" is supposed to be.

Many misread Baudrillard's point, arguing that he was conjuring away the brutal consequences of the war (for example, Christopher Norris who used the occasion of Baudrillard's monograph to mount a furious attack on post-modernist denials of reality).[24] A more nuanced reading must recognize that Baudrillard was suggesting that what war has been – a violent engagement between antagonistic bodies – has been displaced by a clinical slaughter in which one side's technological superiority insulates its warriors form the traditional vulnerabilities of direct combat. Of course, what Baudrillard observed about the first Gulf War was not the first instance of the use of a weapons technology that substitutes slaughter from a distance for what had been the more familiar violent confrontations associated with traditional battlefields. For example, in describing the consequences of the use of the newly invented breach-loading rifle – which could be quickly reloaded and kill at a great distance – at the battle of Omdurman in the Sudan (1898), Sven Lindqvist writes, "the art of killing at a distance became a European specialty early on." Thus, in the "victory" at Omdurman, there were 11,000 Sudanese killed and only 48 British casualties.[25]

Lindqvist's investigation of Europe's genocidal wars in Africa – a literary intervention that re-inflects those wars' interpretive future (grammatically speaking, the future anterior: their will-have-beens) – inspires much of this analysis. As I note in Chapter 1, Lindqvist inter-weaves a personal travel story (interspersed with historical information) with a reprise of Joseph Conrad's *Heart of Darkness* (along with his biography), and adds a commentary on the history of the kind of racial discourses that encouraged and legitimated colonial violence. His multi-genre analysis gives those wars a renewed yet altered presence. Moving back and forth between his personal experiences and perceptions and a history of violent modes of apprehension and action, he chronicles both the way the wars have become present to him (as he achieves a new presence to himself) and the way he wants to make them present to history. Rob Nixon's endorsement on the back of the paperback edition is both apropos and compelling: "Lindqvist's disturbing, brilliant work of historical sleuthing deserves to be taken up in a thousand classrooms."[26] Here Nixon is suggesting that the future presence of war ought to be registered in pedagogical venues. As spaces of alternative (and often more critically self-reflective) media, classrooms are often counter-hegemonic spaces within which futures of the past are radically altered. The literature to which Nixon exposes his students "brings lives into focus"[27] in a very different way from that of the remote spectator who sees the Middle Eastern people, combatants and non-combatants alike, through the eyes of weapons – for example of late, the afore-mentioned Predator drones. Although there is doubtless much to learn about the lives of those who live in the war zones, my focus here is on the way contemporary artistic treatments – which challenge the limits of perception – can bring the lives of those on the U.S. domestic front into focus and thereby affect the ways in which wars will achieve future, interpretive presences.

The limits of perception

Since Baudrillard's skeptical intervention into the first Gulf War, and Nixon's resort to literature in order to evince a history of victimization that rarely achieves public recognition, a variety of artistic genres have generated critical perspectives on the kind of presence manifested by the Gulf and Afghanistan wars. They constitute a growing archive that will participate in a perpetual contest over how those wars will have been. Although Baudrillard's point is well taken – that the war did not take place in the usual way, in what follows I want to take issue with his approach to the (non-)presence of war and summon both some philosophical treatments of the "virtual" that contest his perspective on what is present or actual along with some artistic approaches to war that re-inflect war's presence in critical ways – giving it a variety of actualizations. Inasmuch as wars are susceptible to continual interpretive contestation, their future anteriors (their will-have-beens) are never consummated. Baudrillard's approach to war's non-reality is based on his well-known concept of hyperreality, a situation in which simulacra replace reality such that, in the case of war, one cannot distinguish virtual from actual. For Baudrillard, in our media-saturated world one cannot distinguish actual from simulated events. Thus, as he points out, during the Gulf War one side saw the other through technological prostheses (the U.S. forces) and the other side deployed decoys to mask their presence. The result was an ultimate non-engagement or non-co-presence.

To contest Baudrillard's perspective on the non-presence of contemporary war and thus add to its interpretive future, I want to turn to theories of perception which imply that war has always functioned within what I shall call a *hypo*reality, because perceptual practices evacuate much of what is potentially actual. From the points of view of a variety of approaches to perception – those of Henri Bergson, Jacques Lacan, and Kaja Silverman, for example – however close or distant actual bodily contact may be between antagonists, the attendant interpersonal perceptions – with or without complicated technological mediation – are always partial and in various ways misleading. For example, from a Bergsonian perspective, an Other can never be wholly present because other bodies, like any kind of matter, become available through interest-motivated forms of apprehension. For Bergson, to perceive is to subtract in order to come up with *a* sense of the world, selected from all the possible senses. Moreover, that selection is interest-based inasmuch as the perceiver subtracts – in her/his own interest-based way – some aspects of the aggregate of images rather than others.[28] As is well known, for Bergson that isolating subtraction is based on the ways in which both habitual and pure memory orient perception. When pure memory becomes engaged during the act of perception, the subject purposively selects from the entire stock of recollections. Thus, from Bergson's perspective, the thing or person perceived acquires its identity from both habitual and purposive forms of recognition that mediate the two images (the perceiving body as an image) and the Other or thing-as-image.

Jacques Lacan's indictment of the reality-inflections of perception takes a different form. Distinguishing between the eye and the gaze, he points out that the latter serves as a "phantom force" which controls vision while itself remaining unobserved: "In our relation to things, in so far as this relation is constituted by the way of vision, and ordered in the figures of representation, something slips, passes, is transmitted, from stage to stage, and is always to some degree eluded in it – this is what we call the gaze."[29] While the Bergsonian and Lacanian indictments of the adequacy of perception are restricted to individual observers – and thus leave few critical options for political response – Kaja Silverman provides a collective version of the Lacanian distinction between the eye and the gaze in a way that gestures toward a useful meta-politics of perception. She treats what is prior to the eye, as a "cultural screen" or "repertoire of representations by means of which our culture figures all those many varieties of difference," which mediate not only how we see the object world but also how we locate ourselves.[30]

Aesthetic interventions

A variety of artistic genres articulate the implications of collective as well as individual gazes and thereby respond effectively to the limits of perception. Doubtless the most conspicuous and effective one is cinema, which has capacities that are especially worth noting. Although, as Siegfried Kracauer famously argued, some films are intended to make you believe rather than see critically because they deal primarily in "corroborative images,"[31] others compose their images in ways that turn the spectator into what Gilles Deleuze refers to as a seer (*voyant*) – a reflecting and thus critical subject rather than one simply ready to anticipate the next part of a drama. As Deleuze notes, once cinema – by dint of its direct image of time (created through composition and editing) – creates a break in the "sensory-motor link that gives primacy to action, the viewer 'SEES' and thus asks not what is coming next but rather 'what is there to see in the image'."[32] The cinema of seeing is activated by the critical way cinema works. Specifically, the conditions of possibility for such critical seeing are owed to the composition effects of film form. Rancière has put it well. Cinema is able to achieve what perception (expectancy- and interest-aimed vision) tends to obscure. It does so by undoing "the ordinary work of the human brain [because] its operation is one of restitution [of the reality that the brain has] confiscated."[33]

Walter Benjamin provides a similar analysis of the critical advantages of visual technologies. In his treatment of photography's and cinema's advantages over mere perception, he refers to their capacity for revealing an "optical unconscious" which contains details not available to the naked eye. In particular, "the capacity for montage and shocklike abutment of dissimilars" provides for the apprehension of connections that the perceiving eye cannot assemble.[34] Among the most important concepts that Benjamin lends to the effects of photography and cinema is "distraction." In his dense and complex (and ambiguous) essay, "The Work of Art in the Age of Mechanical Reproduction," Benjamin distinguishes two kinds of reception: concentration and distraction. The latter he saw as an effect of Dada: "The Dadaists," he asserts, "became an instrument of ballistics. It hit the spectator like a bullet, it happened to him, thus acquiring a tactile quality. It promoted a demand for the film, the distracting element of which is also primarily tactile, being based on changes of place and focus which periodically assail the spectator." According to Benjamin, film carries out and generalizes the form of distraction that Dadaism had introduced: "By means of its technical structure, the film has taken the physical shock effect out of the wrappers in which Dadaism had, as it were, kept it inside the moral shock effect."[35] In contrast with a painting, which "invites the spectator to contemplation," film contains a "distracting element ... based on changes of place and focus which periodically assail the spectator." Although both Benjamin and his Weimar friend, Kracauer, addressed the negative aspect of distraction – its tendency to manipulate the masses – they also saw its critical potential. In Kracauer's case, he saw cinema's distraction as an opening to art's critical potential. But he argued that cinema's critical potential – the way its montage of fragments pointed toward social disintegration – was undercut by the large picture palaces, "festooned with drapery," such that they force the fragments back into a misleading unity.[36] To provide an example: both the positive and negative aspects of distraction are the dominant thematics in Jean-Luc Godard's film *Ici et Ailleurs* (*Here and Elsewhere*, 1976). A family is seated watching a television set with split screens: three of which show commodities and commoditized news, while a fourth is flickering with rapidly shifting images related to violence and war. There are quick headshots of Nixon and Kissinger and quick takes of images connected to the Israel–Palestine conflict. That fourth screen – which the family must experience obliquely, tacitly and in a state of positive distraction (inasmuch as it conflicts with the ordinary modes of image consumption) – undercuts the negative distraction of the commoditized world, which distracts a population from apprehending the violence within and on the margins of that world. The film thus shows the inhibition to the reality of violence that everyday media consumption entails, while at the same time demonstrating the positive distraction that cinema can enact as it assails and unsettles the viewer's precognitive awareness. In what follows, I turn to three texts in different genres – photography, cinema, and literature – all of which critically support Cindy Sheehan's above noted political gestures. They inter-articulate war and domestic space, a connection that tends to be conjured away in the discursive practices of defense and security policy (and in the writings of their intellectual agents in mainstream media and academia).

The war and the home 1: Martha Rosler's photomontage

In her "Bringing the War Home: House Beautiful" exhibition, Martha Rosler – a Dada-inspired artist, avowedly influenced by the juxtapositions in Godard's *Ici et Ailleurs* – creates photomontage images that articulate particularly well with Benjamin's and Kracauer's both negative and positive perspectives on distraction.[37] Her images include commodity-saturated domestic interiors in advertisements juxtaposed with violent moments in distant wars, which are brought into the worlds of domesticity. By themselves, the interiors speak to the distracting aspects of entertainment and commodities, the attractions of which distract the residents from the violence in various global venues because of the way they dominate the mediascape. As for the positive effect, through their "abutment of dissimilars," the juxtapositions of the commodity-saturated domestic interiors with war scenes (from the Vietnam War) have an unsettling effect that must engender reflection on the ways in which everyday domestic life is politically insulating. Rosler's images are the epitome of critical art because she distracts the viewer by creating a clash of heterogeneous elements. In a gloss on the politics of aesthetics that applies to Rosler's photomontages, Rancière puts it well: "The main procedure of political or critical art consists in setting out the encounter and possibly the clash of heterogeneous elements. The clash of these heterogeneous elements is supposed to provoke a break in our perception, to disclose some secret connection of things hidden behind the everyday reality."[38]

To offer some specifics: in one of Rosler's photomontages – which has an insertion of news photos of the war in Vietnam in advertising images of American interiors – people are seated in patio chairs in a comfortable home while viewing tanks and shanties. In another, a young Vietnamese woman is carrying a bleeding baby within a richly adorned American home (Figure 8.1a). And in this one (Figure 8.1b) – perhaps her most powerful set of juxtapositions – a couple is relaxing in their suburban home, while two very disparate kinds of images are inserted: a commercial for smart phones (using attractive models, seen in the foreground), and a war raging outside in the background. Although Rosler's photomontages operate under the rubric of "Bringing the War Home," the events to which they are addressed cannot be easily named. One analysis of photography-as-event asserts that "the very ... naming of the event gives it significance".[39] However, in the case of Rosler's photomontages, the possible namings are confounded because two kinds of event are inter-articulated. The photomontages combine the longer-term historical moment of the increasing commoditization of the home and the shorter historical moment of the Vietnam War. As a result, the juxtaposition of the dual events gives a surcharge to the kind of distraction the images evoke because they disturb the complacency one ordinarily achieves by consummating the significance of an experience by naming it. However, while Rosler's photomontage genre introduces a critical temporality

Figures 8.1a and b
Photomontages from Rosler's "Bringing the War Home"

that complicates the presence of war, the cinematic time images are even more able to situate presence critically. As Deleuze has shown, "avant-garde film [creates] ... an aesthetic encounter with duration that generates a complex web of shifting ideas about what constitutes the present."[40] Here I turn to one that does so as it explores the war–home relationship.

The war and the home 2: Paul Haggis's *In the Valley of Elah*

Like Rosler's photomontages, Haggis's film inserts the war into domestic space. While as shown above, in one of Rosler's photomontages (in Figure 8.1b), the smart phone is constructed as an attractive commodity (in the hands of attractive female models who are superimposed into a commodity-rich domestic interior, while outside the home we see a war unnoticed by the home's inhabitants), in *Elah*, the smart phone and web become the technologies that connect the war with the home. The film opens with recovered footage from the cell-phone camera of the young soldier Mike Deerfield (Jonathan Tucker) in combat in Iraq, shown while the credits are running. Once the film's narrative gets underway, the time is November 1, 2004, and the first scene opens in the Deerfield home, with Mike's father Hank (Tommy Lee Jones), sitting on a bed in his underwear as he takes a call informing him that his son – who had recently returned to his New Mexico base – is AWOL. Thereafter, email and phone technologies keep Mike close to the militarized home that his father has fashioned, while the home itself monumentalizes an earlier period – Mike's childhood, articulated through shots of the pictures and artifacts in his room.

After Hank takes the call from the base, the film's drama is launched: Hank hits the road, headed to the New Mexico base to investigate his son's disappearance. But the storyline – which follows twists and turns, as Hank, with the help of a local police detective, Emily Saunders (Charlize Theron), discovers that his son was murdered by his fellow soldiers – is less significant for purposes of this analysis than two separations that the film's images convey. One pertains to the household. The Deerfield home is spatially divided, as becomes evident once the scene in the couple's shared bedroom is followed by scenes in other rooms. Joan Deerfield's (Susan Sarandon) feminized kitchen – with its lace curtains and window-shelf potted plants (Figure 8.2) – contrasts sharply with Hank Deerfield's masculine study, with its metal bookshelf and desk and its plaques and regalia which testify to his career as a military police sergeant. However, the masculine, militarized inflections dominate the household. It's Hank's bodily comportment – as he prepares to drive to his son's (and his former) New Mexico base – that is at the center of the home's protocols. Although it is a comportment that carries in the present, it is evident that he acquired it earlier, during his military career.

At one point, when Joan stands holding a laundry basket while asking, "is there anything you want to tell me," (because she has not been a party to the communications about Mike's disappearance), her question goes unanswered, and her subsequent request to accompany Hank on the drive is rejected. Hank says that the last thing Mike needs is his mother walking in on one of his celebrations. And, as I have noted, Mike's room reflects his childhood. We see it

Figure 8.2
Joan Deerfield's kitchen

when Hank stops to get a recent photo of Mike to bring with him. It has bunk beds and the usual male sports logos and paraphernalia with photos of the two sons: one with a pre-adolescent Mike next to his older brother (who had died in combat) in uniform.

However, it is Hank Deerfield's body and his verbally expressed allegiance to military protocols that convey the ways in which the Deerfield home is militarized. And, as the film narrative progresses the primary separation in evidence is that between Hank's militarized bodily comportment and his face, which registers increasing sadness and perplexity (Figure 8.3). The camera observes that separation by closing in on the work of Hank's hands – as he packs his bag for the drive, creating a careful order in his suitcase, and as he subsequently prepares himself for the day in the motel near the base, buffing his shoes and setting them neatly beside the bed, making his bed with tight square corners, and washing and shaving in an orderly, ritualized set of movements – and by continually providing close-ups of his face, as he learns about the extent to which the young soldiers, his son included, deviate markedly from the military codes to which he is allegiant.

The extraordinary force of Hank's allegiance to those codes becomes evident not only because of the way his body mimes them but also because of the extent to which he resists the evidence that his son was murdered by his fellow soldiers, right up to the moment when one of them confesses to it. Hitherto, his absorption into the regulative ideals of the army he imagines and thinks he has experienced

Figure 8.3
Hank Deerfield

dominate his perceptions: "Anyone who has been in combat together is incapable of such a crime," he asserts when the police detective, Emily Sanders, supplies compelling evidence that Mike's army friends have killed him. And, in a flashback near the end of the film, he is shown rejecting his son's tearful and frantic request to help him get out of a war that has gone wrong. Hank blows him off with the remark, "That's just nerves talking."

Certainly, there is a psychiatric reading that is plausible, for the film shows how the traumatic effects of combat duty can produce young soldiers capable of sudden, seemingly inexplicable murderous violence against their intimates.[41] And an analysis that treats the way the film effectively impugns the myth of the warrior hero and substitutes flawed and damaged young men and women is also plausible.[42] For example, included in the film is a parallel story about a woman whose soldier/husband goes into a murderous rage and drowns the family dog in the bath tub and then – after her unheeded plea for help during an interview with the police detective, Emily Sanders – suffers the same fate as the dog. And a more general problem with the unheroic way "America" is at war is symbolized by scenes at the beginning and end of the film. As Hank heads out on his drive, he stops at a high school to correct the way the American flag is being flown. Hank informs the janitor, who has hung it upside-down, that he has produced what is known as an international distress signal and carefully runs it up the flag pole "correctly." At the end of the film, Hank goes back to the school, sends the flag up upside down, and tapes the ropes to the flagpole to render the distress signal permanent.

However, if we shift our focus to the household's gendered division, the film – with Joan Deerfield's body and words as assists – has something to tell us about the relationship between war and the home. While Hank is an aesthetic subject who combines his role as a father with his role as a military man, respecting the codes of the army throughout the film, his wife Joan is a mother who is trapped in a domestic space that she doesn't control and is ultimately deprived of her two sons by war. Once the parents learn that Mike has been murdered and Joan finally joins Hank at the base in order to view the body, Hank remains entrenched in his former role as a military investigator and treats the venues of the mutilated body as a source of clues while Joan experiences her son's body as something taken from her, something she can no longer see or touch. Not allowed to enter the room in the New Mexico army base where the body parts have been autopsied, she tentatively touches the glass window through which she has seen the remains. After having her request to go in the room denied, the blinds on the window are shut. Thus, the partitioning of the base functions the same way as the partitioning of her home – in both cases constituting the way the military inhibits her contact with her son. While ultimately for Hank, his son's death is a case of a war and its personnel that operate outside of the correct protocols, for Joan her son's death is a result of the way her militarized household left him no option other than to enlist. As she puts it, "Living in this house, he sure never could have felt like a man if he hadn't gone." And she identifies Hank's masculinized/militarized dominance in the home as the source of her losses: "Both of my boys Hank? You could have left me one."

Although Joan has never been able to influence her husband's masculinized models of male comportment and childrearing, his face does register a world in which strong women bear the burdens of war and crime fighting. When Hank first arrives in New Mexico, the first soldiers with whom he must deal to enter Mike's section of the base are women, and the camera lingers on his taking note of that. The local police department, where Emily Sanders's role as a detective is subject to male sexist harassment, is effectively a war zone for her. And after he enlists her assistance in the investigation, Hank's body increasingly registers acceptance of her strength and sagacity and a recognition (that the viewers must begin to share) that she must in effect conduct a war in order to do her job in venues that are male-dominated. The early camera shots in which Hank is shown rigidly facing Emily are gradually supplanted by more side-to-side shots.

Finally, the film subtly registers domestic "America" ("the home of the brave") as a war zone, past and present; for the film's various characters register America's coercive history. The janitor that Hank engages about managing the flying of the flag in the schoolyard on two occasions is a Latino; a bartender Hanks asks about the appearance of his son is a Native American; and one of the initial suspects in Mike's murder, whom Hank beats savagely, is a Mexican American, Robert Ortiez (Victor Wolf). After Hank learns about the actual perpetrators and goes to find Ortiez in order to apologize, Ortiez's first remark is, "Man, you have some serious issues" (Figure 8.4). Certainly Ortiez is correct about the way that Hank's perspective on the events of Mike's murder has been filtered by his "issues" (his blind allegiance to military protocols and his regulative ideals about how soldiers act). However, we can also take the "you" as a reference to a collective, Anglo American blindness, a failure to recognize that their America is a palimpsest. They live complacently and unapologetically in spaces that were acquired though the violent conquest of peoples whose contemporary purchase on those spaces amount to little more than place names.

Figure 8.4 Hank Deerfield and Ortiez

The war and the home 3: Annie Proulx's "Tits-Up in a Ditch"

> Making fictions does not mean telling stories. It means undoing and rearticulating the connections between signs and images, images and times, or signs and space that frame the existing sense of reality.
>
> Jacques Rancière

While Joan Deerfield in Haggis's *Elah* is merely excluded from influence in a patriarchal, militarized home, the protagonist in Annie Proulx's story – Dakotah Lister (who lacks her mother's beauty and sex appeal) – is a devalued ward of her grandparents, who were "stuck with her" when their daughter, Shaina, ran off with a boyfriend: "one of her greasy pals [who] picked her up and headed west for Los Angeles."[43] Dakotah's grandfather, Verl, rules a domestic space that is disparaged by his neighbors, who view him as a "trash rancher," incapable of running his property and livestock effectively. The world of the Listers is screened through their two metaphysical commitments – Jim Bakker's televangelism in the case of the grandmother, Bonita, and the vagaries of fortune, "luck," in the case of Grandfather Verl. While the divergence of their metaphysics creates some marital tension, the significance of their interpretive practices in the story is more important for the way it insulates Dakatoh from the realities of the global world of violence than for how it characterizes the interactions between husband and wife. And most significantly, Verl's version of luck sets up the symbolic montage that structures the story, which connects Verl's local luck with that experienced by Dakotah, after she leaves the household and ends up in Iraq.

After he loses a cow, a pronouncement of Verl's metaphysic supplies the story's title and theme: "Had me some luck today. Goddamn cow got herself tits-up in the ditch couple days ago. Dead time I found her."[44] When Bonita responds: "Not every man would say that is luck," Verl says. "It is, in a way of speakin." Verl's "way of speakin," which is seemingly merely a window into the local vernacular, has a larger significance in the story's gloss on the politics of the war–home relationship. While in the case of *Elah*'s Mike, his movement from the home to the war is largely determined by the home's absorption into a familial military tradition, in Dakotah's case, her movement from the home to the war results from the (bad) luck of a series of contingencies – a loveless home she is eager to escape, a pregnancy she has not planned, and the loss of a job as a result of the store management's unwillingness to continue employing a pregnant woman.

Briefly, because Verl and Bonita offer Dakotah neither affection nor encouragement of any kind (and burden her with endless chores), she accepts a marriage proposal in order to escape their home. But because her treatment by her husband, Sash Hicks, is no improvement on what she had experienced in her grandparents' home, she becomes assertive enough to provoke arguments that lead to a separation. Initially, she can afford the separation because her job has made her self-supporting. However, after her pregnancy and job loss, her grandfather encourages her to enlist – which she does, leaving Baby Verl with her grandparents. At the beginning of her army experience, she establishes her first close friendship. She and her friend Marnie, another female soldier, become military police together in Iraq, after they both fail their EMT training program. At this point, Dakotah has two strong attachments – Marnie and Baby Verl, with whom she stays in touch through the pictures sent by her grandparents. She imagines a future post-army duty living arrangement with both Marnie and her son. However "luck" intervenes. The Humvee in which Dakotah and Marnie are riding gets hit by an IED (improvised explosive device) that hurls their vehicle into a ditch, killing Marnie and maiming one of Dakotah's arms.

During her convalescence at a military hospital, Dakotah learns that her estranged husband, Sash, is there as well because he too has been a victim of an IED episode. Forced to visit him (because she remains listed as his spouse), she finds a body with missing legs, half a face, severe brain damage, and no awareness of who is talking to him. After her convalescence is complete and she returns home, hoping to retrieve her son, she learns that she has had more "luck." Grandfather Verl had let the toddler ride in the truck bed with the dogs. His truck hit a ditch, which bounced little Verl out of the truck and under the wheels, killing him. By the end of the story, Dakotah is back in the Lister household, where she is visited by Sash's parents, who want to learn something about his condition because they can't afford to travel to the hospital where he is vegetating, and the army won't divulge the details of his condition. At this point, the story ends with its title and thematic, which apply to both Sash and Dakotah:

> "Sash," she said at last so softly they could barely hear. "Sash is tits-up in a ditch." They sat frozen like people in the aftermath of an explosion, each silently calculating their survival chances in lives that must grind on. The air vibrated. At last Mrs. Hicks turned her red eyes on Dakotah. "you're his wife," she said. There was no answer to that and Dakotah felt her own hooves slip and the beginning descent into the dark, watery mud.[45]

Although Dakotah's unhappy experiences narrate a singular life, Proulx's story has significance well beyond the circumstances of Dakotah's "luck." The montage effects in the story – as the scene shifts back and forth between the war front and the home front – are like those in modern cinema, which, as Mary Ann Doane puts it, "endow[s] the singular with significance without relinquishing singularity."[46] If we heed Proulx's figuration at the very end of the story – which has the people assembled in the Lister living room, sitting "frozen like people in the aftermath of an explosion" – and note as well the story's other (and most pervasive) figuration, the "ditch," we can discern more than a mere expulsive force, operating to drive young people from the home to the war. We are invited into an *equivalence* in which the home and home front can be as damaging to lives as the war. Ditches abound, and "luck" is involved in who ends up in them.

Conclusion: at home, at war

My first experiences of war took place in my home, shortly after the end of World War II. A family friend, who participated as an infantry soldier in the famous "Battle of the Bulge" (one of the allies' famous last victories), showed up at my house with a shoulder holster and Colonel's hat he had taken from a German officer, who had surrendered at the end of the battle. Both turned out to be terrific props to use when I played childhood war games with the other children in my neighborhood. However, as objects they supplied little by way of testimony to the experiences of the war where they were used. Later, when in 1961 as a young adult I traveled in Europe for the first time, I was able to see that a war which had ended 16 years earlier was still very much visible in European cities. The cars in the Paris *Métro* had reserved seats with signs that read, *Reservé pour Mutilés de Guerre*. And on the UK highways, I saw many three-wheel automobiles that had been manufactured for disabled war veterans to drive. That part of the war initiated me into some of the ways in which it will-have-been. Because, at that time, television had yet to produce documentaries and features that treated the aftermath of war as it had been experienced in everyday life, where it had taken place, what I was able to see in Europe had not yet made it into my home.

Encouraged to analyze the blurred boundary between the war and home fronts after thinking critically about political topologies in response to my early experiences and, at the same time, wanting to interrogate Jean Baudrillard's (in)famous argument that the Gulf War didn't take place, I enacted an "interference" between theoretical and artistic texts in order to address the various ways that war is and will have been present in the home.[47] Certainly, Baudrillard's argument has to provoke reflection on the spatio-temporality of presence in general and specifically on the spatio-temporality of the presence of war. I came to appreciate that the home front is now more than ever connected to the war front, primarily because of contemporary media technologies – because of the documentary and fictional media that enter the home, because some "warriors" use satellite assisted media to fight remotely from their home, and because modern technologies bring the war home, sometimes instantaneously, as soldiers communicate with their families, even in the very moments when they are facing or deploying live fire.

However, rather than merely summarizing the trajectory of my analysis of the presence of war, as it comes from and to the home, I want to reflect on the methodology of this essay. One of the terms that is common to some of the theoretical and artistic works I treat is montage. As I noted, both Benjamin and Kracauer saw montage as the primary basis for cinema's critical capacity; the critical capacity of Rosler's photos to connect the war and the home inheres in their photomontage structures; and Godard's critical commentary on the war–home relationship in his film *Ici et Ailleurs* is also a function of his montage technique. It is also the case that Proulx's story employs a symbolic montage. But to show how the montage structure in "Tits-up in a Ditch" – as is the case with other montage instances – delivers political significance, I want to summon the concept of measure as it is elaborated by Rancière in a discussion of Godard's film *Histoire(s) du Cinema*. Attributing to Godard's film a symbolic montage effect, the creation of a "clash of heterogeneous elements that provides a common measure," Rancière points to the way the film creates an equivalence between "two captivations:"[48] that of the "German crowds by Nazi ideology" and that of the "film crowds by Hollywood."[49]

A common measure is also the result of the symbolic montage that Annie Proulx's "Tits-Up in a Ditch" effects. She creates equivalence between the damage that the war does to bodies and the damage wrought by the sexism and mean-spiritedness of the small Wyoming town. It is not simply the case that Dakotah's home expelled her in the direction of the war front. The home itself kills, demoralizes, and destroys bodies. Proulx's story, like Haggis's film, enlarges the spatio-temporality of war. Both texts disclose not only the way the home front delivers bodies to the war front but also the degree to which war takes place on the home front. They evince an equivalence that frames "war" within a critical politics of aesthetics inasmuch as they repartition the sense of war as they challenge the boundary between war and domesticity. That challenge is articulated as a displacement from the authoritative community of sense that shapes the familiar world of a warring state to a world that expresses another sensibility. The avatars of that world are the aesthetic subjects whose experiences disfigure authoritative subject models and create space for an alternative "community of sense."[50]

Notes

Preface

1 H. Garfinkel, *Studies in Ethnomethodology* (Cambridge, UK: Polity, 1984).
2 *Ibid.*, 11.
3 *Ibid.*, 16.
4 P. Roth, *The Humbling* (New York: Vintage, 2009), 14–15.
5 M. Foucault, "The Confession of the Flesh." A conversation in C. Gordon ed. *Power/ Knowledge: Selected Interviews and Other Writings 1972–1977* trans. C. Gordon, L. Marshall, J. Mepham and K. Soper (New York: Pantheon), 194.
6 The quotation is from J. Rancière's reading of the story in his *The Flesh of Words: The Politics of Writing* trans. C. Mandell (Stanford, CA: Stanford University Press, 2004), 146.
7 H. Garfinkel, *Studies in Ethnomethodology*, 1.
8 G. Deleuze, *Difference and Repetition* trans. P. Patton (New York: Columbia University Press, 1994), 133.
9 M. J. Shapiro, *Cinematic Political Thought* (New York: NYU Press, 1999), 22.
10 M. Blanchot, *The Space of Literature* trans. A. Smock (Lincoln: University of Nebraska Press, 1982), 3.
11 J. Rancière, *The Politics of Aesthetics* trans. G. Rockhill (New York: Continuum, 2004), 13.
12 *Ibid.*
13 M. Foucault, "What is Critique?" in *The Politics of Truth* trans. L. Hochroth and C. Porter (New York: Semiotext(e), 2007), 66.
14 M. J. Shapiro, *Cinematic Political Thought*, 7.
15 L. Althusser, *Philosophy of the Encounter: Later Writings, 1978–1987* trans. G. M. Goshgarian (New York: Verso, 2006), 163–207.
16 *Ibid.*, 167.
17 *Ibid.*, 174.
18 *Ibid.*
19 See M. J. Shapiro, *The Time of the City: Politics, Philosophy and Genre* (New York: Routledge, 2010), 109–17.
20 C. Fuentes, "Writing in Time," *Democracy* 2 (1962), 61.
21 *Ibid.*
22 *Ibid.*, 72
23 This characterization of Deleuze on events belongs to L. R. Bryant, "The Ethics of the Event," in N. Jun and D. W. Smith eds. *Deleuze and Ethics* (Edinburgh, UK: Edinburgh University Press, 2011), 34.
24 *Ibid.*, 37.
25 The quotation is from N. C. Johnson, "From Time Immemorial: Narratives of nationhood and the making of national space," in J. May and N. Thrift eds. *Timespace: Geographies of Temporality* (New York: Routledge, 2001), 89.

26 For a good discussion of Deleuze's Kantian inversion, see S. Shaviro, "The 'Wrenching Duality' of Aesthetics: Kant, Deleuze, and the Theory of the Sensible," on the web at: www.shaviro.com/Othertexts/SPEP.pdf.
27 G. Deleuze and F. Guattari, *What is Philosophy?* trans. H. Tomlinson and G. Burchell (New York: Columbia University Press, 1994), 153.
28 The quotations are from C. Colwell, "Deleuze and Foucault: Series, Event, Genealogy," *Theory & Event* 1: 2 (1997).
29 G. Deleuze, *The Logic of Sense* trans. M. Lester (New York: Columbia University Press: 1990), 161.
30 Deleuze and Guattari, *What is Philosophy?* 65–6.
31 G. Shteyngart, *Super Sad True Love Story* (New York: Random House, 2010).
32 *Ibid.*, 3.
33 *Ibid.*, 5.
34 *Ibid.*, 12.
35 For a treatment of this late antiquity mode of surveillance, see P. Brown, *The Making of Late Antiquity* (Cambridge, MA: Harvard University Press, 1993).
36 See P. Dick, *Do Androids Dream of Electric Sheep?* (New York: Del Ray, 1996). Ridley Scott's film version, *Blade Runner*, came out in 1982.
37 M. Foucault, *The History of Sexuality* trans. R. Hurley (New York: Random House, 1978), 25.
38 See M. Foucault, "Governmentality," in G. Burchell, C. Gordon, and P. Miller eds. *The Foucault Effect* (Chicago: University of Chicago Press, 1991), 87–104.
39 G. Shteyngart, *Super Sad True Love Story*, 329.

1 Philosophy, method, and the arts

1 Here I am influenced by Gilles Deleuze's succinct remarks about the philosophical world that Kantianism disturbed. See his lecture on Kant, 14/3/78. On the web at: http://www.webdeleuze.com/php/texte.php?cle=66&groupe=Kant&langue=2 (obtained 1/20/2010). Deleuze says, "with Kant a radically new understanding of the notion of phenomenon emerges. Namely that the phenomenon will no longer at all be appearance. The difference is fundamental, this idea alone was enough for philosophy to enter into a new element, which is to say I think that if there is a founder of phenomenology it is Kant ... The conceptual landscape has literally changed completely, the problem is absolutely no longer the same, the problem has become phenomenological. For the disjunctive couple appearance/essence, Kant will substitute the conjunctive couple, what appears/conditions of apparition. Everything is new in this."
2 *Ibid.*
3 S. Wolin, "Political Theory as a Vocation," *American Political Science Review* 63: 4 (Dec., 1969), 1062–82.
4 *Ibid.*, p. 1064.
5 See I. Kant, *The Critique of Pure Reason*. And for a discussion of the delicate balance between passivity and activity in the Kantian subject, see G. Deleuze, *Kant's Critical Philosophy* trans. H. Tomlinson and B. Habberjam (Minneapolis: University of Minnesota Press, 1984), pp. 14–15.
6 See I. Kant, *The Critique of Judgment,* trans. J. H. Bernard (Amherst, NY: Prometheus Books, 2000), 119. And see my discussion of Kant's struggle to hold onto his notion of subjective necessity in the face of the disconfirming implications he discovers in his "analytic of the sublime": M. J. Shapiro, *Cinematic Geopolitics* (London: Routledge, 2009), 94–9.
7 This example is drawn from my discussion of Panofsky in M. J. Shapiro, *Deforming American Political Thought: Ethnicity, Facticity and Genre* (Lexington: University Press of Kentucky, 2006), 108–9. The text I analyze is I. Panofsky, *Gothic Architecture and Scholasticism* (New York: Meridian, 1958).

8 M. Foucault, *Manet and the Object of Painting*, trans. M. Barr (London: Tate, 2009).

9 *Ibid.*, 32.

10 The quotation is from N. Bourriaud's introduction to Foucault's Manet lectures, "Michel Foucault: Manet and the Birth of the Viewer," in *Ibid.*, 16.

11 J. Crary, *Suspensions of Perception: Attention, Spectacle, and Modern Culture* (Cambridge, MA: MIT Press, 1999), 87.

12 C. Selltiz, M. Jahoda, M. Deutsch, S. Cook, *Research Methods in Social Relations* Revised edition (London: Methuen, 1965), 9.

13 See for example W. Phillips Shively's much-adopted, *The Craft of Political Research* 8th edition (Englewood Cliffs, NJ: Prentice Hall, 2010).

14 P. Gilroy, *Darker Than Blue: On the Moral Economies of Black Atlantic Culture* (Cambridge, MA; Harvard University Press, 2010), 27.

15 R. Crooks, "From the Far Side of the Urban Frontier: The Detective Fiction of Chester Himes and Walter Mosley," *College Literature* 22: 3 (October, 1995), 68.

16 M. Foucault, *The Archaeology of Knowledge,* trans. A. M. Sheridan-Smith (New York: Pantheon, 1972), 120.

17 M. DeLanda, *A New Philosophy of Society: Assemblage Theory and Social Complexity* (New York: Continuum, 2006), 3.

18 C. Woods, *Development Arrested: Race, Power, and the Blues in the Mississippi* (New York: Verso, 1998), 96–7.

19 *Ibid.*, 30.

20 *Ibid.*, 19.

21 *Ibid.*, 50.

22 See A. Gussow, *It Seems Like Murder Here* (Chicago: University of Chicago Press, 2002), 161.

23 See T. W. Adorno, E. Frenkel Brunswik, D. J. Levinson, D. J. and R. Nevitt Sanford, *The Authoritarian Personality* Parts One and Two (New York: John Wiley & Sons, 1964), H. J. Eysenck, *Psychology of Politics* (London: Routledge & Kegan Paul, 1954), and M. Rokeach, *The Open and the Closed Mind* (New York: Basic Books, 1973).

24 See M. J. Shapiro, "Introduction," in M. J. Shapiro and H. Alker eds. *Challenging Boundaries* (Minneapolis: University of Minnesota Press, 1996), xix.

25 A. Césaire, *Discourse on Colonialism*, trans. J. Pinkham (New York: Monthly Review Press, 1972), 14.

26 G. Deleuze and F. Guattari, *What is Philosophy?*, trans. H. Tomlinson and B. Habberjam (New York: Columbia University Press, 1994), 18.

27 M. Foucault, *The Use of Pleasure*, trans. R. Hurley (New York: Pantheon, 1985), 3.

28 *Ibid.*, 10.

29 *Ibid.*, 9.

30 M. Foucault, "Questions of Method," in G. Burchell, C. Gordon, and P. Miller eds. *The Foucault Effect* (London: Harvester/Wheatsheaf, 1991), 75.

31 M. Foucault, *Discipline and Punish: The Birth of the Prison*, trans. A. Sheridan (New York: Pantheon, 1977, 272.

32 One such privilege-affirming investigation belongs to J. Q. Wilson and R. Herrnstein *Crime and Human Nature* (New York, Simon & Schuster, 1985).

33 P. Gootenberg, "Talking about the Flow: Drugs, Borders, and the Discourse of Drug Control," *Cultural Critique* 71 (Winter, 2009), 14.

34 *Ibid.*, 15.

35 M. Foucault, "Intellectuals and Power," in D. F. Bouchard ed. *Language, Counter-Memory, Practice* (Ithaca, NY: Cornell University Press, 1977), 214.

36 I. Kant, "An Answer to the Question: What is Enlightenment (1784)." On the web at: http://www.english.upenn.edu/~mgamer/Etexts/kant.html.

37 M. Foucault, "What is Enlightenment?" trans. C. Porter in R, Rabinow and W. M. Sullivan eds, *Interpretive Social Science: A Second Look* (Berkeley: University of California Press, 1987), 167.

38 I am quoting here from another version of Foucault's essay, "What is Enlightenment?" in *The Politics of Truth* trans. L. Hochroth and C. Porter (New York: Semiotext(e), 2007), 113–14.

39 M. Foucault, "What is Critique?" in *The Politics of Truth*, 59.

40 M. Foucault, "What is Enlightenment?" in *The Politics of Truth*, 117.

41 M. Foucault, "The Subject and Power," in H. Dreyfus and P. Rabinow, *Michel Foucault: Beyond Structuralism and Hermeneutics* (Chicago: University of Chicago Press, 1982), 216.

42 F. Guattari, *Chaosmosis: An Ethico-Aesthetic Paradigm* (Bloomington: Indiana University Press, 1995), 13.

43 J. Rancière, "Aesthetic Separation, Aesthetic Community: Scenes from the Aesthetic Regime of Art," *Art & Research* 2: 1 (Summer 2008) on the web at: http://artandresearch.org.uk/v2n1/ranciere.html Obtained 8/30/2010.

44 For a critical treatment of this kind of psychologizing, see E. Herman, *The Romance of American Psychology* (Berkeley: University of California Press, 1995), 82–123.

45 See B. Lopez, *Arctic Dreams* (New York: Scribners, 1986), 201.

46 See M. J. Shapiro, *Reading the Postmodern Polity* (Minneapolis: University of Minnesota Press, 1992), 127.

47 *Ibid.*, 128.

48 E. Herman, *The Romance of American Psychology,* 235–6.

49 See *The Oak Ridge National Laboratory Review* (Vol 25, Nos 3 and 4) on the web at http://www.ornl.gov/info/ornlreview/rev25–34/net625.html (obtained 2//15/09).

50 D. B. Bobrow and A. R. Wilcox, "Dimensions of Defense Opinion: The American Public," *Papers of the Peace Research Society (International)*, Vol VI, (1966), 140.

51 *Ibid.*

52 The quotations are from M. J. Shapiro, *For Moral Ambiguity: National Culture and the Politics of the Family* (Minneapolis: University of Minnesota Press, 2001), 18.

53 See L. Bersani and U. Dutoit, *Forms of Being* (London: BFI, 2004), 21–2.

54 R. Nixon, "The Hidden Lives of Oil," *The Chronicle of Higher Education* April 5, 2002, B 7.

55 *Ibid.*, B 8.

56 A. Munif, *Cities of Salt* trans. P. Theroux (Boston: Cape Cod Scriveners, 1987), 85.

57 S. Lindqvist, *"Exterminate All the Brutes"* trans. J. Tate (New York: The New Press, 1992), 124.

58 *Ibid.*, 24–5.

59 *Ibid.*, ix.

60 The quoted expression is the title of a book by V. Y. Mudimbe, *The Invention of Africa: Gnosis, Philosophy and the Order of Knowledge* (Bloomington: Indiana University Press, 1988).

61 C. Young, *Ideology and Development in Africa* (New Haven, CT: Yale University Press, 1982), xiii.

62 A. Mbembe, *On the Postcolony* (Berkeley, CA: University of California Press, 2001), 3.

63 A. Mbembe, "African Self-Writing," *Public Culture* 14: 1 (Winter, 2002), 272.

64 I want to note however that there remain significant problems of "development" that should not be ignored. As James Ferguson points out, "For all their manifold failings, the developmental narratives that have long dominated Africa's place-in-the-world – narratives that explicitly rank the countries from high to low, from more to less 'developed' – do at least acknowledge (and promise to remedy) the grievances of political-economic inequality and low global status in relation to other places." And while he recognizes the ways in which the old narrative of political development only allows Africa a form of lack, "a culturized and relativized notion of modernity tends to allow the material and social inequalities that have long been at the heart of African aspirations to modernity drop out of the picture." See J. Ferguson, *Global Shadows* (Durham, NC: Duke University Press, 2006), 33–4.

65   A. Mbembe, *On the Postcolony*, 9.
66   The quotation is from C. Achebe, "The African Writer and the English Language," in R. Spillman ed. *Gods and Soldiers* (New York: Penguin, 2009), 12.
67   S. O. Opondo, "Genre and the African City: The Politics and Poetics of Urban Rhythms," *Journal for Cultural Research* 12: 1 (January, 2008), 66.
68   The concept of inbetweenness, developed by Homi Bhabha, construes the negotiation of cultural identity as a continuing exchange of cultural performances in a "liminal space" of "hybrid" identity formation. See H. Bhabha, *The Location of Culture* (New York: Routledge, 1994). The other quotations in the sentence are from Jorge Fernandes's analysis of Okri's novel: J. L. A. Fernandes, *Challenging Euro-America's Politics of Identity: The Return of the Native* (New York: Routledge, 2008), 134.
69   Fernandes, *Challenging Euro-America's Politics of Identity: The Return of the Native*, 135.
70   B. Okri quoted in O. Ogunsanwo, "Intertextuality and Post-Colonial Literature in Ben Okri's 'The Famished Road'," *Research in African Literatures* 26: 1 (Spring, 1995), 40.
71   The quotation is from S. K. Desai's reading of the novel: "The Theme of Childhood in Commonwealth Fiction," in C. D. Narasimjaiah ed. *Commonwealth Literature: Problems of Response* (Madras, India: Macmillan India, 1981), 45.
72   O. Ogunsanwo, "Intertextuality and Post-Colonial Literature," 43.
73   B. Okri, *The Famished Road* (New York: Doubleday, 1991), 307.
74   O. Ogunsanwo, "Intertextuality and Post-Colonial Literature," 42.
75   J. L. A. Fernandes, *Challenging Euro-America's Politics of Identity: The Return of the Native*, 135.
76   M. M. Bakhtin, "Author and Hero in Aesthetic Activity," in *Art and Answerability*, trans V. Liapunov (Austin: University of Texas Press, 1990), 13.
77   F. Fanon, *Black Skin, White Masks*, trans. R. Philcox (New York: Grove Press, 2008), 111.
78   *Ibid.*, 112.
79   K. Reeves, *Voting Hopes or Fears? White Voters, Black Candidates and Racial Politics in America* (New York: Oxford University Press, 1997).
80   *Ibid.*, 32.
81   H. Spillers, "Mama's Baby, Papa's Maybe: An American Grammar Book," *diacritics* 17 (1987), 66.
82   *Ibid.*
83   The expression belongs to R. D. G. Kelley, "How the West Was One; The African Diaspora and the Re-Mapping of U.S. History," in T. Bender ed. *Rethinking American History in a Global Age* (Ewing, NJ: University of California Press, 2002), 123.
84   R. Banks, *Continental Drift* (New York: Harper and Row, 1985), 64.
85   Ibid., 145.
86   See C. Joyce, "The Salon Interview: Russell Banks," on the web at: http://www.salon.com/books/int/1998/01/cov_si_05int3.html. Obtained 7/26/10.
87   See G. Lukács, *The Historical Novel* trans. H. Mitchell and S,. Mitchell (Lincoln: University of Nebraska Press, 1983), 35, for the phrase, historical-social type[s]. The other quotations, based on a methodological adaptation of Lukács's on the historical novel, are from M. O. Ortiz, *The Novel as Event* (Ann Arbor: University of Michigan Press, 2010), 29.
88   H. Kunzru, *The Impressionist* (New York: Plume, 2002), 181.
89   F. Kafka, "A Report to an Academy," in N. Glatzer ed. *The Complete Stories* (New York: Schocken, 1946), 258.
90   H. Kunzru, *The Impressionist*, 182.
91   *Ibid.*, 256.
92   *Ibid.*, 258.
93   See the interview with Hari Kunzu by Will Doig in *N'Nerve: Love.Sex.Culture.* On the web at: http://www.nerve.com/content/anti-matters.html. Obtained 7/26/10.
94   A. Garfinkel, *Forms of Explanation* (New Haven, CT: Yale University Press, 1981), 91.
95   *Ibid.*, 95.

96 *Ibid.*, 96.

97 The quotation is from an analysis of the Australian government's policy paper. See C. Tatz, "The Politics of Aboriginal Health," *Politics* (The Journal of the Australian Political Studies Association), 7: 2 (November, 1972), 3.

98 *Ibid.*, 8.

99 M. Foucault, *The History of Sexuality* Vol 1, trans. R. Hurley (New York: Pantheon, 1978), 25.

100 M. Foucault, *The Birth of the Clinic: An Archaeology of Medical Perception* trans. A. Sheridan (New York: Pantheon, 1973), 38.

101 *Ibid.*, 31.

102 *Ibid.*, 109.

103 M. Foucault, *Security, Territory, Population,* trans. G. Burchell (New York: Palgrave Macmillan, 2007), 75.

104 *Ibid.*, 76–7.

105 M. Foucault, "Questions of Method," in G. Burchell, C. Gordon and P. Miller, *The Foucault Effect* (Chicago: University of Chicago Press, 1991), 74.

106 The quotations are from C. Allen, *Art in Australia: From Colonization to Postmodernism* (London: Thames and Hudson, 1997), 12.

107 *Ibid.*, 68.

108 I have "spatial expression" in quotes because I have been edified by its use in Daniel Morgan's interpretation of Andre Bazin on Jean Renoir's film *Le Crime de Monsieur Lange* (1936): D. Morgan, "Rethinking Bazin: Ontology and Realist Aesthetics," *Critical Inquiry* 32, (2006), 460.

109 G. Deleuze, *Cinema 2: The Time Image* trans. H. Tomlinson and R. Galeta, (Minneapolis: University of Minnesota Press, 1989), 272.

110 See S. Kracauer, *Theory of Film: The Redemption of Physical Reality* (Princeton, NJ: Princeton University Press, 1960), 306.

111 See G. Deleuze, *Cinema 1: The Movement Image,* trans. H. Tomlinson and B. Habberjam (Minneapolis: University of Minnesota Press, 1986), 58 and 86.

112 The quotations are from D. Pye's reading of the film, *Lusty Men* (1952), in "Movies and Point of View," *Movie* 36, (2000), 27.

113 See M. M. Bakhtin, "Forms of Time and Chronotope in the Novel," in C. Emerson and M. Holquist, trans., *The Dialogic Imagination* (Austin: University of Texas Press, 1981), 243.

114 G. Deleuze, *Cinema 2*, 116.

115 C. Fuentes, "Writing in Time," 72.

116 See also Lobo Antunes earlier novel (first published in 1979) *The Land at the End of the World* trans. M. J. Costa (New York: W. W. Norton, 2011).

117 See G. J. Bender, *Angola under the Portuguese: The Myth and the Reality* (Berkeley: University of California Press, 1978), 226.

118 See R. Minder, "Portugal Turns to Former Colony for Growth," *New York Times* on the web at: http://www.nytimes.com/2010/07/14/business/global/14angolabiz. html?_r=1&scp=1&sq=portugal%20turns%20to%20former%20colony&st=cse. Obtained 7/15/10.

119 C. Casarino, "Philopoesis: A Theoretico-Methodological Manifesto," *boundary 2* (2002), 86.

120 *Ibid.*, 67. The internal quotations are from Deleuze and Guattari, *What is Philosophy?*

121 C. Casarino, *Modernity at Sea: Melville, Marx, Conrad in Crisis* (Minneapolis: University of Minnesota Press, 2002), xxv.

122 G. Deleuze, *Francis Bacon: The Logic of Sensation*, trans. D. W. Smith (Minneapolis: University of Minnesota Press, 2003), 71.

123 *Ibid.*, 71–2.

124 S. Bernardi, "Rossellini's Landscapes: Naure, Myth, History," in D. Forgacsm, S. Lutton and G. Nowell-Smith eds. *Roberto Rosselini: Magician of the Real* (London: BFI, 2001), 51.

125 See D. Sylvester, *The Brutality of Fact: Interviews with Francis Bacon* (New York: Thames and Hudson, 1981), 40.

126 M. Alzira Seixo, "Still Facts and Living Fictions: The Literary Work of Antonio Lobo Antunes, An Introduction," in V. K. Mendes ed. *Facts and Fictions of Antonio Lobo Antunes* (Dartmouth, MA: Tagus Press, 2011), 21.

127 The quotation is from R. Helgerson, *Forms of Nationhood* (Chicago: University of Chicago Press), 155.

128 A. Lobo Antunes, *The Return of the Caravels*, trans. G. Rabassa (New York: Grove Press, 2002), 4.

129 The quotations are from a novel: R. Powers *Generosity: An Enhancement* (New York: Farrar, Straus and Giroux, 2009), 168.

130 The quotation is from M. A. Seixo, "Rewriting the fiction of history: Camões's *The Lusiads* and Lobo Antunes's *The Return of the Caravels,*" *Journal of Romance Studies* 3: 3 (2003), 79. My discussion of Lobo Antunes's novels benefits greatly from Seixo's reading.

131 *Ibid.*, 77.

132 Lobo Antunes, *The Return of the Caravels*, 28–9.

133 See for example J. Rancière, *The Politics of Aesthetics* trans. G. Rockhill (New York: Continuum, 2004).

134 The quotation is from Davide Panagia's Rancière-inspired work on the politics of sensation; see D. Panagia, *The Political Life of Sensation* (Durham, NC: Duke University Press, 2009), 7.

135 W. Benjamin, "The Work of Art in the Age of Mechanical Reproduction," in H. Arendt ed. *Illuminations* (New York: Schocken, 1968), 217–52.

136 W. Benjamin, "Program of the Coming Philosophy," trans. M. Ritter in G. Smith ed. *Benjamin: Philosophy, History, Aesthetics* (Chicago: University of Chicago Press, 1989), 3.

137 For a thorough treatment of this aspect of Benjamin's revision of the Kantian model of experience, which explores the many texts within which the ideas are touched upon, see H. Caygill, *Walter Benjamin: The Colour of Experience* (New York: Routledge, 1998), 1–33.

138 See W. Benjamin, "On Perception Itself," in M. P. Bullock, M. W. Jennings, H. Eiland and G. Smith eds. *Selected Writings 1931–1934* (Cambridge, MA: Harvard University Press, 2005), 667. And for a perceptive reading of that aspect of Benjamin's neo-Kantian rendering of a philosophy of experience, see P. A. Quadrio, "Benjamin Contra Kant on Experience: Philosophizing beyond Philosophy," *philament.* On the web at: http://sudney.edu.au/arts/publications/philament/issue 1_PhilQuadrio.hmt. Obtained 8/8/2010.

139 R. Gasché, "Objective Diversions: On Some Kantian themes in Benjamin's 'The Work of Art in the Age of Mechanical Reproduction'," in A. Benjamin and P. Osborne eds. *Walter Benjamin's Philosophy: Destruction and Experience* (New York: Routledge, 1994), 195.

140 The quotation is from K. Arens, "*Stadtwollen*: Benjamin's *Arcades Project* and the Problem of Method," *PLMA* 122: 1 (January, 2007), 7.

141 W. Benjamin, *The Arcades Project* trans. H. Eiland and K. McLaughlin (Cambridge, MA; Harvard University Press, 199), 460.

142 *Ibid.*, 463.

143 *Ibid.*, 470.

144 *Ibid.*, 461.

145 The quotation is from H. U. Gumbrecht, *Making Sense in Life and Literature* trans. G. Burns (Minneapolis: University of Minnesota Press, 1992), 12.

146 D. Wellbery, "Introduction," to Friedrich Kittler, *Discourse Networks 1800/1900* (Stanford, CA: Stanford University Press, 1990), ix.

147 *Ibid.*, 12.

148 The phrase, "the production of presence," is taken from H. U. Gumbrecht's post-hermeneutic approach in his *The Production of Presence* (Stanford, CA: Stanford University Press, 2004).

149 See for example Terry Eagleton's discussion of the historical origin of aesthetics: T. Eagleton, *Ideology of the Aesthetic ,* (Cambridge, MA: Basil Blackwell, 1990), 13.

150 J. Rancière, "The Sublime from Lyotard to Schiller," *Radical Philosophy* 126 (July/August, 2004), 9.

151 The quotation is from J. Rancière, "Thinking between disciplines: an aesthetics of knowledge," *Parrhesia* No. 1 (2006), 1.

152 G. Deleuze, *Difference and Repetition* trans. P. Patton (New York: Columbia University Press, 1994), 139.

153 J. Rancière "The Politics of Aesthetics" at http://theater.kein.org/node/99 (Obtained 5/18/05).

154 The quotation on politics as re-partitioning is from J. Rancière, "The Thinking of Dissensus, politics and aesthetics," A paper presented at the conference 'Fidelity to the Disagreement: Jacques Rancière and the Politics, Goldsmith College, London, 16–17 September 2003.

155 J. Rancière, "The Politics of Aesthetics."

156 J. Rancière, "Aesthetic Separation, Aesthetic Community: Scenes from the Aesthetic Regime of Art," *Art & Research: A Journal of Ideas, Contexts and Methods* (Summer, 2008) On the web at: http://www.artandresearch.org.uk/v2n1/ranciere. hmtl. Obtained 8/16/2010.

157 W. Benjamin, *The Arcades Project*, 460.

158 J. Rancière, "The Politics of Aesthetics."

159 See the interview with Rancière in *Art & Research* 2 (2008), on the web at http://www,artandresearch.org.uk/v2n1jrinterview.html. Obtained 6/23/2009.

160 C. Casarino, "Philopoesis: A Theoretico-Methodological Manifesto," *boundary 2* (2002), 73. The quotation from Deleuze is from G. Deleuze, *Foucault*, trans. S. Hand (Minneapolis: University of Minnesota Press, 1988), 86.

2 The moralized economy in hard times

1 For an extended treatment of automobility, a term initiated by James Flink, who referred to it as a complex that included the vehicle, the industry, the road or highway, and the emotional significance it has for Americans, see C. Seiler, *Republic of Drivers: A Cultural History of Automobility in America* (Chicago: University of Chicago Press, 2008).

2 L. Birken, *Consuming Desire* (Ithaca, NY: Cornell University Press, 1988), 28–9.

3 The expression, "land of desire" comes from William Leach's study of the development of the American department store in the twentieth century, with a focus on Wannamaker's in Philadelphia: W. Leach, *Land of Desire: Merchants, Power, and the Rise of a New American Culture* (New York: Pantheon, 1993).

4 F. Braudel, *The Wheels of Commerce: Civilization and Capitalism, 15th –18th Century* Vol 2 (New York: Harper & Row, 1982).

5 The concept of "sign function value" is developed by Jean Baudrillard: J. Baudrillard, "Sign Function and Class Logic," in *For a Critique of the Political Economy of the Sign* trans. C. Levin (St Louis, MO: Telos Press, 1981), 29–62.

6 The quoted expression is from I. Kopytoff, "The Cultural Biography of Things: Commoditization as Process" in A. Appadurai, ed. *The Social Life of Things* (New York: Cambridge University Press, 1986), 89.

7 *Ibid.*, 89–90.

8 The quotation is from D. Dudley, "The Vanishing Mercury Class," *New York Times*, Week in Review, (June 13, 2010), 12.

9 The expression "color-line century" is in P. Gilroy, *Darker Than Blue: On the Moral Economies of Black Atlantic Culture* (Cambridge, MA; Harvard University Press, 2010), 27.

10 J. Crary, *Techniques of the Observer* (Cambridge, MA: MIT Press, 1991), 10.
11 See P. J. Deloria, *Indians in Unexpected Places* (Lawrence: University of Kansas Press, 2006).
12 For a treatment of the role of the automobile in women's liberation, see Seiler, *Republic of Drivers*, 50–60.
13 P. Gilroy, *Darker Than Blue*, 13.
14 Of course that process was anything but smooth. The drama that Doctorow stages in his novel *Ragtime* features racist reactions to the African American, Coalhouse Walker Jr.'s owning of a Model T, which begins when the father of the family where Walker comes in his car to visit the mother of his child, Sarah, who is employed in the house, thinks that Walker's confident car ownership implies that he is stepping out of his identity, that he "didn't know he was a Negro": E. L. Doctorow, *Ragtime*. (New York: Random House, 1975), 185.
15 See M. S. Moore, *Yankee Blues: Musical Culture and American Identity*. (Bloomington: Indiana University Press, 1985).
16 R. Peterson, *Creating Country Music: Fabricating Authenticity* (Chicago: University of Chicago Press, 1997), 60.
17 The quotations are from A. Kempton, *Boogaloo* (New York: Pantheon, 2003), 17.
18 *Ibid.*, 166.
19 P. Gilroy, *Darker Than Blue*, 15.
20 *Ibid.*
21 *Ibid.*
22 B. C. Snell, "American Ground Transportation: A Proposal for Restructuring the Automobile, Truck, Bus & Rail Industries" (The Original 1974 U.S. Government Report) on the web at: http://www.worldcarfree.net/resources/freesources/American.htm. Obtained 4/30/2010.
23 The quotation is from an analysis of Snell's "American Ground Transportation" report. See "The Third Rail," online at: http://thethridrail.net/9905/agt3.htm. Obtained 5/7/2010.
24 The expression "radical monopoly" belongs to Ivan Illich, who laments the way that the monopolization of traffic and the domination of the landscape by a motorscape has compromised what he calls conviviality, "autonomous and creative intercourse among persons": I. Illich, *Tools for Conviviality* (New York: Harper & Row, 1973), 11.
25 The quotations are from R. Everman and O. Lofgren, "Romancing the Road: Road Movies and Images of Mobility," *Theory, Culture and Society* 12 (1995), 59.
26 J. Bonham, "Transport: Disciplining the Body that Travels," in S. Bohm *et al.* eds. *Against Automobility* (Malden, MA: Blackwell, 2006), 59.
27 *Ibid.*, 58.
28 See R. Brandon, *Auto Mobile* (London: Macmillan, 2002), 130–1.
29 *Ibid.*, 70.
30 See D. H. Lumley, *Breaking the Banks in Motor City* (Jefferson, NC: McFarland & Co, 2009), 38.
31 C. Dickens, *Hard Times* (New York: Barnes & Noble Classics, 2004 [originally published in 1854]).
32 See *International Herald Tribune* (June 3, 2010), 3.
33 The quotation is from the *New York Times* on the web: http://www.nytimes.com/2010/04/28/business/28goldman.html?scp=2&sq=goldman&st=cse. Obtained 4/28/10.
34 *Ibid.*
35 G. W. F. Hegel, *Natural Law* trans. T. M. Knox. (Philadelphia: University of Pennsylvania Press, 1975).
36 I. Kopytoff, "The Cultural Biography of Things ," 64.
37 J. O. Appleby, *Economic Thought and Ideology in Seventeenth-Century England* (Princeton, NJ: Princeton University Press, 1978), 52.

38 *Ibid.*, 56.
39 *Ibid.*, 71.
40 *Ibid.*, 245.
41 *Ibid.*, 279.
42 See S. Maza, "Only Connect: Family Values in the Age of Sentiment," *Eighteenth Century Studies* 30 (1997), 207–12.
43 The quotation is from M. J. Shapiro, *For Moral Ambiguity: National Culture and the Politics of the Family* (Minneapolis: University of Minnesota Press, 2001), 35.
44 The quotation is from E. T. Bannet, "The Marriage Act of 1753: 'A Most Cruel Law for the Fair Sex'," *Eighteenth Century Studies* 30 (1997), 240.
45 See G. Simmel, "Money in Modern Culture," *Theory, Culture & Society* 8 (1991), 18.
46 J. Urry, "Inhabiting the Car," in E. R. Larreta, ed. *Collective Imagination and Beyond* (Rio de Janeiro: UNESCO.ISSC.EDUCAM, 2001), 279.
47 *Ibid.*, 291.
48 J. Eugenides, *Middlesex* (New York: Picador, 2002), 158–9.
49 J. G. Ballard, *Crash* (New York: Picador, 1973), 78.
50 *Ibid.*, 134.
51 *Ibid.*, 45.
52 See A. R. Stone, "Split Subjects, Not Atoms; or, How I Fell in Love with My Prosthesis," *Configurations* 2 (1994), 178.
53 See M. Selzer, *Bodies and Machines* (New York: Routledge. 1992), 6.
54 Stone, "Split Subjects, Not Atoms; or, How I Fell in Love with My Prosthesis," 183.
55 H. Brown, "The Status of the Automobile," *Yale Law Journal* 17 (1908), 14.
56 The quotation is from C. Seiler, *Republic of Drivers*, 37.
57 H. Adams, *The Education of Henry Adams* (Boston: Houghton Mifflin, 1961), 380.
58 Urry, "Inhabiting the Car," 282–3.
59 *Ibid.*, 291.
60 *Ibid.*, 279.
61 C. Ware, "Frank King's *Gasoline Alley*," in H. Katz ed. *Cartoon America* (New York: Abrams, 2006), 162.
62 The quoted expression is from D. Markstein, "Toonopedia: Gasoline Alley," on the web at: http://www.toonopedia.com/gasalley.htm . Obtained 4/12/2010.
63 F. O. King, *Walt & Skeezix 1921 & 1922* (Montreal: Drawn and Quarterly Books, 2005).
64 See R. Denney, *The Astonished Muse* (Chicago: University of Chicago Press, 1957), 142. In effect, Denney's observation, which refers to *Gasoline Alley*'s witnessing of change in the culture of automobility, anticipates Pierre Bourdieu's conception of "distinction." Denney's concept of "marginal differentiation" applied to the way autos were differentiated to serve as identity markers for "particular leisure interest groups," is very much like Bourdieu's insight about the way commodities are located in a social logic of class distinction: P. Bourdieu, *Distinction: A Social Critique of the Judgment of Taste* (London: Routledge Classics, 2010).
65 J. Updike, *Rabbit is Rich* (New York, Alfred A. Knopf, 1981), 34.
66 The term "dromocracy" belongs to P. Virilio, *Speed and Politics,* trans. M. Polizzotti (New York: Semiotext(e), 1986).
67 J. Updike, *Rabbit is Rich*, 3.
68 *Ibid.*, 15–16.
69 J. Updike, *Rabbit at Rest* (New York: Ballantine, 1996), 28.
70 The quoted expression is from D. Brooks, "Bailout to nowhere," an op-ed in the *New York Times*. On the web at: http://www.nytimes.com/2008/11/14opinion/14brooks. html. Obtained 5/22/10.
71 The quotation is from A. Abdel-Sahed, "Unnecessary Moral Hazards: The Auto Bailout," in *Islamic Insights* on the web at: http://www.islamicinsights.com.news/ opinion/unnecessary-moral-hazards-the-auto-bailout.htm. Obtained 5/22/10.

72 The quotation is from E. Weber, "Ethics and the Economy: The Moral Implications of an Auto Industry Bailout," *EverydayEthics* on the web at: http://everyday-ethics-org/2008/12/ethics-and-the-economy-the-moral-implications-of-an-auto-industry-bailout.htm. Obtained 5/22/10.

73 P. Johnson, "*Hard Times* and the Structure of Industrialism: The Novel as Factory," *Studies in the Novel* 21 (1989), 130.

74 C. Dickens, *Hard Times*, 1.

75 Dickens's approach thus contrasts interestingly with Marx's. Whereas Marx shows the ways in which the working body is sequestered within the thing (e.g., factory machines as congealed labor), Dickens reverses the relationship and shows the thing in the working body.

76 J. Bennett, *Empathic Vision: Affect, Trauma, and Contemporary Art* (Stanford, CA: Stanford University Press, 2004).

77 The quotation is from G. Deleuze, *Spinoza: Practical Philosophy* trans. R. Hurley, (San Francisco: City Lights), 23.

78 See G. Deleuze, *Cinema 1: The Movement Image* trans. H. Tomlinson and B. Habberjam (Minneapolis: University of Minnesota Press, 1986), 58 and 86.

79 G. Deleuze, *Cinema 2: The Time Image* trans. H. Tomlinson and R. Galeta (Minneapolis: University of Minnesota Press, 1989), 280.

80 *Ibid.*

81 Nigel Reynolds quoted in M. Barker, J. Arthurs and R. Harindranath, *The Crash Controversy: Censorship Campaigns and Film Reception* (London: Wallflower Press, 2001), 16.

82 See for example T. Harpold, "Dry Leatherette: Cronenberg's *Crash*," *Postmodern Culture* 7 (1997). On the web: muse.jhu.edu/journals/postmodern_culture/v007/7.3r_harpold.html

83 L. Kristensen, reviewing *Friend of the Deceased* in *KinoKultura* online at: http://www.kinoKultura.com/specials/9/friendofdeceased.shtml obtained 6/10/2010.

84 J. Rancière, *The Politics of Aesthetics* trans. G. Rockhill (London: Continuum, 2004), 21.

85 See G. Deleuze and F. Guattari, *What is Philosophy?* trans. H. Tomlinson and G. Burchell (New York: Columbia University Press, 2004), 2.

86 The study is reported in the *British Medical Journal*. Online at http://bmj.bmjjournals.com/cgi/content/extract/319/7208/468/a?ck=nck. Obtained 6/10/2010.

87 The quotation is from L. Berlant, "Intimacy: A Special Issue," *Critical Inquiry* 24 (1998),

88 J. Derrida, *Politics of Friendship* trans. G. Collins (London: Verso, 1997), 19.

3 The blues subject

1 R. D. G. Kelley, "Check the Technique: Black Urban Culture and the Predicament of Social Science" in N. B. Dirks, ed. *In Near Ruins* (Minneapolis: University of Minnesota Press), 47.

2 *Ibid.*, 46.

3 J. Merod, "Singing in the Shower: Ralph Ellison and the Blues," *La Folia* online at: http://www.lafolia.com/archive/merod200204ellison.html. Obyaine 6/20/2010.

4 A. Gussow, *It Seems Like Murder Here* (Chicago: University of Chicago Press, 2002), 161.

5 P. Gilroy, *Darker Than Blue*, 27.

6 R. Crooks, "From the Far Side of the Urban Frontier: The Detective Fiction of Chester Himes and Walter Mosley," *College Literature* 22 (1995), 68.

7 See M. S. Moore, *Yankee Blues: Musical Culture and American Identity* (Bloomington: Indiana University Press, 1985).

8 For the development of the term "ethnogenesis," see W. Boelhower, *Through a Glass Darkly: Ethnic Semiosis and American Literature* (New York: Oxford University Press, 1986).

9　J. Burr, "Notes" in *Copland Connotations: Studies and Interviews (review)* 60 (2002), 27.

10　A. Baraka, *Blues People: Negro Music in White America* (New York: Harper, 1999).

11　C. Woods, *Development Arrested: Race, Power and the Blues in the Mississippi Delta* (New York: Verso, 1998).

12　*Ibid.*, 30.

13　A. Murray, *The Hero and the Blues* (New York: Vintage, 1996).

14　J. E. Wideman, *Brothers and Keepers* (Boston: Houghton Mifflin, 2005), 28–9.

15　R. Ellison, "An Extravagance of Laughter," in *Going to the Territory* (New York: Vintage, 1986), 148.

16　*Ibid.*, 160.

17　*Ibid.*, 161.

18　B. B. King, *Blues All Around Me* (New York: Avon, 1996), 66.

19　*Ibid.*, 127.

20　R. Ellison, "Richard Wright's Blues," *Antioch Review* 50 (1992), 62.

21　M. E. Mengeling, "Whitman and Ellison: Older Symbols in a Modern Mainstream," in J. F. Trimmer ed. *A Casebook on Ralph Ellison's* Invisible Man, (New York: Thomas Crowell, 1972), 269.

22　*Ibid.*, 270.

23　*Ibid.*

24　R. Ellison, *Invisible Man* (New York: Vintage, 1980), 119.

25　*Ibid.*, 116.

26　H. A. Baker, Jr. "Figurations for a New American Literary History," in S. Berkovitch and M. Jehlen eds. *Ideology and Classic American Literature* (New York: Cambridge University Press, 1986), 33–6.

27　G. Deleuze and F. Guattari, *Kafka: Toward a Minor Literature* trans. D. Polan (Minneapolis: University of Minnesota Press, 1986).

28　A. Hwang, "What is a Minor Literature," *Immanent Terrain* on the web at: http://immanentterrain.wordpress.com/2011/04/26/what-is-a-minor-literature–3/ Obtained 6/13/2011.

29　*Ibid.*

30　W. Mosley, *Devil in a Blue Dress* (New York: Washington Square Press, 1990), 45.

31　R. Chandler, *Farewell My Lovely* (New York: Vintage, 1992).

32　W. Mosley, *Devil in a Blue Dress*, 63.

33　S. F. Soitos, *The Blues Detective* (Amherst, MA: University of Massachusetts Press, 1996), 3.

34　H. A. Baker, Jr. "Figurations for a New American Literary History," 160.

35　*Ibid.*

37　J. L. A. Fernandes, *Challenging Euro-America's Politics of Identity: The Return of the Native*, 119.

37　E. Lott, "Love and Theft: The Racial Unconscious of Blackface Minstrelsy," *Representations* 39 (1992), 27.

38　*Ibid.*, 120–1.

39　Mosley, *Devil in a Blue* Dress, 263.

40　L. Bersani and U. Dutoit, *Forms of Being*, 6.

41　The quotation is from the book jacket of W. Mosley, *RL's Dream* (New York: W. W. Norton, 1992).

42　*Ibid.*, 99–100.

43　*Ibid.*, 143–4.

44　*Ibid.*, 130.

45　*Ibid.*, 131.

46　B. L. Pearson, and B. McCulloch, *Robert Johnson* (Urbana: University of Illinois Press, 2003), 46.

47　Mosley, *RL's Dream*, 143.

48 C. Levecq, "Blues Poetics and Blues Politics in Walter Mosley's *RL's Dream*," *African American Review* 38(2) (2004), 251.
49 S. Alexie, *Reservation Blues* (New York: Warner Books, 1996).
50 *Ibid.*, 174.
51 J. Troutman, *Indian Blues: American Indians and the Politics of Music 1879–1934* (Norman: University of Oklahoma Press, 2009), 206.
52 M. J. Shapiro, *Deforming American Political Thought: Ethnicity, Facticity, and Genre* (Lexington: University Press of Kentucky, 2006), 156.
53 T. Morrison, "Unspeakable Things Unspoken: The Afro-American Presence in American Literature," *Michigan Quarterly Review*, 28 (1989): 150.
54 C. Moses, "The Blues Aesthetic in Toni Morrison's *The Bluest Eye*," *African American Review* 33 (1999), 623.
55 T. Leclair, "'The Language Must Not Sweat': A Conversation with Toni Morrison," in H. L. Gates, Jr., and K. A. Appiah, *Toni Morrison: Critical Perspectives Past and Present* (New York: Amistad, 1993), 371.
56 C. Moses, "The Blues Aesthetic in Toni Morrison's *The Bluest Eye*," 630.
57 T. Morrison, *The Bluest Eye* (New York: Vintage, 1970), 26.
58 *Ibid.*, 58.
59 T. Morrison, "Unspeakable Things Unspoken," 147.
60 *Ibid.*, 150.
61 T. Leclair, "The Language Must Not Sweat," 373.
62 R. G. O'Meally, *Living with Music: Ralph Ellison's Jazz Writings* (New York: Modern Library, 2002), xxxii.
63 D. B. Gibson, 1993. "Text and Countertext in *The Bluest Eye*" in Gates, Jr. and Appiah, *Toni Morrison: Critical Perspectives Past and Present*, 159–160.
64 C. Moses, "The Blues Aesthetic in Toni Morrison's *The Bluest Eye*."
65 *Ibid.*
66 P.G. Eckard, "The Interplay of Music, Language, and Narrative in Toni Morrison's *Jazz*," *CLA Journal* 38 (1994), 11.
67 *Ibid.*, 13.
68 See M. M. Bakhtin, "Discourse and the Novel," trans. C. Emerson in M. Holquist ed. *The Dialogic Imagination* (Austin: University of Texas Press, 1981), 259–422.
69 T. Morrison, *Jazz* (New York: Alfred A, Knopf, 1992), 45.
70 H. L. Gates, Jr., "Jazz," in Gates, Jr. and Appiah, *Toni Morrison: Critical Perspectives Past and Present*, 53–4.
71 T. Morrison, *Jazz*, 3.
72 L. Hughes, *The Collected Poems of Langston Hughes* ed. A. Rampersad, (New York: Vintage, 1994), 50.
73 R. Rubenstein, "Singing the Blues / Reclaiming Jazz: Toni Morrison and Cultural Mourning," *Mosaic* 31 (1998), 149.
74 T. Morrison, *Jazz*, 33.
75 *Ibid.*, 50–1.
76 A. Amin and N. Thrift, *Cities: Reimagining the Urban* (Malden, MA: Polity Press, 2002), 31.
77 T. Morrison, *Jazz,* 120.
78 A-M Paquet-Deyris, "Toni Morrison's Jazz and the City," *African American Review* 35 (2001), 223.
79 P. Gilroy, *Darker Than Blue*, 55.
80 *Ibid.*, 57.
81 *Ibid.*, 59.
82 L. Bunch, III and S. R. Crew, "A Historian's Eye: Jacob Lawrence, Historical Reality and the Migration Series," in E. H. Turner, ed. *Jacob Lawrence: The Migration Series* (Washington D.C.: The Rappahannack Press, 1993), 25–6.
83 R. Ellison, "An Extravagance of Laughter," 148.
84 Morrison, *Jazz*, 9.

85 *Ibid.*, 54.
86 H. Lefebvre, "The Right to the City," in E. Kofman and E. Lebas eds and trans. *Writings on Cities: Henri Lefebvre* (New York: Wiley-Blackwell, 1996), 158.
87 *Ibid.*, 154.
88 A.-M. Paquet-Deyris, "Toni Morrison's Jazz and the City," 228.
89 *Ibid.*, 221.
90 R. Rubenstein, "Singing the Blues / Reclaiming Jazz," 289.
91 A. Carabi, "Interview with Toni Morrison." *Belles Lettres* 10 (1995), 41.
92 H. G. Cohen, "Duke Ellington and *Black, Brown and Beige*," *American Quarterly* 56 (2004), 2006.
93 A. Murray, *Stomping the Blues* (New York: McGraw-Hill, 1976).
94 A. Murray, *The Hero and the Blues,* 19.
95 A. Murray, *The Blue Devils of Nada: A Contemporary American Approach to Aesthetic Statement* (New York: Vintage, 1997), 15.
96 M. Peress, *Dvorak to Duke Ellington: A Conductor Explores America's Music* (New York: Oxford University Press, 2004), 186.
97 *Ibid.*, 188.
98 D. Ellington, "Interview in Los Angeles: On *Jump for Joy*, Opera and Dissonance," in M. Tucker, ed. *The Duke Ellington Reader* (New York: Oxford University Press, 1995), 151.
99 *Ibid.*, 150.

4 Zones of justice

1   M. Énard, *Zone*, trans. C. Mandell (Rochester, NY: Open Letter, 2010), 145.
2   *Ibid.*, 72–3.
3   M. Foucault, "The Confession of the Flesh, A Conversation" in C. Gordon ed. *Power/Knowledge* (New York: Pantheon, 1980), 194.
4   G. Deleuze and F. Guattari, *What is Philosophy?*, 21.
5   F. Moretti, *Atlas of the European Novel: 1800–1900* (London: Verso, 1998), 22.
6   C. Casarino, "Philopoesis: A Methodological Manifesto," 86.
7   *Ibid.*, 67.
8   G. Deleuze, *Cinema 2: The Time Image*, 280.
9   C. Casarino, *Modernity at Sea*, xxii.
10 G. Deleuze and F. Guattari, *What is Philosophy?*, 19.
11 C. Casarino, "Philopoesis: A Methodological Manifesto," 86.
12 *Ibid.*, 79.
13 C. Malabou, *Plasticity at the Dusk of Writing,* trans. C. Shread (New York: Columbia University Press, 2010), 2.
14 M. M. Bakhtin, "Author and Hero in Aesthetic Activity," in *Art and Answerability* (Austin: University of Texas Press, 1986), 13.
15 C. Malabou, *Plasticity at the Dusk of Writing*, 14.
16 *Ibid.*, 33.
17 *Ibid.*, 3.
18 C. Malabou, *Counterpath: Traveling with Jacques Derrida* trans. D. Wills (Stanford, CA.: Stanford University Press, 2004), 186.
19 *Ibid.*, 5.
20 C. Malabou, *What Should We Do with Our Brain?* trans. M. Jeannerod (New York: Fordham University Press, 2008), 80.
21 *Ibid.*, 81.
22 M. M. Bakhtin, "Epic and Novel," in *The Dialogic Imagination*, 39.
23 *Ibid.*
24 M. M. Bakhtin, "The *Bildungsroman* and Its Significance in the History of Realism (Toward a Historical Typology of the Novel)," in *Speech Genres and Other Late Essays* trans. V. W. McGee (Austin: University of Texas Press, 1986), 10.

25   *Ibid.*, 23.
26   C. Malabou, *Counterpath*, 16.
27   G. Deleuze and F. Guattari, *What is Philosophy?*, 61–83.
28   M. J. Shapiro, *The Time of the City: Politics, Philosophy and Genre* (London: Routledge, 2010), 7.
29   G. Deleuze and F. Guattari, *What is Philosophy?*, 65.
30   J. Rancière, "Afterword," in G. Rockhill and P. Watts, eds. *Jacques Rancière* (Durham, NC: Duke University Press, 2009), 278–9.
31   C. Malabou, *Plasticity at the Dusk of Writing*.
32   M. M. Bakhtin.
33   M. Énard, *Zone*.
34   B. Everson, "Introduction," to *Zone*, ix.
35   M. M. Bakhtin, "Epic and Novel," 3.
36   *Ibid.*, 5.
37   M. Énard, *Zone*, 251.
38   Malabou, *Counterpath*, 4.
39   *Ibid.*, 6.
40   S. Tsirkas, *Drifting Cities*, trans. K. Cicellis (New York: Knopf, 1974).
41   M. Énard, *Zone*, 104–5.
42   *Ibid.*, 212.
43   *Ibid.*, 207.
44   The quotations are from A. de Lange, "'Reading' and 'Constructing' Space, Gender and Race: Joseph Conrad's *Lord Jim* and J. M. Coetzee's *Foe*", in A. de Lange *et al.* eds. *Literary Landscapes* (London: Palgrave MacMillan, 2008), 113.
45   M. M. Bakhtin, "The *Bildungsroman* and Its Significance in the History of Realism," 23.
46   M. Énard, *Zone*, 21–2.
47   *Ibid.*, 23.
48   A. Mbembe, "Necropolitics," *Public Culture* 15 (2003), 33.
49   M. Énard, *Zone*, 174–5.
50   S. O'Sullivan, *Art Encounters: Deleuze and Guattari* (New York: Palgrave Macmillan, 2006), 50.
51   R. H. Brown and B. Davis-Brown, "The making of Memory: The Politics of Archives, Libraries and Museums," *History of the Human Sciences* 11 (1998), 17.
52   M. Foucault, *The Archaeology of Knowledge*, 129.
53   M. Énard, *Zone*, 127.
54   S. Lindqvist, "*Exterminate All the Brutes*," trans. J. Tate (New York: The New Press, 1992).
55   M. Énard, *Zone*, 150.
56   *Ibid.*, 75.
57   V. Harris, *Archives and Justice: A South African Perspective* (Chicago: SAA. 2007), 5.
58   J. Derrida, *Archive Fever*, trans. E. Prenowitz (Chicago: University of Chicago Press, 1996), 15.
59   W. Hamacher, "Guilt History: Benjamin's Sketch 'Capitalism as Religion'," *Diacritics* 32 (2002), 82.
60   *Ibid.*, 81.
61   *Ibid.*, 84 [quoting Benjamin].
62   W. Benjamin, "Two Poems by Friedrich Holderlin," trans. S. Corngold in *Walter Benjamin: Selected Writings 1913–1926* (Cambridge, MA: Harvard University Press, 1996), 31.
63   *Ibid.*, 34.
64   P. Fenves, *The Messianic Reduction: Walter Benjamin and the Shape of Time* (Stanford, CA: Stanford University Press, 2011), 3.
65   J. Skoller, *Shadows, Specters, Shards: History in Avant-Garde Film* (Minneapolis: University of Minnesota Press, 2005), 4.

66 W. Benjamin, "On the Concept of History," trans. E. Jephcott in *Walter Benjamin: Selected Writings 1938–1940* (Cambridge, MA: Harvard University Press, 2003), 397.
67 V. Harris, *Archives and Justice*, 13.
68 *Ibid.*
69 M. Énard, *Zone*, 21.
70 *Ibid.*, 73.
71 G. Deleuze, *Spinoza: Practical Philosophy* trans. R. Hurley (San Francisco: City Lights, 1988), 23.
72 M. J. Shapiro, "Slow Looking: The Ethics and Politics of Aesthetics" a review essay in *Millennium* 37 (2008), 196.
73 M-A. Oaknin, *The Burnt Book: Reading the Talmud* trans. L. Brown (Princeton, NJ: Princeton University Press, 1995), xiv–xv.
74 M. J. Shapiro, *Deforming American Political Thought*, 7.
75 W. Apess, *On Our Own Ground: The Complete Writings of William Apess* (Amherst: University of Massachusetts Press, 1992), 1–90.
76 *Ibid.*, 277–310.
77 B. O'Connell, "Introduction" to W. Apess, *On Our Own Ground*, xxi.
78 J. Kincaid, "The Little Revenge from the Periphery," *Transition* 73 (1997), 70.
79 See M.-A. Oaknin, *The Burnt Book*, 33.
80 T. Hunter, "Putting an Antebellum Myth to Rest," *New York Times*, August 2 (2011), A21.
81 D. Ellington, "Interview in Los Angeles: On *Jump for Joy*, Opera and Dissonance," 151.
82 W. Benjamin, "Critique of Violence," in *Reflections* trans. P. Demetz (New York: Schocken, 1986), 279–95.
83 D. Ellington, "Interview in Los Angeles: On *Jump for Joy*, Opera and Dissonance," 150.
84 R. H. Brown and B. Davis-Brown, "The Making of Memory: The Politics of Archives, Libraries and Museums," 17.

5 For an anti-fascist aesthetics

1 G. Deleuze, *Two Regimes of Madness* trans. A. Hodges and M. Taormina (New York: Semiotext(e), 2007), 138.
2 See for example, B. Bettleheim, Interview *New York Times*, Book Review, (October 5, 1986), 12.
3 D. DeLillo, *Libra* (New York: Viking, 1988), 148.
4 *Ibid.*, 321.
5 M. J. Shapiro, *Reading the Postmodern Polity* (Minneapolis: University of Minnesota Press), 80.
6 S. Sontag, "Fascinating Fascism," *New York Review of Books* On the web at: http://www.nybooks.com/articles/archives/1975/feb/06/fascinating-fascism/. Obtained 4/10/10.
7 D. Delillo, *White Noise* (New York: Viking-Penguin, 1985), 25–6.
8 R. B. Heberle, *From Democracy to Nazism: A Regional Case Study on Political Parties in Germany* (Baton Rouge: Louisiana State University Press, 1945), 6.
9 *Ibid.*, 9.
10 P. Henisch, *Negatives of My Father,* trans. A. C. Ulmer (Riverside, CA: Ariadne Press, 1990), 50.
11 J. T. Schnapp, "Fascinating Fascism," *Journal of Contemporary History* 31 (1996), 236.
12 K. Ravetto, *The Unmaking of Fascist Aesthetics* (Minneapolis: University of Minnesota Press, 2001), 5.
13 S. Eisenstein, "On Fascism, German Cinema and Real Life: Open Letter to the German Minister of Propaganda," in *Eisenstein Writings* ed. R. Taylor Vol 1 (Bloomington: Indiana University Press, 1988), 280.
14 J. Rancière, *Film Fables*, trans. E. Battista (Oxford: Berg, 2006), 29.

15 *Ibid.*, 30.
16 W. Benjamin, "The Work of Art in the Age of Mechanical Reproduction," 238.
17 *Ibid.*, 241.
18 G. Deleuze, *Two Regimes of Madness*, 168.
19 D. M. Lasansky, *The Renaissance Perfected: Architecture, Spectacle, and Tourism in Fascist Italy* (University Park: Pennsylvania State University Press, 2004), 107.
20 *Ibid.*, 117.
21 *Ibid.*, 99.
22 J. Rancière, *The Politics of Aesthetics*, 65.
23 H.-J. Syberberg, *Hitler: A Film from Germany*, trans. J. Neugroschel (New York: Farrar, Straus and Giroux, 1982), 18.
24 R. Mueller, "Hans-Jürgen Syberberg's *Hitler* an Interview-Montage," *Discourse* 2 (1980), 60.
25 S. Sontag, "Syberberg's Hitler," in *Under the Sign of Saturn* (New York: Farrar, Straus and Giroux, 1973), 143.
26 H.-J. Syberberg, *Hitler: A Film from Germany*, 13.
27 D. DeLillo, *Running Dog* (New York: Vintage, 1978), 236–7.
28 S. Sontag, "Syberberg's Hitler," 148.
29 E. L. Santner, *Mourning, Memory and Film in Postwar Germany* (Ithaca, NY: Cornell University Press, 1990), 143.
30 Quoted in *Ibid.*, 116.
31 S. Sontag, "Syberberg's Hitler," 155.
32 G. Deleuze, *Francis Bacon: The Logic of Sensation*, 71.
33 *Ibid.*, 71–2.
34 H.-J. Syberberg, *Hitler, Ein Film aus Deutschland* (Reinbek, 1978), 81.
35 G. Deleuze, *Cinema 2*, 264.
36 See G. Deleuze and F. Guattari, *A Thousand Plateaus*, trans. B. Massumi (Minneapolis: University of Minnesota Press, 1987).
37 The Amiel perspective articulated here is explicated in J. Game, "Cinematic Bodies," *Studies in French Cinema* 10 (2001), 4.
38 V. Amiel, *Le Corps au Cinema: Keaton, Bresson, Cassavetes* (Paris: Presses Universitaires de France, 1998), 51.
39 *Ibid.*, 7.
40 W. Benjamin, "The Work of Art in the Age of Mechanical Reproduction," 232.
41 M. Hansen, "Benjamin, Cinema and Experience: The Blue Flower in the Land of Technology," *New German Critique* 40 (1987), 204.
42 W. Benjamin quoted in *Ibid.*, 205.
43 F. Jameson, *Brecht and Method* (New York: Verso, 1998), 58.
44 K. Ravetto, *The Unmaking of Fascist Aesthetics*, 227.
45 J. Rancière, *The Politics of Aesthetics*, 65.
46 G. Deleuze, "Postscript on Societies of Control," *October* 59 (1992), 5.
47 G. Deleuze, and F. Guattari, *A Thousand Plateaus*, 215–16.
48 *Ibid.*, 208–31.
49 P. Dick, *Minority Report* (New York: Pantheon, 2002), 45.
50 V. Amiel, *Le Corps au Cinema*, 7.
51 M. J. Shapiro, "Introduction," in M. J. Shapiro and H. Alker eds. *Challenging Boundaries* (Minneapolis: University of Minnesota Press, 1996), xix.
52 T. W. Adorno, E. Frenkel Brunswik, D. J. Levinson, and R. Nevitt Sanford, *The Authoritarian Personality* Part One (New York: John Wiley & Sons, 1964), 1.
53 J. H. Eysenck, *The Psychology of Politics* (London: Routledge & Kegan Paul, 1954), 147.
54 M. Rokeach, *The Open and the Closed Mind* (New York: Basic Books, 1973).
55 T. W. E. Adorno *et al.*, *The Authoritarian Personality* Part Two (New York: John Wiley & Sons, 1964), 891–970.
56 M. Foucault, "The Confession of the Flesh," in C. Gordon, ed. *Power/Knowledge: Selected Interviews and Other Writings 1972–1977* (New York: Pantheon, 1980), 194.

6 The micro-politics of justice

1 For a review of this research paradigm, see H. Gilman, "What's Law Got to Do with It? Judicial Behaviorists Test the 'Legal Model' of Judicial Decision Making," *Law and Society Inquiry* 26 (2001), 465–504.

2 "Aesthetics," as Terry Eagleton puts it, is "born as a discourse of the body": T. Eagleton, *The Ideology of the Aesthetic* (London: Basil Blackwell, 1990), 13.

3 H. Melville, "Bartleby, the Scrivener: A Story of Wall Street," online at: http://www.bartleby.com/129/.

4 G. Deleuze, "Bartleby; or The Formula," in *Essays Critical and Clinical* trans. D. W. Smith and M. S. Greco (Minneapolis: University of Minnesota Press, 1997), 68–90.

5 The first quotation is from *Ibid.*, p. 71 and the second from J. Rancière, "Deleuze, Bartleby, and the Literary Formula." in *The Flesh of Words: The Politics of Writing* trans. C. Mandell (Stanford, CA: Stanford University Press, 2004), 146.

6 G. Deleuze, "Bartleby; or The Formula," 73.

7 *Ibid.*

8 *Ibid.*

9 *Ibid.*, 74.

10 The quotations are from J. Rancière and D. Panagia, "Dissenting Words: A Conversation with Jacques Rancière," *Diacritics* 30 (2000), 115.

11 T. Morrison, "Nobel Lecture," December 7, 1993. On the web at: http://nobelprize.org/nobel_prizes/literature/laureates/1993/morrison-lecture.html. Obtained 8/5/08.

12 V. Amiel, *Le Corps au Cinema: Keaton, Bresson, Cassavetes,* 7 (my translation).

13 See P. Virno on idle talk in his *A Grammar of the Multitude* trans. I. Bertolleti, J. Cascaito, and A. Casson (New York: Semiotext(e), 2004), 89.

14 As J.-F. Lyotard has argued, "all legal injustice [involves] linguistic domination." The quotation is from a treatment of Lyotard by H. Ruthrof, "Differend and Agonistics: A Transcendental Argument?" *Philosophy Today* 36 (1992), 331.

15 M. Foucault, *The Birth of the Clinic: An Archaeology of Medical Perception* trans. A. Sheridan Smith, (New York: Pantheon, 1973), 15.

16 *Ibid.*, 19.

17 The quotations are from *Ibid.*

18 M. Foucault, *The Use of Pleasure* trans. R. Hurley (New York: Pantheon, 1985), 3.

19 P. Veyne, "The Inventory of Differences," trans. E. Kingdom, *Economy and Society* 11 (1982), 176.

20 See G. Agamben, *Homo Sacer: Sovereign Power and Bare Life* trans. D. Heller-Roazen (Stanford, CA: Stanford University Press, 1998).

21 *Njals Saga,* trans. R. Cook, (New York: Penguin, 2002).

22 See F. Braudel, *Afterthoughts on Material Civilization and Capitalism* trans. P. M. Ranum (Baltimore: Johns Hopkins University Press, 1977).

23 The quoted expression is from S. Truby, *Exit Architecture: Between War and Peace* trans. R. Payne (Vienna: Stringer-Verlag, 2008), 43.

24 The quotation is from T. Harshaw, "Assassinating Americans, Killing the Constitution?" on the web at: http://opinionator.blogs.nytimes.com/2010/02/05/assassinating-americans-killing-the-constitution/?scp=1&sq=assassinating%20americans&st=cse (obtained 2/6/2010).

25 *Ibid.*

26 See J.-F. Lyotard, *The Differend: Phrases in Dispute* trans. G. Van Den Abbeele (Minneapolis: University of Minnesota Press, 1988).

27 Williams's concept of a "structure of feeling" is developed in his *The Long Revolution* (1961) but is elaborated in his *Marxism and Literature* (1977), from which the quotation is taken. See R. Williams, *Marxism and Literature* (Oxford, UK: Oxford University Press, 1977), 132.

28 The quotation is from R. Williams, *The Long Revolution* (London: Chatto and Windus, 1961), 49.

29 L. Sciascia, *The Day of the Owl* trans. A. Colquhoun and A. Oliver (New York: Jonathan Cape, 2003), 95.
30 The quotation is from D. M. Engel, "Litigation Across Space and Time: Courts, Conflict, and Social Change," *Law & Society Review* 24 (1990), 337.
31 *Ibid.*, 338.
32 *Ibid.*, 339.
33 *Ibid.*, 340.
34 This discussion of Sciascia's novelistic grammar is inspired by Slavoj Žižek's analysis of Henry James's style: See his "Kate's Choice, or, The Materialism of Henry James," in S. Žižek ed. *Lacan: The Silent Partners* (London: Verso, 2006), 288.
35 L. Sciascia, *The Day of the Owl*, 9.
36 *Ibid.*, 10.
37 G. Scialabba, "Introduction" to *The Day of the Owl*, ix.
38 *Ibid.*
39 *Ibid.*, x.
40 L. Sciascia, *The Day of the Owl*, 17.
41 See I. Kant, *Critique of Practical Reason*, trans. W. S. Pluhar (Indianapolis: Hackett, 2002).
42 The quotations are from J.-F. Lyotard, "The Sign of History," in A. Benjamin ed. *The Lyotard Reader* (New York: Basil Blackwell, 1989), 93.
43 *Ibid.*, 106.
44 Lyotard, *The Differend: Phrases in Dispute* trans. G. Van Den Abeele (Minneapolis: University of Minnesota Press), xi.
45 The quotations are from *Ibid.*, 128.
46 See M. M. Bakhtin, "Discourse and the Novel," in *The Dialogic Imagination*, trans. C. Emerson and M. Holquist (Austin: University of Texas Press, 1981), 259–422.
47 J-F. Sciascia, *The Day of the Owl*, 62–3.
48 *Ibid.*, 63.
49 *Ibid.*, 29.
50 *Ibid.*
51 M. Foucault, *Discipline and Punish: The Birth of the Prison* trans. A. Sheridan Smith (New York: Pantheon, 1977), 272.
52 L. Sciascia, *The Day of the Owl*, 30.
53 *Ibid.*, 28.
54 *Ibid.*
55 C. Lucarelli, "Preface," in *Carte Blanche*, trans. M. Reynolds (New York: Europa Editions, 2006), 10–11.
56 *Ibid.*, 11. Lucarelli's "Preface" is repeated in the other two novels in the trilogy. See also *The Damned Season* trans. M. Reynolds (New York: Europe Editions, 2007) and *Via Delle Oche* trans. M. Reynolds (New York: Europe Editions, 2008).
57 L. Sciascia, *The Day of the Owl*, 15.
58 G. Scialabba, "Introduction" to *The Day of the Owl*, xi.
59 L. Sciascia, *The Day of the Owl*, 102–3.
60 *Ibid.*, 115.
61 J. Rancière, "The Politics of Aesthetics," on the web at: http://theater.kein.org/node/99 (accessed 5/18/2005). Nancy Fraser raises a similar question about justice claims, noting that there are instances of "abnormal justice" where there is a lack of shared "ontological assumptions about the kind(s) of actors who are entitled to make such claims." N. Fraser, "Abnormal Justice," on the web at: http://www.law.yale.edu/documents/pdf/Intellectual_Life/ltw_fraser.pdf (obtained 3/2/2010).
62 L. Sciascia, *The Day of the Owl*, 117.
63 See F. Jameson, "The Existence of Italy," in *Signatures of the Visible* (New York: Routledge, 1992), 155–229.
64 R. D. Putnam, *Making Democracy Work: Civic Traditions in Modern Italy* (Princeton, NJ: Princeton University Press, 1993).
65 *Ibid.*, 12.

7 A continuing violent cartography

1 M. J. Shapiro, *Deforming American Political Thought: Ethnicity, Facticity and Genre* (Lexington: University Press of Kentucky 2006), 59.
2 A. Rosenus, *General Vallejo and the Advent of the Americans* (Berkeley, CA: University of California Press, 1995), 90–1.
3 J. M. Lynch, "'A Distinct Place in America Where All *Mestizos* Reside': Landscape and Identity in Ana Castillo's *Scapogonia* and Diana Chang's *The Frontiers of Love*," *Melus* 26 (2001), 120.
4 J. D. Saldivar, "Nuestra America's Borders," in J. Belnap and R. Fernandez eds. *Jose Marti's 'Our American'* (Durham, NC: Duke University Press, 1998), 156.
5 R. Sanchez and B. Pita, "Introduction" to M. A. Ruiz de Burton, *The Squatter and the Don* (Houston: Arte Publico Press, 1997), 7.
6 M. A. Ruiz de Burton, *The Squatter and the Don*, 66.
7 E. Zilberg, "Falling Down in El Norte: A Cultural Politics and Spatial Poetics of the ReLatinization of Los Angeles," *Wide Angle* 20 (1998), 183–209.
8 C. Fuentes, *The Crystal Frontier*, trans. A. MacAdam (New York: Farrar, Straus and Giroux, 1995), 57.
9 See S. P. Huntington, "The Clash of Civilizations," *Foreign Affairs* 20 (1993), 22–49 and *The Clash of Civilizations and the Remaking of World Order* (New York: Touchstone Books, 1998).
10 See J. Bale, "The Victims of the Border Vigilantes," *Socialist Worker*. On the web at: http://socialistworker.org/2005–1/541/541_02_Vigilantes.shtml. Obtained 10/5/2010.
11 J. C. Cremony, *Life Among the Apaches* (New York: Indian Head Books, 1991), 13–14.
12 D. West, and J. M. West, "Borders and Boundaries: An Interview with John Sayles," *Cineaste* 22: 3. On the web at: http://www.en.utexas.edu/Classes/Bremen/e316k/316kprivate/scans/sayles_lonestar.html. Obtained 10/6/2010.
13 See J. Rancière, "Rethinking Aesthetics: Contemporary Art and the Politics of Aeshetics," in B. Hindlerlitter *et al.*, *Communities of Sense* (Durham, NC: Duke University Press, 2009).
14 G. Deleuze, *Cinema 1*, trans. H. Tomlinson and B. Habberjam (Minneapolis: University of Minnesota Press, 1986), 146.
15 S. Kollin, "Genre and the Geographies of Violence: Cormac McCarthy and the Contemporary Western," *Contemporary Literature* 42 (2001), 562.
16 See J. Jones, "A House is not a Home," *Frieze Magazine Online*. Available at: http://www.frieze.com/issue/print_article/a_house_is_not_a_home/. Obtained 10/17/11.
17 See C. McCarthy, *Blood Meridian: Or the Evening Redness in the West* (New York: Vintage, 1992), the book jacket.
18 See J. Sepich, *Notes on Blood Meridian* 2nd edition (Austin: University of Texas Press, 2008).
19 The expression belongs to W. Boelhower, *Through a Glass Darkly: Ethnic Semiosis and American Literature* (New York: Oxford University Press, 1986).
20 S. Scheckel, *The Insistence of the Indian* (Princeton, NJ: Princeton University Press, 1998), 19.
21 *Ibid.*
22 T. Goddu, *Gothic America: Narrative, History, and Nation* (New York: Columbia University Press, 1997), 56.
23 M. J. Shapiro, *Methods and Nations: Cultural Governance and the Indigenous Subject* (New York: Routledge, 2004), 187.
24 *Ibid.*, 188.
25 *Ibid.*, 189.
26 A. Baricco, *City*, trans. A. Goldstein (New York: Vintage, 2003), 158–9.
27 V. W. Wexman, "The Family on the Land," in D. Bernardi ed., *The Birth of Whiteness: Race and the Emergence of U.S. Cinema* (New Brunswick, NJ: Rutgers University Press, 1996), 131.

28 N. F. Cott, *Public Vows: A History of Marriage and the Nation* (Cambridge, MA: Harvard University Press, 2000), 10.
29 *Ibid.*, 25.
30 N. Campbell, *The Rhizomatic West* (Lincoln: University of Nebraska Press, 2008).
31 *Ibid.*, the book jacket.
32 G. Deleuze, *Francis Bacon: The Logic of Sensation* (Minneapolis: University of Minnesota Press, 2003), 71.
33 *Ibid.*, 71–2.
34 M. J. Shapiro, *Deforming American Political Thought*, 83–4.
35 R. Slotkin, *Gunfighter Nation* (Norman: University of Oklahoma Press, 1992), 752.
36 C. McCarthy, *Blood Meridian*, 3.
37 *Ibid.*, 4.
38 *Ibid.*
39 W. Wright, *Six Guns and Society* (Berkeley, CA: University of California Press, 1977).
40 A. Nadel, *Containment Culture: American Narratives, Postmodernism, and the Atomic Age* (Durham, NC: Duke University Press, 1995), 195.
41 T. Gallagher, "Angels Gambol Where They May: John Ford's Indians," in J. Kitses and G. Rickman eds. *The Western Reader* (New York: Limelight, 1998), 273.
42 C. McCarthy, *Blood Meridian*, 198.
43 *Ibid.*, 199.
44 *Ibid.*, 116.
45 *Ibid.*, 56.
46 *Ibid.*, 47.
47 *Ibid.*, 48.
48 *Ibid.*
49 *Ibid.*, 34.
50 *Ibid.*, 123.
51 F. Nietzsche, *Thus Spake Zarathustra*, trans. A. Tille (New York, Dutton, 1960), 153.
52 C. McCarthy, *Blood Meridian*, 327.
53 *Ibid.*
54 M. J. Shapiro, "Slow Looking: The Ethics and Politics of Aesthetics," 196.
55 J. Rancière, *The Politics of Aesthetics*, (New York: Continuum, 2004).
56 J. Akers, "Vigilantes at the Border: The New War on Immigrants," *International Socialist Review* 43 (2005), 1.
57 M. Coleman, "A Geopolitics of Engagement: Neoliberalism, the War on Terrorism, and the Reconfiguration of US Immigrant Enforcement," *Geopolitics* 12 (2007), 608.
58 L. A. Herzog, *Where North Meets South: Cities, Space and Politics on the U.S – Mexican Border*, (Austin: University of Texas Press, 1990), 619.
59 *Ibid.*, 627.
60 L. Gilbert, "Resistance in the Neoliberal City," *City: Analysis of Urban Trends, Culture, Theory, Policy, Action* 9 (2005), 23–32.
61 E. Alliez, *Capital Times* trans. G. Van Den Abbeele (Minneapolis: University of Minnesota Press. 1996), 6.
62 M. J. Shapiro, *The Time of the City: Politics, Philosophy and Genre* (London: Routledge, 2010).
63 L.Gilbert, "Resistance in the Neoliberal City," 31.
64 V. Talavera *et al.*, "Deportation in the U.S.–Mexico Borderlands: Anticipation, Experience, and Memory," in N. De Genova and N. Peutz, *The Deportation Regime* (Durham, NC: Duke University Press, 2006), 166.
65 *Ibid.*, 172.
66 R. Doty, "Crossroads of Death," in C. Masters and E, Dauphinée eds. *The Logics of Biopower and the War on Terror* (London: Palgrave Macmillan, 2006), 6.
67 *Ibid.*, 17.

68 See for example C. Bowdon and A. L. Briggs, *Dreamland: The Way Out of Juarez* (Austin: University of Texas Press, 2010) and G. Thompson, "U.S. Agents Aided Mexican Drug Trafficker to Infiltrate His Criminal Ring," *New York Times International,* Monday, January 9 (2012), A5.
69 L. Savage, "Justice for Janitors: Scales of Organizing and Representing Workers," *Antipode* 38 (2006), 647.
70 My treatment of the film is revised from a version I do in Shapiro, *The Time of the City,* 40–5.
71 The quotation is from J. Auerbach, *Dark Borders: Film Noir and American Citizenship* (Durham, NC: Duke University Press, 2011), 137.
72 H. Lefebvre, *The Production of Space* trans. D. Nicholson-Smith (Cambridge, MA: Blackwell, 1991), 49.
73 See H. Lefebvre, *The Urban Revolution* trans. R. Bononno (Minneapolis: University of Minnesota Press, 2003).
74 A. Ong, "A Bio-Cartography: Maids, Neo-Slavery, and NGOs," in S. Benhabib and J. Resnik eds. *Migrations and Mobilities: Citizenship, Borders, and Gender* (New York: NYU Press, 2009).
75 See R. D. Abrahams, *Everyday Life: A Poetics of Vernacular Practices* (Philadelphia: University of Pennsylvania Press, 2005), 139–48.

8 The presence of war

1 There are quotations marks around "Here and Elsewhere" because I am taking the subtitle from Jean-Luc Goddard's film, *Ici et Ailleurs* (1976).
2 See F. Nietzsche, *Untimely Meditations* trans. R. Hollingdale (New York: Cambridge University Press, 1983). My remarks on untimeliness are also edified by Giorgio Agamben's Nietzsche-inspired essay, "What is the Contemporary?" in G. Agamben, *What is an Apparatus?* trans. D. Kishik and S. Pedatella (Stanford, CA; Stanford University Press, 2009), 40–41.
3 J. Rancière, "Who is the Subject of the Rights of Man?" *The South Atlantic Quarterly.* 103 (2004), 297.
4 *Ibid.*
5 H. Arendt, "Understanding and Politics," *Partisan Review* 20 (1953), 379.
6 H. Arendt, *The Human Condition* (Chicago: University of Chicago Press, 1958), 27.
7 *Ibid.,* 31.
8 *Ibid.*
9 *Ibid.,* 28.
10 C. Sheehan, "Address to Veterans For Peace Convention," on the web at http://www.truthout.org/docs_2005/printer_B081005.shtml obtained 8/5/2006.
11 "War Critic Buys Land in Same Town as President Bush's Ranch, *New York Times* on the web at: http://www.nytimes.com/2006/07/28/us/28brfs-004.html?ex=1157774400 &en=9f12c9da473082bf&ei=5070 obtained 8/5/2006.
12 H. Arendt, "Understanding and Politics".
13 For a critical analysis of the history of the mothers–war relationship, see J. Elshtain, *Women and War* (Chicago: University of Chicago Press, revised edition, 1995).
14 J. Rancière, "The Politics of Aesthetics," on the web at: http://theater.kein.org/node/view/99 (Obtained 3/23/05).
15 H. Arendt, *The Human Condition,* 177.
16 H. Arendt, "Understanding and Politics," 288.
17 J. Rancière, *Dis-agreement* trans. J. Rose (Minneapolis: University of Minnesota Press, 1999), 39.
18 International relations theorists have also addressed the implications of war's increasing virtuality. See for example J. Der Derian, "The Virtualization of Violence and the Disappearance of War," *Cultural Values* 1 (1997): 203–18.

19 P. Singer, *Wired for War: The Robotic Revolution and Conflict in the 21st Century* (New York: Penguin, 2009).

20 P. Virilio, *War and Cinema* trans. P. Camillera (New York: Verso, 1989).

21 J. Baudrillard, *The Gulf War did not Take Place*. trans. P. Patton (Bloomington: Indiana University Press, 1991), 26.

22 St. Augustine, *The Confessions* trans. J. K. Ryan (New York: Doubleday, 1960), 288.

23 Of course among contemporary philosophers, no one has more convincingly established the philosophical complexities attending the relationships between grammar and presence than Jacques Derrida, beginning with one of his earliest texts, *Speech and Phenomena and Other Essays on Husserl's Theory of Signs* trans. D. B. Allison (Evanston, IL: Northwestern University Press, 1973).

24 See P. Patton's "Introduction" to Baudrillard, *The Gulf War did not Take Place*.

25 S. Lindqvist,*"Exterminate all the Brutes"*, 46.

26 R. Nixon, "The Hidden Lives of Oil," B 7.

27 *Ibid.*, B 8.

28 See H. Bergson, *Matter and Memory* trans. N. M. Paul and W. S. Palmer (New York: Macmillan, 1929).

29 J. Lacan, "The Eye and the Gaze," in *Four Fundamental Concepts of Psycho-Analysis* trans. A. Sheridan (London: Penguin, 1979), 73.

30 See K. Silverman, *The Threshold of the Visible World* (New York: Routledge, 1996).

31 S. Kracauer, *Theory of Film: The Redemption of Physical Reality* (Princeton, NJ: Princeton University Press, 1960), 306.

32 G. Deleuze, *Cinema 2*, 272.

33 J. Rancière, *Film Fables,* 111.

34 The quotation in the sentence belongs to M. Taussig, "Tactility and Distraction," *Cultural Anthropology* 6 (1991): 149.

35 W. Benjamin, "The Work of Art in the Age of Mechanical Reproduction," 238.

35 S. Kracauer, "The Cult of Distraction" in *The Mass Ornament* trans. T. Y. Levin (Cambridge, MA: Harvard University Press, 1995), 327–8.

37 See the images at: http://images.google.com/images?hl=en&source=hp&q=martha+r osler+bringing+the+war+home&gbv=2&aq=0&aqi=g1&aql=&oq=martha+rosler.

38 J. Rancière, "The Politics of Aesthetics."

39 D. Sutton, *Photography, Cinema, Memory: The Crystal Image* (Minneapolis: University of Minnesota Press, 2009), 8.

40 The quotation about Deleuze's approach is from J. Skoller, *Shadows, Specters, Shards*, xix.

41 For a psychiatric reading, see N. Keltner, "Real Reels," *Perspectives in Psychiatric Care* 44 (2008), 298–300.

42 For this kind of emphasis, see K. Wilz, "Richard's Story: The Present Referent in *In the Valley of Elah*," *Global Media Journal*. On the web at: http://lass.calumet.purdue. edu/cca/gmj/fa09/graduate/gmj-fa09-grad-wilz.htm. Obtained 6/11/2010.

43 A. Proulx, "Tits Up in a Ditch" in *Fine Just the Way It Is* (New York: Scribners, 2008), 179.

44 *Ibid.*, 182.

45 *Ibid.*, 221.

46 M. A. Doane, *The Emergence of Cinematic Time* (Cambridge, MA: Harvard University Press, 2008). 202.

47 As in other chapters, the concept of interference I use here is inspired by Cesare Casarino's analysis of the way philosophical concepts illuminate artistic text by interfering with them: Casarino, "Philopoesis: A Theoretico-Methodological Manifesto," 86.

48 J. Rancière, *The Future of the Image* trans. G. Elliot (New York: Verso, 2007), 55.

49 *Ibid.*, 53.

50 J. Rancière, *The Flesh of Words*, 159.

Bibliography

Abdel-Sahed, A., "Unnecessary Moral Hazards: The Auto Bailout," in *Islamic Insights* on the web at: http://www.islamicinsights.com.news/opinion/unnecessary-moral-hazards-the-auto-bailout.htm (obtained 5/22/10).

Abrahams, R. D., *Everyday Life: A Poetics of Vernacular Practices* (Philadelphia: University of Pennsylvania Press, 2005).

Achebe, C., "The African Writer and the English Language," in R. Spillman ed. *Gods and Soldiers* (New York: Penguin, 2009).

Adams, H., *The Education of Henry Adams* (Boston: Houghton Mifflin, 1961).

Adorno, T. W., E. Frenkel Brunswik, D. J. Levinson, and R. Nevitt Sanford, *The Authoritarian Personality* Parts One and Two (New York: John Wiley & Sons, 1964).

Agamben, G., *Homo Sacer: Sovereign Power and Bare Life*. trans. D. Heller-Roazen (Stanford, CA: Stanford University Press, 1998).

Agamben, G., *What is an Apparatus?* trans. D. Kishik and S. Pedatella (Stanford, CA; Stanford University Press, 2009).

Akers, J., "Vigilantes at the Border: The New War on Immigrants," *International Socialist Review* 43 (2005) online: http://www.isreview.org/issues/43/minutemen.shtml

Alexie, S., *Reservation Blues* (New York: Warner Books, 1996).

Allen, C., *Art in Australia: From Colonization to Postmodernism* (London: Thames and Hudson, 1997).

Alliez, E., *Capital Times*. trans. G. Van Den Abbeele (Minneapolis: University of Minnesota Press, 1996).

Althusser, L., *Philosophy of the Encounter: Later Writings, 1978–1987*. trans. G. M. Goshgarian (New York: Verso, 2006).

Alzira Seixo, M., "Still Facts and Living Fictions: The Literary Work of Antonio Lobo Antunes, An Introduction," in V. K. Mendes ed. *Facts and Fictions of Antonio Lobo Antunes* (Dartmouth, MA: Tagus Press, 2011), 19–43.

Amiel, V., *Le Corps au Cinema: Keaton, Bresson, Cassavetes* (Paris: Presses Universitaires de France, 1998).

Amin, A. and N. Thrift, *Cities: Reimagining the Urban* (Malden, MA: Polity Press, 2002).

Apess, W., *On Our Own Ground: The Complete Writings of William Apess* (Amherst: University of Massachusetts Press 1992).

Appleby, J. O., *Economic Thought and Ideology in Seventeenth-Century England* (Princeton, NJ: Princeton University Press, 1978).

Arendt, H., "Understanding and Politics," *Partisan Review* 20 (1953), 377–92.

Arendt, H., *The Human Condition* (Chicago: University of Chicago Press, 1958).

Arens, K., "*Stadtwollen*: Benjamin's *Arcades Project* and the Problem of Method," *PLMA* 122: 1 ((January, 2007), 43–60.

Auerbach, J., *Dark Borders: Film Noir and American Citizenship* (Durham, NC: Duke University Press, 2011).

St. Augustine, *The Confessions.* trans. J. K. Ryan (New York: Doubleday, 1960).

Baker, Jr., H. A., "Figurations for a New American Literary History," in S. Berkovitch and M. Jehlen eds. *Ideology and Classic American Literature* (New York: Cambridge University Press, 1986), 33–6.

Bakhtin, M. M., "Discourse and the Novel," trans. C. Emerson in M. Holquist ed. *The Dialogic Imagination* (Austin: University of Texas Press, 1981), 259–422.

Bakhtin, M. M., "Epic and Novel," in M. Holquist ed. *The Dialogic Imagination* (Austin: University of Texas Press, 1981), 3–40.

Bakhtin, M. M., "Forms of Time and Chronotope in the Novel," in C. Emerson and M. Holquist trans. *The Dialogic Imagination* (Austin: University of Texas Press, 1981), 84–258.

Bakhtin, M. M., "The *Bildungsroman* and Its Significance in the History of Realism (Toward a Historical Typology of the Novel) in *Speech Genres and Other Late Essays* trans. V. W. McGee, (Austin: University of Texas Press, 1986), 10–59.

Bakhtin, M. M., "Author and Hero in Aesthetic Activity," in *Art and Answerability*, trans V. Liapunov (Austin: University of Texas Press, 1990), 4–256.

Bale, J., "The Victims of the Border Vigilantes," *The Socialistworker.org* on the web at: http://socialistworker.org/2005–1/541/541_02_Vigilantes.shtml (obtained 10/5/2010).

Ballard, J. G., *Crash* (New York: Picador, 1973).

Bannet, E. T., "The Marriage Act of 1753: 'A Most Cruel Law for the Fair Sex'," *Eighteenth Century Studies* 30 (1997), 237–51.

Banks, R., *Continental Drift* (New York: Harper and Row, 1985).

Baraka, A., *Blues People: Negro Music in White America* (New York: Harper, 1999).

Barker, M., J. Arthurs and R. Harindranath, *The Crash Controversy Censorship Campaigns and Film Reception* (London: Wallflower Press, 2001).

Baudrillard, J., "Sign Function and Class Logic," in *For a Critique of the Political Economy of the Sign.* trans. C. Levin (St Louis, MO: Telos Press, 1981), 29–62.

Baudrillard, J., *The Gulf War did not Take Place.* trans. P. Patton (Bloomington: Indiana University Press, 1991).

Bender, G. J., *Angola under the Portuguese: The Myth and the Reality* (Berkeley: University of California Press, 1978).

Benjamin, W., "The Work of Art in the Age of Mechanical Reproduction," in H. Arendt ed. *Illuminations* (New York: Schocken, 1968), 217–52.

Benjamin, W., "Critique of Violence," in *Reflections.* trans. P. Demetz (New York: Schocken, 1986), 279–95.

Benjamin, W., "Program of the Coming Philosophy," trans. M. Ritter in G. Smith ed. *Benjamin: Philosophy, History, Aesthetics* (Chicago: University of Chicago Press, 1989), 1–12.

Benjamin, W., "Two Poems by Friedrich Holderlin," trans. S. Corngold in *Walter Benjamin: Selected Writings 1913–1926* (Cambridge, MA: Harvard University Press, 1996), 18–36.

Benjamin, W., *The Arcades Project.* trans. H. Eiland and K. McLaughlin (Cambridge, MA; Harvard University Press, 2002).

Benjamin, W., "On the Concept of History," trans. E. Jephcott in *Walter Benjamin: Selected Writings 1938–1940* (Cambridge, MA: Harvard University Press, 2003), 389–400.

Bennett, J., *Empathic Vision: Affect, Trauma, and Contemporary Art* (Stanford, CA: Stanford University Press, 2004).

Bergson, H., *Matter and Memory.* trans. N. M. Paul and W. S. Palmer (New York: Macmillan, 1929).

Berlant, L., "Intimacy: A Special Issue," *Critical Inquiry* 24 (1998), 1–10.

Bernardi, S., "Rossellini's Landscapes: Nature, Myth, History," in D. Forgacs, S. Lutton and G. Nowell-Smith eds. *Roberto Rosselini: Magician of the Real* (London: BFI, 2001), 50–63.

Bersani, L., and U. Dutoit, *Forms of Being* (London, BFI, 2004).

Bettleheim, B., Interview, *New York Times*, Book Review (October 5, 1986), 11–13.

Bhabha, H., *The Location of Culture* (New York: Routledge, 1994).

Birken, L., *Consuming Desire* (Ithaca, NY: Cornell University Press, 1988).

Blanchot, M., *The Space of Literature.* trans. A. Smock (Lincoln: University of Nebraska Press, 1982).

Boelhower, W., *Through a Glass Darkly: Ethnic Semiosis and American Literature* (New York: Oxford University Press, 1986).

Bonham, J., "Transport: Disciplining the Body that Travels," in S. Bohm *et al.* eds. *Against Automobility* (Malden, MA: Blackwell, 2006), 57–74.

Bowdon C., and A. L. Briggs *Dreamland: The Way Out of Juarez* (Austin: University of Texas Press, 2010).

Brandon, R., *Auto Mobile* (London: Macmillan, 2002).

Braudel, F., *Afterthoughts on Material Civilization and Capitalism.* trans. P. M. Ranum (Baltimore: Johns Hopkins University Press, 1977).

Braudel, F., *The Wheels of Commerce: Civilization & Capitalism, 15th –18th Century* Vol 2 (New York: Harper & Row, 1982).

Brooks, D., "Bailout to Nowhere," an op-ed in the *New York Times.* On the web at: http://www.nytimes.com/2008/11/14opinion/14brooks.html (obtained 5/22/10).

Brown, P., *The Making of Late Antiquity* (Cambridge, MA: Harvard University Press, 1993).

Brown, R. H., and B. Davis-Brown, "The Making of Memory: The Politics of Archives, Libraries and Museums," *History of the Human Sciences* 11: 4 (November, 1998), 17–32.

Bunch III, L., and S. R. Crew, "A Historian's Eye: Jacob Lawrence, Historical Reality and the Migration Series," in E. H. Turner, ed, *Jacob Lawrence: The Migration Series* (Washington D.C.: The Rappahannack Press, 1993), 23–32.

Burr, J. "Notes" in *Copland Connotations: Studies and Interviews (review)* 60 (2002), 22–8.

Campbell, N., *The Rhizomatic West* (Lincoln: University of Nebraska Press, 2008).

Carabi, A., "Interview with Toni Morrison." *Belles Lettres* 10 (1995), 40–3.

Casarino, C., "Philopoesis: A Theoretico-Methodological Manifesto," *boundary 2* (2002*a*), 65–96.

Casarino, C., *Modernity at Sea: Melville, Marx, Conrad in Crisis* (Minneapolis: University of Minnesota Press, 2002).

Caygill, H., *Walter Benjamin: The Colour of Experience* (New York: Routledge, 1998).

Césaire, A., *Discourse on Colonialism.* trans. J. Pinkham (New York: Monthly Review Press, 1972).

Chandler, R., *Farewell My Lovely* (New York: Vintage, 1992).

Cohen, H. G., "Duke Ellington and *Black, Brown and Beige*," *American Quarterly* 56 (2004), 1003–34.

Coleman, M., "A Geopolitics of Engagement: Neoliberalism, the War on Terrorism, and the Reconfiguration of US Immigrant Enforcement," *Geopolitics* 12 (2007), 607–34.

Colwell, C., "Deleuze and Foucault: Series, Event, Genealogy," *Theory & Event* 1: 2 (1997).

Cott, N. F., *Public Vows: A History of Marriage and the Nation* (Cambridge, MA: Harvard University Press, 2000).

Crary, J., *Techniques of the Observer* (Cambridge, MA: MIT Press, 1991).

Crary, J., *Suspensions of Perception: Attention, Spectacle, and Modern Culture* (Cambridge, MA: MIT Press, 1999).

Cremony, J. C., *Life Among the Apaches* (New York: Indian Head Books, 1991).

Crooks, R., "From the Far Side of the Urban Frontier: The Detective Fiction of Chester Himes and Walter Mosley," *College Literature* 22: 3 (October, 1995), 175–99.

DeLanda, M., *A New Philosophy of Society: Assemblage Theory and Social Complexity* (New York: Continuum, 2006), 3.

Deleuze, G., *Kant's Critical Philosophy*. trans. H. Tomlinson and B. Habberjam (Minneapolis: University of Minnesota Press, 1984).

Deleuze, G., *Cinema 1: The Movement Image*. trans. H. Tomlinson and B. Habberjam (Minneapolis: University of Minnesota Press, 1986).

Deleuze, G., *Foucault*. trans. S. Hand (Minneapolis: University of Minnesota Press, 1988).

Deleuze, G., *Cinema 2: The Time Image*. trans. H. Tomlinson and R. Galeta, (Minneapolis: University of Minnesota Press, 1989).

Deleuze, G., *The Logic of Sense*. trans. M. Lester (New York: Columbia University Press: 1990).

Deleuze, G., "Postscript on Societies of Control," *October* 59 (1992), 3–7.

Deleuze, G., *Difference and Repetition*. trans. P. Patton (New York: Columbia University Press, 1994).

Deleuze, G., "Bartleby; or The Formula." in *Essays Critical and Clinical* trans. D. W. Smith and M. S. Greco (Minneapolis: University of Minnesota Press, 1997), 68–90.

Deleuze, G., *Spinoza: Practical Philosophy*. trans. R. Hurley (San Francisco: City Lights, 2001).

Deleuze, G., *Francis Bacon: The Logic of Sensation*. trans. D. W. Smith (Minneapolis: University of Minnesota Press, 2003).

Deleuze, G., *Two Regimes of Madness*. trans. A. Hodges and M. Taormina (New York: Semiotext(e), 2007).

Deleuze, G., Lecture on Kant, 14/3/78. On the web at: http://www.webdeleuze.com/php/texte.php?cle=66&groupe=Kant&langue=2 (obtained 1/20/2010).

Deleuze, G., and F. Guattari, *Kafka: Toward a Minor Literature*. trans. D. Polan (Minneapolis: University of Minnesota Press, 1986).

Deleuze, G., and F. Guattari, *A Thousand Plateaus*. trans. B. Massumi (Minneapolis: University of Minnesota Press, 1987).

Deleuze, G., and F. Guattari, *What is Philosophy?*. trans. H. Tomlinson and B. Habberjam (New York: Columbia University Press, 1994).

DeLillo, D., *Running Dog* (New York: Vintage, 1978).

DeLillo, D., *White Noise* (New York: Viking-Penguin, 1985).

DeLillo, D., *Libra* (New York: Viking, 1988).

Deloria, P. J., *Indians in Unexpected Places* (Lawrence: University of Kansas Press, 2006).

Denney, R., *The Astonished Muse* (Chicago: University of Chicago Press, 1957).

Der Derian, J., "The Virtualization of Violence and the Disappearance of War," *Cultural Values* 1 (1997): 203–18.

Derrida, J., *Speech and Phenomena and Other Essays on Husserl's Theory of Signs*. trans. D. B. Allison (Evanston, IL: Northwestern University Press, 1973).

Derrida, J., *Archive Fever*. trans. E. Prenowitz (Chicago: University of Chicago Press, 1996).

Derrida, J., *Politics of Friendship*. trans. G. Collins (London: Verso, 1997).

Dick, P., *Do Androids Dream of Electric Sheep?* (New York: Del Ray, 1996).

Dick, P., *Minority Report* (New York: Pantheon, 2002).

Dickens, C., *Hard Times* (New York: Barnes & Noble Classics, 2004 [originally published in 1854]).

Doane, M. A., *The Emergence of Cinematic Time* (Cambridge, MA: Harvard University Press, 2008).

Doctorow, E. L., *Ragtime* (New York: Random House, 1975).

Doty, R., "Crossroads of Death," in C. Masters and E, Dauphinee eds. *The Logics of Biopower and the War on Terror* (London: Palgrave Macmillan, 2006), 4–18.

Dudley, D., "The Vanishing Mercury Class," *New York Times*, Week in Review, (June 13, 2010), 12.

Eagleton, T., *Ideology of the Aesthetic* (Cambridge, MA: Basil Blackwell, 1990).

Eckard, P.G. "The Interplay of Music, Language, and Narrative in Toni Morrison's *Jazz*," *CLA Journal* 38 (1994), 11–19.

Eisenstein, S., "On Fascism, German Cinema and Real Life: Open Letter to the German Minister of Propaganda," in *Eisenstein Writings* ed. R. Taylor Vol 1 (Bloomington: Indiana University Press, 1988), 280.

Ellington, D., "Interview in Los Angeles: On *Jump for Joy*, Opera and Dissonance, in M. Tucker, ed. *The Duke Ellington Reader* (New York: Oxford University Press, 1995), 148–51.

Ellison, R., *Invisible Man* (New York: Vintage, 1980).

Ellison, R., "An Extravagance of Laughter," in *Going to the Territory* (New York: Vintage, 1986), 145–59.

Ellison, R., "Richard Wright's Blues," *Antioch Review* 50 (1992), 61–74.

Elshtain, J., *Women and War* (Chicago: University of Chicago Press, revised edition, 1995).

Énard, M., *Zone*. trans. C. Mandell (Rochester, NY: Open Letter, 2010).

Engel, D. M., "Litigation Across Space and Time: Courts, Conflict, and Social Change," *Law & Society Review* 24 (1990), 333–44.

Eugenides, J., *Middlesex* (New York: Picador, 2002).

Everman R., and O. Lofgren, "Romancing the Road: Road Movies and Images of Mobility," *Theory, Culture and Society* 12 (1995), 53–79.

Eysenck, H. J., *Psychology of Politics* (London: Routledge & Kegan Paul, 1954).

Fanon, F., *Black Skin, White Masks*. trans. R. Philcox (New York: Grove Press, 2008).

Fenves, P., *The Messianic Reduction: Walter Benjamin and the Shape of Time* (Stanford, CA: Stanford University Press, 2011).

Ferguson, J., *Global Shadows* (Durham, NC: Duke University Press, 2006).

Fernandes, J. L. A., *Challenging Euro-America's Politics of Identity: The Return of the Native* (New York: Routledge, 2008).

Foucault, M., *The Archaeology of Knowledge*. trans. A. M. Sheridan-Smith (New York: Pantheon, 1972).

Foucault, M., *The Birth of the Clinic: An Archaeology of Medical Perception*. trans. A. Sheridan (New York: Pantheon, 1973).

Foucault, M., *Discipline and Punish: The Birth of the Prison*. trans. A. Sheridan Smith (New York: Pantheon, 1977).

Foucault, M., "Intellectuals and Power," in D. F. Bouchard ed. *Language, Counter-Memory, Practice* (Ithaca, NY: Cornell University Press, 1977), 205–17.

Foucault, M., *The History of Sexuality*. trans. R. Hurley (New York: Random House, 1978).

Foucault, M., "The Confession of the Flesh. A Conversation" in C. Gordon ed. *Power/ Knowledge: Selected Interviews and Other Writings 1972–1977.* trans. C. Gordon, L. Marshall, J., Mepham and K. Soper (New York: Pantheon, 1980), 194–228.

Foucault, M., "The Subject and Power," in H. Dreyfus and P. Rabinow, *Michel Foucault: Beyond Structuralism and Hermeneutics* (Chicago: University of Chicago Press, 1982), 215–22.

Foucault, M., *The Use of Pleasure.* trans. R. Hurley (New York: Pantheon, 1985).

Foucault, M., "What is Enlightenment?". trans. C. Porter in R, Rabinow and W. M. Sullivan eds, *Interpretive Social Science: A Second Look* (Berkeley: University of California Press, 1987), 157–176.

Foucault, M., "Governmentality," in G. Burchell, C. Gordon, and P. Miller eds. *The Foucault Effect* (Chicago: University of Chicago Press, 1991*a*), 87–104.

Foucault, M., "Questions of Method," in G. Burchell, C. Gordon and P. Miller, *The Foucault Effect* (Chicago: University of Chicago Press, 1991*b*), 73–86.

Foucault, M., "What is Critique?" in *The Politics of Truth.* trans. L. Hochroth and C. Porter (New York: Semiotext(e), 2004), 41–53.

Foucault, M., *Security, Territory, Population.* trans. G. Burchell (New York: Palgrave Macmillan, 2007).

Foucault, M., *Manet and the Object of Painting.* trans. M. Barr (London: Tate, 2009).

Fraser, N., "Abnormal Justice," on the web at: http://www.law.yale.edu/documents/pdf/ Intellectual_Life/ltw_fraser.pdf (obtained 3/2/2010).

Fuentes, C., "Writing in Time," *Democracy* 2 (1962), 69–77.

Fuentes, C., *The Crystal Frontier.* trans. A. MacAdam (New York: Farrar, Straus and Giroux, 1995).

Gallagher, T., "Angels Gambol Where They May: John Ford's Indians," in J. Kitses and G. Rickman eds. *The Western Reader* (New York: Limelight, 1998), 269–76.

Game, J., "Cinematic Bodies," *Studies in French Cinema* 10 (2001), 4–11.

Garfinkel, A., *Forms of Explanation* (New Haven, CT: Yale University Press, 1981).

Garfinkel, H., *Studies in Ethnomethodology* (Cambridge, UK: Polity, 1984).

Gasché, R., "Objective Diversions: On Some Kantian Themes in Benjamin's 'The Work of Art in the Age of Mechanical Reproduction'," in A. Benjamin and P. Osborne eds. *Walter Benjamin's Philosophy: Destruction and Experience* (New York: Routledge, 1994), 194–212.

Gates, Jr., H. L., "Jazz," in H. L. Gates, Jr. and K. Appiah, *Toni Morrison: Critical Perspectives Past and Present* (New York: Amistad, 1993), 53–4.

Gibson, D. B., "Text and Countertext in *The Bluest Eye*," in H. L. Gates, Jr., and K. A. Appiah, *Toni Morrison: Critical Perspectives Past and Present* (New York: Amistad, 1993), 159–60.

Gilbert, L., "Resistance in the Neoliberal City," *City: analysis of urban trends, culture, theory, policy, action* 9 (2005), 23–32.

Gilman, H., "What's Law Got to Do with It? Judicial Behaviorists Test the 'Legal Model' of Judicial Decision Making," *Law and Society Inquiry* 26 (2001), 465–504.

Gilroy, P., *Darker Than Blue: On the Moral Economies of Black Atlantic Culture* (Cambridge, MA; Harvard University Press, 2010).

Goddu, T., *Gothic America: Narrative, History, and Nation* (New York: Columbia University Press, 1997).

Gootenberg, P., "Talking about the Flow: Drugs, Borders, and the Discourse of Drug Control," *Cultural Critique* 71 (Winter, 2009), 13–46.

Guattari, F., *Chaosmosis: An Ethico-Aesthetic Paradigm* (Bloomington: Indiana University Press, 1995).

Gumbrecht, H. U., *Making Sense in Life and Literature*. trans. G. Burns (Minneapolis: University of Minnesota Press, 1992).

Gumbrecht, H. U., *The Production of Presence* (Stanford, CA: Stanford University Press, 2004).

Gussow, A., *It Seems Like Murder Here* (Chicago: University of Chicago Press, 2002).

Hamacher, W., "Guilt History: Benjamin's Sketch 'Capitalism as Religion'," *Diacritics* 32: (2002), 81–106.

Hansen, M., "Benjamin, Cinema and Experience: The Blue Flower in the Land of Technology," *New German Critique* 40 (1987), 179–224.

Harpold, T., "Dry Leatherette: Cronenberg's *Crash*," *Postmodern Culture* 7 (1997). On the web at: muse.jhu.edu/journals/postmodern_culture/v007/7.3r_harpold.html

Harris, V., *Archives and Justice: A South African Perspective* (Chicago: SAA, 2007).

Harshaw, T., "Assassinating Americans, Killing the Constitution?" on the web at: http://opinionator.blogs.nytimes.com/2010/02/05/assassinating-americans-killing-the-constitution/?scp=1&sq=assassinating%20americans&st=cse (obtained 2/6/2010).

Heberle, R. B., *From Democracy to Nazism: A Regional Case Study on Political Parties in Germany* (Baton Rouge: Louisiana State University Press, 1945).

Hegel, G. W. F., *Natural Law*. trans. T. M. Knox (Philadelphia: University of Pennsylvania Press, 1975).

Helgerson, R., *Forms of Nationhood* (Chicago: University of Chicago Press).

Henisch, P., *Negatives of My Father*. trans. A. C. Ulmer (Riverside, CA: Ariadne Press, 1990).

Herman, E., *The Romance of American Psychology* (Berkeley: University of California Press, 1995).

Herzog, L. A., *Where North Meets South: Cities, Space and Politics on the U.S – Mexican Border*, (Austin: University of Texas Press, 1990).

Hughes, L., *The Collected Poems of Langston Hughes* ed. A. Rampersad (New York: Vintage, 1994).

Hunter, T., "Putting an Antebellum Myth to Rest," *New York Times*, August 2 (2011), A21.

Huntington, S. P., "The Clash of Civilizations," *Foreign Affairs* 20 (1993), 22–49.

Huntington, S. P., *The Clash of Civilizations and the Remaking of World Order* (New York: Touchstone Books, 1998).

Hwang, A., "What is a Minor Literature," *Immanent Terrain* on the web at: http://immanentterrain.wordpress.com/2011/04/26/what-is-a-minor-literature–3/ (obtained 6/13/2011).

Illich, I., *Tools for Conviviality* (New York: Harper & Row, 1973).

Jameson, F., "The Existence of Italy," in *Signatures of the Visible* (New York: Routledge, 1992), 155–229.

Jameson, F., *Brecht and Method* (New York: Verso, 1998).

Johnson, N. C., "From Time Immemorial: Narratives of Nationhood and the Making of National Space," in J. May and N. Thrift eds. *Timespace: Geographies of Temporality* (New York: Routledge, 2001), 89–105.

Johnson, P., "*Hard Times* and the Structure of Industrialism: The Novel as Factory," *Studies in the Novel* 21 (1989), 117–33.

Jones, J., "A House is not a Home," *Frieze Magazine* online at: http://www.frieze.com/issue/print_article/a_house_is_not_a_home/ (obtained 10/17/11).

Joyce, C., "The Salon Interview: Russell Banks," on the web at: http://www.salon.com/books/int/1998/01/cov_si_05int3.html (obtained 7/26/10).

Jun, N., and D. W. Smith eds. *Deleuze and Ethics* (Edinburgh, UK: Edinburgh University Press, 2011).

Kafka, F., "A Report to an Academy," in N. Glatzer ed. *The Complete Stories* (New York: Schocken, 1946), 256–9.

Kant, I., "An Answer to the Question: What is Enlightenment?" (1784). On the web at: http://www.english.upenn.edu/~mgamer/Etexts/kant.html

Kant, I., *The Critique of Judgment*. trans. J. H. Bernard (Amherst, NY: Prometheus Books, 2000).

Kant, I., *Critique of Practical Reason*. trans. W. S. Pluhar (Indianapolis: Hackett, 2002).

Kelley, R. D. G., "Check the Technique: Black Urban Culture and the Predicament of Social Science" in N. B. Dirks, ed. *In Near Ruins* (Minneapolis: University of Minnesota Press, 1998), 39–66.

Kelley, R. D. G., "How the West Was One; The African Diaspora and the Re-Mapping of U.S. History," in T. Bender ed. *Rethinking American History in a Global Age* (Ewing, NJ: University of California Press, 2002), 123–47.

Keltner, N., "Real Reels," *Perspectives in Psychiatric Care* 44 (2008), 298–300.

Kempton, A., *Boogaloo* (New York: Pantheon, 2003).

Kincaid, J., "The Little Revenge from the Periphery," *Transition* 73 (1997), 68–73.

King, B. B., *Blues All Around Me* (New York: Avon, 1996).

King, F. O., *Walt & Skeezix 1921 & 1922* (Montreal: Drawn and Quarterly Books, 2005).

Kollin, S., "Genre and the Geographies of Violence: Cormac McCarthy and the Contemporary Western," *Contemporary Literature* 42 (2001), 557–88.

Kopytoff, I., "The Cultural Biography of Things: Commoditization as Process" in A. Appadurai, ed. *The Social Life of Things* (New York: Cambridge University Press, 1986), 64–94.

Kracauer, S., *Theory of Film: The Redemption of Physical Reality* (Princeton, NJ: Princeton University Press, 1960), 306.

Kracauer, S., *The Mass Ornament*. trans. T. Y. Levin. (Cambridge, MA: Harvard University Press, 1995).

Kristensen, L., reviewing *Friend of the Deceased* in *KinoKultura* online at: http://www.kinoKultura.com/specials/9/friendofdeceased.shtml (obtained 6/10/2010).

Kunzru, H., *The Impressionist* (New York: Plume, 2002).

Lacan, J., *Four Fundamental Concepts of Psycho-Analysis*. trans. A. Sheridan (London: Penguin, 1979).

Lange, A. de, "'Reading' and 'Constructing' Space, Gender and Race: Joseph Conrad's *Lord Jim* and J. M. Coetzee's *Foe*, in A. de Lange *et al.* eds. *Literary Landscapes* (London: Palgrave MacMillan, 2008), 109–24.

Lasansky, D. M., *The Renaissance Perfected: Architecture, Spectacle, and Tourism in Fascist Italy* (University Park: Pennsylvania State University Press, 2004).

Leach, W., *Land of Desire: Merchants, Power, and the Rise of a New American Culture* (New York: Pantheon, 1993).

Leclair, T., "The Language Must Not Sweat": A Conversation with Toni Morrison," in H. L. Gates, Jr., and K. A. Appiah, *Toni Morrison: Critical Perspectives Past and Present* (New York: Amistad, 1993), 370–1.

Lefebvre, H., *The Production of Space*. trans. D. Nicholson-Smith (Cambridge, MA: Blackwell, 1991).

Lefebvre, H., "The Right to the City," in E. Kofman and E. Lebas eds and trans. *Writings on Cities: Henri Lefebvre* (New York: Wiley-Blackwell, 1996). 147–59.

Lefebvre, H., *The Urban Revolution*. trans. R. Bononno (Minneapolis: University of Minnesota Press, 2003).

Lindqvist, S., *"Exterminate All the Brutes"* trans. J. Tate (New York: The New Press, 1992).

Lobo Antunes, A., *The Return of the Caravels*. trans. G. Rabassa (New York: Grove Press, 2002).

Lobo Antunes, A., *The Land at the End of the World*. trans. M. J. Costa (New York: W. W. Norton, 2011).

Lopez, B., *Arctic Dreams* (New York: Scribners, 1986).

Lott, E., "Love and Theft: The Racial Unconscious of Blackface Minstrelsy," *Representations* 39 (1992), 23–50.

Lucarelli, C., *Carte Blanche*. trans. M. Reynolds (New York: Europa Editions, 2006).

Lucarelli, C., *The Damned Season*. trans. M. Reynolds (New York: Europe Editions, 2007).

Lucarelli, C., *Via Delle Oche*. trans. M. Reynolds (New York: Europe Editions, 2008).

Lukács, G., *The Historical Novel*. trans. H. Mitchell and S. Mitchell (Lincoln: University of Nebraska Press, 1983).

Lumley, D. H., *Breaking the Banks in Motor City* (Jefferson, NC: McFarland & Co, 2009).

Lyotard, J.-F., *The Differend: Phrases in Dispute*. trans. G. Van Den Abbeele (Minneapolis: University of Minnesota Press, 1988).

Lyotard, J.-F., "The Sign of History," in A. Benjamin ed. *The Lyotard Reader* (New York: Basil Blackwell, 1989), 393–411.

Lynch, J. M., "'A Distinct Place in America Where All *Mestizos* Reside:' Landscape and Identity in Ana Castillo's *Scapogonia* and Diana Chang's *The Frontiers of Love*," *Melus* 26 (2001), 119–44.

Malabou, C., *Counterpath: Traveling with Jacques Derrida*. trans. D. Wills (Stanford, CA: Stanford University Press, 2004).

Malabou, C., *What Should We Do with Our Brain?* trans. M. Jeannerod (New York: Fordham University Press, 2008).

Malabou, C., *Plasticity at the Dusk of Writing*. trans. C. Shread (New York: Columbia University Press, 2010).

Markstein, D., "Toonopedia: Gasoline Alley," on the web at: http://www.toonopedia.com/gasalley.htm (obtained 4/12/2010).

Maza, S., "Only Connect: Family Values in the Age of Sentiment," *Eighteenth Century Studies* 30 (1997), 207–12.

Mbembe, A., *On the Postcolony* (Berkeley, CA: University of California Press, 2001).

Mbembe, A., "African Self-Writing," *Public Culture* 14: 1 (Winter, 2002), 239–73.

Mbembe, A., "Necropolitics," *Public Culture* 15 (2003), 11–40.

McCarthy, C., *Blood Meridian* (New York: Vintage, 1992).

Melville, H., "Bartleby, the Scrivener: A Story of Wall Street," online at: http://www.bartleby.com/129/

Mengeling, M. E., "Whitman and Ellison: Older Symbols in a Modern Mainstream," in J. F. Trimmer ed. *A Casebook on Ralph Ellison's* Invisible Man, (New York: Thomas Crowell, 1972), 268–77.

Merod, J., "Singing in the Shower: Ralph Ellison and the Blues." *La Folia* online at: http://www.lafolia.com/archive/merod200204ellison.html (obtained 6/20/2010).

Minder, R., "Portugal Turns to Former Colony for Growth," *New York Times* on the web at: http://www.nytimes.com/2010/07/14/business/global/14angolabiz.html?r=1&scp=1&sq=portugal%20turns%20to%20former%20colony&st=cse (obtained 7/15/10).

Moretti, F., *Atlas of the European Novel: 1800–1900* (London: Verso, 1998).

Moore, M. S., *Yankee Blues: Musical Culture and American Identity*. (Bloomington: Indiana University Press, 1985).

Morgan, D., "Rethinking Bazin: Ontology and Realist Aesthetics," *Critical Inquiry* 32, (2006), 443–71.

Morrison, T., *The Bluest Eye* (New York: Vintage, 1970).

Morrison, T., "Unspeakable Things Unspoken: The Afro-American Presence in American Literature," *Michigan Quarterly Review*, 28 (1989), 1–163.

Morrison, T., *Jazz* (New York: Alfred A, Knopf, 1992).

Morrison, T., "Nobel Lecture," December 7, 1993. On the web at: http://nobelprize.org/ nobel_prizes/literature/laureates/1993/morrison-lecture.html (obtained 8/5/08).

Moses, C., "The Blues Aesthetic in Toni Morrison's *The Bluest Eye*," *African American Review* 33 (1999), 623–637.

Mosley, W., *Devil in a Blue Dress* (New York: Washington Square Press, 1990).

Mosley, W., *RL's Dream* (New York: Washington Square Press, 1996).

Mudimbe, V. Y., *The Invention of Africa: Gnosis, Philosophy and the Order of Knowledge* (Bloomington: Indiana University Press, 1988).

Mueller, R., "Hans-Jürgen Syberberg's *Hitler* an Interview-Montage," *Discourse* 2 (1980), 60–3.

Munif, A., *Cities of Salt*. trans. P. Theroux (Boston: Cape Cod Scriveners, 1987).

Murray, A., *Stomping the Blues* (New York: McGraw-Hill, 1976).

Murray, A., *The Hero and the Blues* (New York: Vintage, 1995).

Murray, A., *The Blue Devils of Nada: A Contemporary American Approach to Aesthetic Statement* (New York: Vintage, 1997).

Nadel, A., *Containment Culture: American Narratives, Postmodernism, and the Atomic Age* (Durham, NC: Duke University Press, 1995).

Narasimjaiah, C. D., ed. *Commonwealth Literature: Problems of Response* (Madras, India: Macmillan India, 1981).

Nietzsche, F., *Thus Spake Zarathustra*. trans. A. Tille (New York, Dutton: 1960).

Nietzsche, F., *Untimely Meditations* trans. R. Hollingdale (New York: Cambridge University Press, 1983).

Njals Saga. trans. R. Cook (New York: Penguin, 2002).

Oaknin, M-A., *The Burnt Book: Reading the Talmud*. trans. L. Brown (Princeton, NJ: Princeton University Press, 1995).

Ogunsanwo, O., "Intertextuality and Post-Colonial Literature in Ben Okri's 'The Famished Road'," *Research in African Literatures* 26: 1 (Spring, 1995), 40–52.

Okri, B., *The Famished Road* (New York: Doubleday, 1991).

O'Meally, R. G., *Living with Music: Ralph Ellison's Jazz Writings* (New York: Modern Library, 2002).

Ong, A., "A Bio-Cartography: Maids, Neo-Slavery, and NGOs," in S. Benhabib and J. Resnik eds. *Migrations and Mobilities: Citizenship, Borders, and Gender* (New York: NYU Press, 2009), 157–86.

Opondo, S. O., "Genre and the African City: The Politics and Poetics of Urban Rhythms," *Journal for Cultural Research* 12: 1 (January, 2008), 59–79.

O'Sullivan, S., *Art Encounters: Deleuze and Guattari* (New York: Palgrave Macmillan, 2006).

Panagia, D., "Dissenting Words: A Conversation with Jacques Rancière," *Diacritics* 30 (2000), 113–26.

Panagia, D., *The Political Life of Sensation* (Durham, NC: Duke University Press, 2009).

Panofsky, I., *Gothic Architecture and Scholasticism* (New York: Meridian, 1958).

Paquet-Deyris, A.-M., "Toni Morrison's Jazz and the City," *African American Review* 35 (2001), 219–31.

Pearson, B. L., and B. McCulloch, *Robert Johnson* (Urbana: University of Illinois Press, 2003).

Peress, M., *Dvorak to Duke Ellington: A Conductor Explores America's Music* (New York: Oxford University Press, 2004).

Peterson, R., *Creating Country Music: Fabricating Authenticity* (Chicago: University of Chicago Press, 1997).

Powers R., *Generosity: An Enhancement* (New York: Farrar, Straus and Giroux, 2009).

Proulx, A., *Fine Just the Way It Is* (New York: Scribners, 2008).

Putnam, R. D., *Making Democracy Work: Civic Traditions in Modern Italy* (Princeton, NJ: Princeton University Press, 1993).

Quadrio, P. A., "Benjamin Contra Kant on Experience: Philosophizing beyond Philosophy," *Philament* On the web at: http://sudney.edu.au/arts/publications/philament/issue 1_PhilQuadrio.hmt (obtained 8/8/2010).

Rancière, J., *Dis-agreement*. trans. J. Rose (Minneapolis: University of Minnesota Press, 1999).

Rancière, J., *The Flesh of Words: The Politics of Writing*. trans. C. Mandell (Stanford, CA: Stanford University Press, 2004).

Rancière, J., *The Politics of Aesthetics*. trans. G. Rockhill (New York: Continuum, 2004).

Rancière, J., "The Sublime from Lyotard to Schiller," *Radical Philosophy* 126 (July/August, 2004), 6–17.

Rancière, J., "Who is the Subject of the Rights of Man?" *The South Atlantic Quarterly*. 103 (2004), 297–310.

Rancière, J., *Film Fables*. trans. E. Battista (Oxford: Berg, 2006).

Rancière, J., "Thinking between disciplines: an aesthetics of knowledge," *Parrhesia* 1 (2006), 1–12.

Rancière, J., *The Future of the Image*. trans. G. Elliot (New York: Verso, 2007).

Rancière, J., "Aesthetic Separation, Aesthetic Community: Scenes from the Aesthetic Regime of Art," *Art & Research: A Journal of Ideas, Contexts and Methods* (Summer, 2008) On the web at: http://www.artandresearch.org.uk/v2n1/ranciere.hmtl (obtained 8/16/2010).

Rancière, J., "Afterword," in G. Rockhill and P. Watts, eds. *Jacques Rancière* (Durham, NC: Duke University Press, 2009), 278–9.

Rancière, J., "Rethinking Aesthetics: Contemporary Art and the Politics of Aeshetics," in Hindlerlitter, B., *et al.*, *Communities of Sense* (Durham, NC: Duke University Press, 2009), 31–50.

Ravetto, K., *The Unmaking of Fascist Aesthetics* (Minneapolis: University of Minnesota Press, 2001).

Reeves, K., *Voting Hopes or Fears? White Voters, Black Candidates and Racial Politics in America* (New York: Oxford University Press, 1997), 1095–111.

Rokeach, M., *The Open and the Closed Mind* (New York: Basic Books, 1973).

Rosenus, A., *General Vallejo and the Advent of the Americans* (Berkeley, CA: University of California Press, 1995).

Roth, P., *The Humbling* (New York: Vintage, 2009).

Rubenstein, R., "Singing the Blues / Reclaiming Jazz: Toni Morrison and Cultural Mourning," *Mosaic* 31 (1998), 147–63.

Ruiz de Burton, M. A., *The Squatter and the Don* (Houston: Arte Publico Press, 1997).

Ruthrof, H., "Differend and Agonistics: A Transcendental Argument?" *Philosophy Today* 36 (1992), 329–41.

Saldivar, J. D., "Nuestra America's Borders," in J. Belnap and R. Fernandez eds. *Jose Marti's 'Our American'* (Durham, NC: Duke University Press, 1998), 145–78

Santner, E. L., *Mourning, Memory and Film in Postwar Germany* (Ithaca, NY: Cornell University Press, 1990).

Savage, L., "Justice for Janitors: Scales of Organizing and Representing Workers," *Antipode* 38 (2006), 645–66.

Scheckel, S., *The Insistence of the Indian* (Princeton, NJ: Princeton University Press, 1998).

Schnapp, J. T., "Fascinating Fascism," *Journal of Contemporary History* 31 (1996), 235–44.

Sciascia, L., *The Day of the Owl*. trans. A. Colquhoun and A. Oliver (New York: Jonathan Cape, 2003).

Seiler, C., *Republic of Drivers: A Cultural History of Automobility in America* (Chicago: University of Chicago Press, 2008).

Seixo, M. A., "Rewriting the Fiction of History: Camões's *The Lusiads* and Lobo Antunes's *The Return of the Caravels*," *Journal of Romance Studies* 3: 3 (2003), 75–93.

Seixo, M. A., "Still Facts and Living Fictions: The Literary Work of Antonio Lobo Antunes, An Introduction," in V. K. Mendes ed. *Facts and Fictions of Antonio Lobo Antunes* (Dartmouth, MA: Tagus Press, 2011).

Selltiz, C., M. Jahoda, M. Deutsch, S. Cook, *Research Methods in Social Relations* Revised edition (London: Methuen, 1965).

Selzer, M., *Bodies and Machines* (New York: Routledge, 1992).

Sepich, J., *Notes on Blood Meridian* 2nd edition (Austin: University of Texas Press, 2008).

Shapiro, M. J., *Reading the Postmodern Polity* (Minneapolis: University of Minnesota Press, 1992).

Shapiro, M. J., "Introduction," in M. J. Shapiro and H. Alker eds. *Challenging Boundaries* (Minneapolis: University of Minnesota Press, 1996), iii–xvi.

Shapiro, M. J., *Cinematic Political Thought* (New York: NYU Press, 1999).

Shapiro, M. J., *For Moral Ambiguity: National Culture and the Politics of the Family* (Minneapolis: University of Minnesota Press, 2001).

Shapiro, M. J., *Methods and Nations: Cultural Governance and the Indigenous Subject* (New York: Routledge, 2004).

Shapiro, M. J., *Deforming American Political Thought: Ethnicity, Facticity and Genre* (Lexington: University Press of Kentucky, 2006).

Shapiro, M. J., "Slow Looking: The Ethics and Politics of Aesthetics" a review essay in *Millennium* 37: (2008), 181–97.

Shapiro, M. J., *The Time of the City: Politics, Philosophy and Genre* (New York: Routledge, 2010).

Shaviro, S., "The 'Wrenching Duality' of Aesthetics: Kant, Deleuze, and the Theory of the Sensible," on the web at: www.shaviro.com/Othertexts/SPEP.pdf

Sheehan, C., "Address to Veterans For Peace Convention," on the web at http://www.truthout.org/docs_2005/printer_B081005.shtml (obtained 8/5/2006).

Shteyngart, G., *Super Sad True Love Story* (New York: Random House, 2010).

Silverman, K., *The Threshold of the Visible World* (New York: Routledge, 1996)

Simmel, G., "Money in Modern Culture," *Theory, Culture & Society* 8 (1991), 15–21.

Singer, P., *Wired for War: The Robotic Revolution and Conflict in the 21st Century* (New York: Penguin, 2009).

Skoller, J., *Shadows, Specters, Shards: History in Avant-Garde Film* (Minneapolis: University of Minnesota Press, 2005).

Slotkin, R., *Gunfighter Nation* (Norman: University of Oklahoma Press, 1992).

Snell, B. C., "American Ground Transportation: A Proposal for Restructuring the Automobile, Truck, Bus & Rail Industries" (The Original 1974 U.S. Government Report) on the web at: http://www.worldcarfree.net/resources/freesources/American.htm (obtained 4/30/2010).

Soitos, S. F., *The Blues Detective* (Amherst, MA: University of Massachusetts Press, 1996).

Sontag, S., "Fascinating Fascism," *New York Review of Books* On the web at: http://www.nybooks.com/articles/archives/1975/feb/06/fascinating-fascism/

Sontag, S., "Syberberg's Hitler," in *Under the Sign of Saturn* (New York: Farrar, Straus and Giroux, 1973), 73–108.

Spillers, H., "Mama's Baby, Papa's Maybe: An American Grammar Book," *diacritics* 17 (1987), 64–81.

Stone, A. R., "Split Subjects, Not Atoms; or, How I Fell in Love with My Prosthesis," *Configurations* 2 (1994), 173–190.

Sutton, D., *Photography, Cinema, Memory: The Crystal Image of Time* (Minneapolis: University of Minnesota Press, 2009).

Syberberg, H.-J., *Hitler, Ein Film aus Deutschland* (Reinbek, 1978).

Syberberg, H.-J., *Hitler: A Film from Germany*. trans. J. Neugroschel (New York: Farrar, Straus and Giroux, 1982).

Sylvester, D., *The Brutality of Fact: Interviews with Francis Bacon* (New York: Thames and Hudson, 1981).

Talavera V., *et al.*, "Deportation in the U.S.-Mexico Borderlands: Anticipation, Experience, and Memory," in N. De Genova and N. Peutz, *The Deportation Regime* (Durham, NC: Duke University Press, 2006), 166–93.

Tatz, C., "The Politics of Aboriginal Health," *Politics* (The Journal of the Australian Political Studies Association), 7: 2 (November, 1972), 3–23.

Taussig, M., "Tactility and Distraction," *Cultural Anthropology* 6 (1991): 147–53.

Thompson, G., "U.S. Agents Aided Mexican Drug Trafficker to Infiltrate His Criminal Ring," *New York Times International* Monday, January 9 (2012), A5.

Troutman, J., *Indian Blues: American Indians and the Politics of Music 1879–1934* (Norman: University of Oklahoma Press, 2009).

Truby, S., *Exit Architecture: Between War and Peace*. trans. R. Payne (Vienna: Stringer-Verlag, 2008).

Tsirkas, S., *Drifting Cities*. trans. K. Cicellis (New York: Knopf, 1974).

Updike, J., *Rabbit is Rich* (New York, Alfred A. Knopf, 1981).

Updike, J., *Rabbit at Rest* (New York: Ballantine, 1996).

Urry, J., "Inhabiting the Car," in E. R. Larreta, ed. *Collective Imagination and Beyond* (Rio de Janeiro: UNESCO.ISSC.EDUCAM, 2001), 277–93.

Veyne, P., "The Inventory of Differences," trans. E. Kingdom, *Economy and Society* 11 (1982), 173–98.

Virilio, P., *Speed and Politics*. trans. M. Polizzotti. (New York: Semiotext(e), 1986).

Virilio, P., *War and Cinema*. trans. P. Camillera (New York: Verso, 1989).

Virno, P., *A Grammar of the Multitude*. trans. I. Bertolleti, J. Cascaito, and A. Casson (New York: Semiotext(e), 2004).

Ware, C., "Frank King's *Gasoline Alley*," in H. Katz ed. *Cartoon America*. (New York: Abrams, 2006), 161–8.

Weber, E., "Ethics and the Economy: The Moral Implications of an Auto Industry Bailout," *EverydayEthics* on the web at: http://everyday-ethics-org/2008/12/ethics-and-the-economy-the-moral-implications-of-an-auto-industry-bailout.htm (obtained 5/22/10).

Wellbery, D., "Introduction," to F. Kittler, *Discourse Networks 1800/1900* (Stanford, CA: Stanford University Press, 1990).

West, D., and J. M. West, "Borders and Boundaries: An Interview with John Sayles," *Cineaste* 22: 3. On the web at: http://www.en.utexas.edu/Classes/Bremen/e316k/316kprivate/scans/sayles_lonestar.html (obtained 10/6/2010).

Wexman, V. W., "The Family on the Land," in D. Bernardi ed., *The Birth of Whiteness: Race and the Emergence of U.S. Cinema* (New Brunswick, NJ: Rutgers University Press, 1996), 129–69.

White, T., "A Man out of Time Beats the Clock," *Musician* (magazine) 60 (October 1983), 52.)

Wideman, J. E., *Brothers and Keepers* (Boston: Houghton Mifflin, 2005).

Williams, R., *The Long Revolution* (London: Chatto and Windus, 1961).

Williams, R., *Marxism and Literature* (Oxford, UK: Oxford University Press, 1977).

Wilson J. Q., and R. Herrnstein *Crime and Human Nature* (New York, Simon & Schuster, 1985).

Wilz, K., "Richard's Story: The Present Referent in *In the Valley of Elah*," *Global Media Journal.* On the web at: http://lass.calumet.purdue.edu/cca/gmj/fa09/graduate/gmj-fa09-grad-wilz.htm (obtained 6/11/2010).

Wolin, S., "Political Theory as a Vocation," *American Political Science Review* 63: 4 (Dec., 1969), 1062–82.

Woods, C., *Development Arrested: Race, Power, and the Blues in the Mississippi* (New York: Verso, 1998).

Wright, W. *Six Guns and Society* (Berkeley, CA: University of California Press, 1977).

Young, C. *Ideology and Development in Africa* (New Haven, CT: Yale University Press, 1982).

Zilberg, E., "Falling Down in El Norte: A Cultural Politics and Spatial Poetics of the ReLatinization of Los Angeles," *Wide Angle* 20 (1998), 183–209.

Žižek S., ed. *Lacan: The Silent Partners* (London: Verso, 2006).

Index

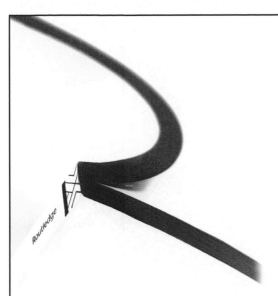